AF480910

Engineering Physics

As per the syllabus of

Gujarat Technological University
Bachelor of Engineering

Subject Code: BE01000021
Subject: Physics
B.E. 1st YEAR

Authors:

Prof. (Dr.) Amitkumar J. Patel
Assistant Prof (Physics)
Government Engineering College-Godhra

Prof. (Dr.) Sanjay K. Singhal
Associate Prof (Physics)
Government Engineering College-Palanpur

Prof. (Dr.) Maheshkumar K. Patel
Assistant Prof (Physics)
Government Engineering College-Godhra

Prof. (Dr.) Rajeshkumar P. Khatri
Assistant Prof (Physics)
Government Engineering College-Modasa

Prof. (Dr.) Dipak H. Sahay
Assistant Prof (Physics)
Government Engineering College-Modasa

Prof. (Dr.) Pratik M. Gadhvi
Assistant Prof (Physics)
Government Engineering College-Gandhinagar

: Preface :

From very beginning, it has been proved that, without understanding of fundamental principles of physics, exploration of technology is not possible. We are very glad to present this book for undergraduate students of engineering and technology especially for the students of Gujarat Technological University, Gujarat state. In this book, subject matter explained with the help of pictures, diagrams, and various examples in very simple easy and lucid language, so students of first year can easily understand.

Following are our key features

→ Complete syllabus covered as described by GTU

→ Simple and easiest way of presentation

→ Rich pedagogy

→ Learning goals

→ Key points to remember

→ Solved and unsolved numericals

→ Short and descriptive questions

→ Model question papers

This book contained six different topics such as Properties of matter, Wave motion & acoustics, Optics, Quantum Physics, Laser and New engineering materials.

All suggestions given by our mentors, academic friends and students have been incorporated to make a complete book. We are sure that, this book will meet all the needs of engineering students, who want to learn and updates their knowledge on fundamental and technical aspects both.

In spite our best effort some misprinting and omission might have crept at some place for which authors owe an apology to the reader. Authors shall be very thankful to the readers for their valuables and constructive suggestions for the enhancement of quality of this book. Readers can send their valuable suggestions in the comment section at https://ajphygtu.wixsite.com/gecg. We will definitely incorporate it in our next edition.

: Acknowledgement :

First of all, we take this opportunity to place on record our indebtedness to a large number of relevant books which we consulted during preparation of this book.

We pay our special thanks to Prof. (Dr.) Kirti M. Korot (GEC-Palanpur), Prof. (Dr.) Harshad Bhutadiya (GEC-Patan), Prof. (Dr.) Ashok Chaudhari (GEC-Patan) Prof. (Dr.) Nilesh Pandya (GEC-Bhavnagar), Prof. (Dr.) Sagar Ambavale (VGEC-Chandkheda), Prof. Jigar Chaudhari (VGEC-Chandkheda) and Prof. Snehal Paladiya (VGEC-Chandkheda) for their encouragement for the preparation of this book.

We are sincerely indebted to the faculty members from our institute; Prof. Hitesh Baria, Prof. L. S. Narsigani, Prof. S. Y. Pathan, Prof. J. N. Sutariya and Prof. G. A. Rathva for their inspiration, direction and continuous support during preparation of this book.

We are thankful to the management team for all kind of support in the publication of this book.

Prof. (Dr.) Amitkumar J. Patel

Prof. (Dr.) Sanjay K. Singhal

Prof. (Dr.) Maheshkumar K. Patel

Prof. (Dr.) Rajeshkumar P. Khatri

Prof. (Dr.) Dipak H. Sahay

Prof. (Dr.) Pratik M. Gadhvi

: Table of content :

CHAPTER-I PROPERTIES OF MATTER

Learning goals:

At the end of this chapter reader will be able to

✓ Calculate various modulus of elasticity by applying the concepts of load, stress, strain, twisting couple, Hooke's law, twisting couple, bending of beam etc.
✓ Explain the stress-strain diagram.
✓ Explain I shaped girder.
✓ Calculate the rigidity of a wire using torsional pendulum.

PREREQUISITES

Force

Force is an interaction between two objects which if unopposed than changes the state of motion of objects. It is represented by a symbol "F" and its SI unit is N.

Deforming force

Deforming force is the external force acting on a body which can change the form of dimensions of the body.

Rigid body

If relative position of the constituent particles of a body remain unchanged in spite of any amount of deforming force is applied than such body is called rigid body.

Elasticity

Elasticity is the property of solid material to return to its original shape or size after being deformed when external applied force is removed.

Elastic limit

Elastic limit is the maximum stress after the application of which a material is able to regain its original shape or size.

1.1 INTRODUCTION

The practical applications of engineering materials in manufacturing and construction engineering depend on the thorough knowledge of their particular properties under a wide range of conditions. The properties of material that determine its behaviour under applied forces are known as properties of matter. These properties are expressed as functions of stress, strain etc. A sound knowledge of mechanical properties of materials provides the basis for predicting behaviour of materials under different load conditions and designing the components out of them for various kinds of applications.

1.2 CONCEPT OF LOAD, STRESS AND STRAIN

Almost every engineering object is subjected to external force under which objects are expected to serve a particular application. If the object is in equilibrium, resultant external force will be zero but; all such forces collectively apply a load on the object. SI unit of load is *Newton.*

There are a number of different ways in which load can be applied to an object.

→ **Static or dead loads**, i.e. non-fluctuating loads, generally caused by gravity effects.
→ **Live loads**, as produced by, for example, vehicles crossing a bridge.
→ **Impact or shock loads** caused by sudden blows.
→ **Fatigue, fluctuating or alternating loads**, where magnitude and sign of the load changes with time.

A load can simply be divided in two types as direct pull or push, technically known as **Tension** and **Compression**.

1.3 STRESS

Every object tends to deform as a result of application of external force. Degree of deformation of an object depends upon the nature of molecular attraction of object. As soon as the object starts deforming, molecular displacement in object takes place and internal forces comes in to play to oppose and counter balance the external force and restore the object back to its original condition. Magnitude of such internal or restoring forces depends on the degree of deformation caused. Such restoring force per unit area developed inside the object is called stress. Unit of stress are $N \cdot m^{-2}$ and Pa. It is denoted by the symbol **"σ"**.

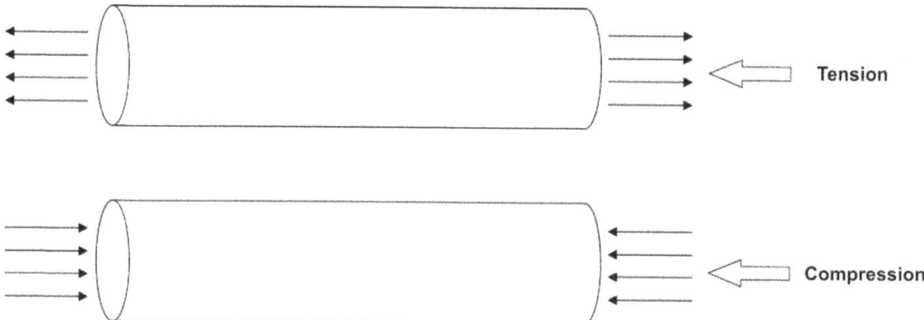

Figure 1.1: Graphical representation of tension and compression.

Stress is the restoring force per unit area developed in the object to oppose the deformation of object under external force.

$$\text{Stress} = \frac{\text{restoring force}}{\text{area of cross} - \text{section}}$$

At equilibrium, restoring force is equal to deforming force, therefore

$$\text{Stress} = \frac{\text{deforming force}}{\text{area of cross} - \text{section}} = \frac{F}{A}$$

Stress can be classified as normal stress (tensile/compressive), shearing stress, and bulk stress.

1.3.1 Normal stress

Normal stress may be tensile or compressive according to increase or decrease in the volume of an object under external force. It is also known as **longitudinal stress**.

Tensile stress

Tensile stress is the restoring force developed per unit area of cross section of an object when the length of an object increases along the direction of applied external force.

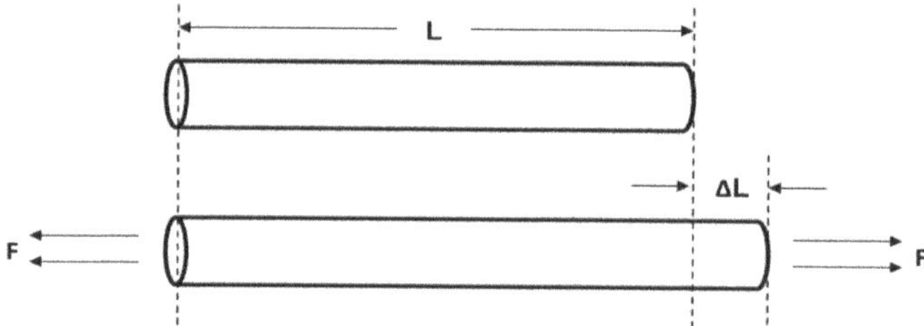

Figure 1.2: Tensile stress.

Compressive stress

Compressive stress is the restoring force developed per unit area of cross section of an object when the length of an object decreases along the direction of applied external force.

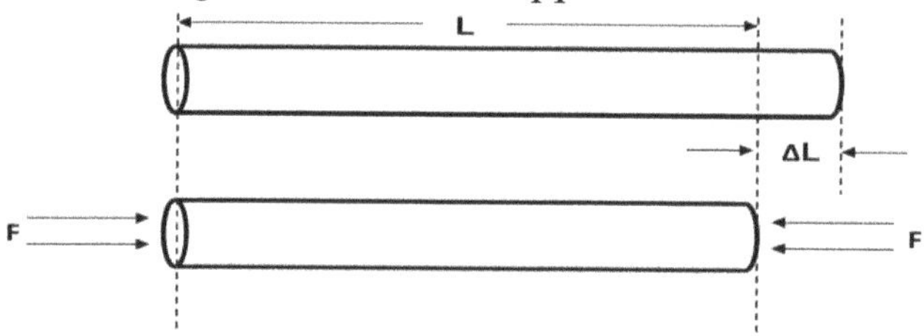

Figure 1.3: Compressive stress.

1.3.2 Shearing stress

When external force acts tangentially over an area of an object, then the object gets sheared through a certain angle. Such a stress is called shearing or tangential stress.

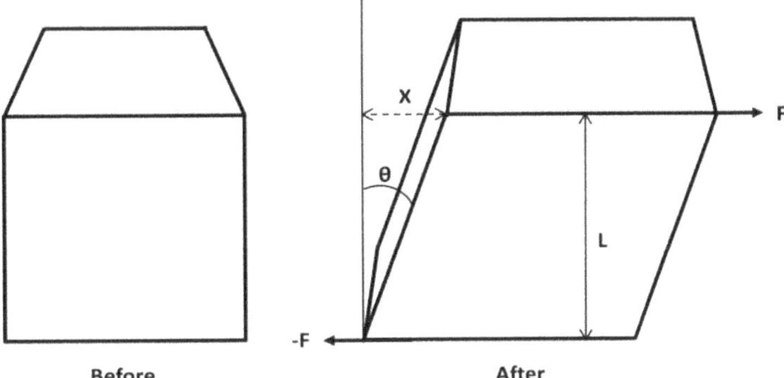

Figure 1.4: Shearing stress.

1.3.3 Bulk stress

When a solid is immersed in a liquid, it gets compressed uniformly in all directions. The force applied by the fluid acts perpendicularly at every point on the surface of solid and solid is said to be under compression. This leads to change in the volume of solid without any change in its geometrical shape. Thus when external force acts normally from all the sides of object, the object gets compressed without any change in its geometrical shape. Such a stress is called bulk stress.

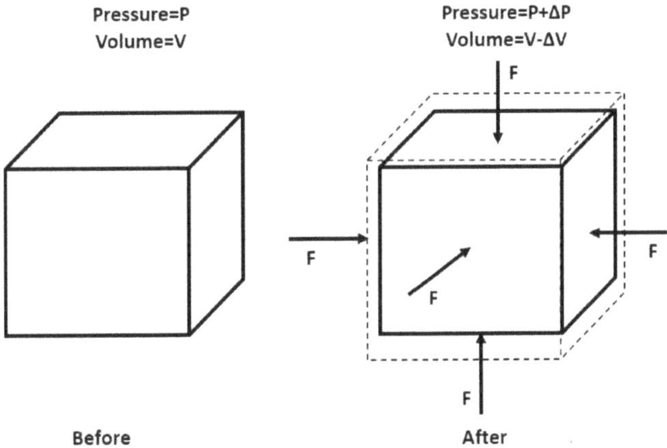

Figure 1.5: Bulk stress.

1.4 STRAIN

When an external force acts on an object, it produces molecular realignment. This leads to the deformation in shape of the object and the object is said to be in strained state. Strain is thus a measure of the deformation of the object.

Strain in a material is defined as the ratio of change in dimension to the original dimension of object under external force.

Strain is a dimensionless quantity. It is denoted by the symbol "ε". Strain is of three types depending upon the change produced in a body and the stress applied. It can be classified in to three types depending on the change produced in a body.

1.4.1 Longitudinal strain

It is the ratio of the change in length of a body to the original length of the body. If L is the original length of a wire or a rod and the final length of the wire or the rod is L+ΔL under the action of a normal stress, the change in length is ΔL.

$$\textbf{Longitudinal Strain} = \frac{\textbf{Change in the length}}{\textbf{Original length}} = \frac{\Delta L}{L}$$

If the length increases due to tensile stress, the corresponding strain is called tensile strain. If the length decreases due to compressive stress, the strain is called compressive strain.

1.4.2 Shearing strain

It is the angle through which a face originally perpendicular to the fixed face is turned. (or) It is the ratio of the displacement of a layer to its distance from the fixed layer.

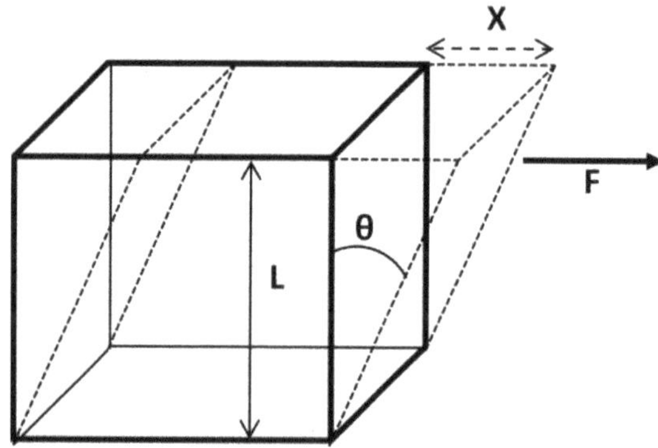

Figure 1.6: Displacement of layer through an angle.

As shown in Figure1.6 the relative displacement of layers is 'x' in an object having length 'L'. Therefore

$$\textbf{Shearing Strain} = \frac{x}{L} = \tan\theta$$

Usually angle θ is very small, therefore $\tan\theta \approx \theta$ and we can write

$$\textbf{Shearing Strain} = \tan\theta \approx \theta$$

1.4.3 Volume strain

It is the ratio of the change in volume of a body to its original volume. If V is the original volume of a body and V-ΔV is the volume of the body under the action of a normal stress, the change in volume is ΔV.

$$\textbf{Volume Strain} = \frac{\textbf{Change in the volume}}{\textbf{Original volume}} = \frac{\Delta V}{V}$$

1.5 HOOKE'S LAW

Hooke's Law states that Strain is Proportional to the Stress which produced it.

$$k = \frac{\textbf{Stress}}{\textbf{Strain}}$$

Here the constant 'k' is coefficient of elasticity and is known as modulus of elasticity. Its units are $N{\cdot}m^{-2}$ and Pa. Hooke's law is obeyed within certain limits by most ferrous alloys and can usually be assumed to apply with sufficient accuracy to other Engineering Materials such as timber, concrete and non-ferrous alloys. In general a material is said to be **Elastic** if it obeys Hooke's Law.

- Ratio of longitudinal stress over longitudinal strain is **Young's modulus (E).**
- Ratio of shear stress over shear strain is **Modulus of rigidity (C, N or G),** also called **Shear modulus.**
- Ratio of bulk stress over bulk strain is **Bulk modulus (K).**

Significance of calculating stress and strain

By calculating stress we can examine various properties of materials like **yield point, ultimate tensile strength** etc. by getting values of these properties we can select the material to be used for particular application.

By determining stress and strain we can predict the **endurance limit**, which tells us the life of a material or we can say the period after which it may fail.

- Where a number of Loads are acting together on an Elastic Material, the **Principle of Superposition** states that the resultant Strain will be the sum of the individual Strains caused by each Load separately.

1.6 STRESS-STRAIN DIAGRAM

It is a curve between stress and strain. A graph is plotted between the stress (which is equal in magnitude to the applied force per unit area) and the strain produced. Stress-Strain diagram shown in Figure1.7 helps us to understand how a given material deforms with increasing loads.

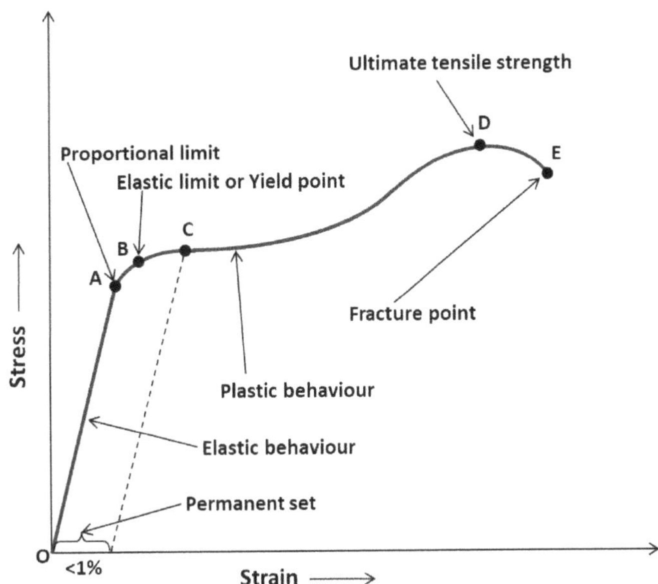

Figure 1.7: Stress-Strain diagram.

→ The curve between O and A, is a straight line. This means stress is directly proportional to strain. In this region Hooke's Law is applicable. In this region the material behaves like an elastic body.

→ In the region from A to B, stress and strain are not directly proportional. But still the material returns to its original dimension after the force is removed. They exhibit elastic properties.

→ The point B in the curve is known as **yield point** (also known as elastic limit) which means till this point the material will be elastic in behaviour and the stress corresponding to point B is known as yield strength of the material.

→ The region between O and B is called as **Elastic region.**

→ From point B to point D we can see that strain increases rapidly even for small change in stress. Even if we remove the force the material does not come back to its original position. At this point stress is zero but strain is not zero as body has changed its shape. The material has undergone **plastic deformation**. The material is said to be **permanent set**.

→ The stress corresponding to point D on the graph is known as ultimate tensile strength of the material.

→ From D to E we can see that stress decreases even if strain increases.

→ Finally at point E fracture occurs. This means the body breaks.

Conclusion

➢ An object is brittle if D and E are very close. This means fracture point is near to tensile strength. i.e. Glass which is brittle.

➢ An object is ductile if D and E are very far apart from each other. This means fracture point is far away from tensile strength. i.e. Metals, Gold and silver etc.

Elastic substances like rubber have larger elastic region. i.e. spring, catapult, tissue of aorta etc.

1.7 ELASTIC BEHAVIOR OF SOLIDS

The following elastic behaviors are observed in almost all solids.

Elastic after effect

When an elastic body is stretched and applied deforming force is removed then the body is expected to return to its original configuration instantaneously. But sometimes some materials take some time to return to its original configuration. This temporary delay in achieving its original configuration is termed as elastic after effect. This elastic after effect is very short for quartz fiber. But elastic after effect is more for glass. Therefore, quartz fiber is used in galvanometer coil.

Elastically fatigue

Elastically fatigue state of an elastic body refers to a tired state of the body due to exposure to continuous alternating deforming forces. Due to these alternating forces any elastic body gradually loses its elastic property and finally reaches a state after which the body cannot regain its original configuration. This state of elastic body represents elastically fatigue.

Elastic hysteresis

Certain elastic materials follow one curve (path) on stretching when the stress is increased and follows another path while regaining its original configuration. This particular behavior of the elastic material is called elastic hysteresis (Figure 1.18). The work evolved during regaining its original configuration is less than the work done in the body while stretching. This property of elastic material enables it to absorb vibrations. So, materials like vulcanized rubber are often used as shock absorbers.

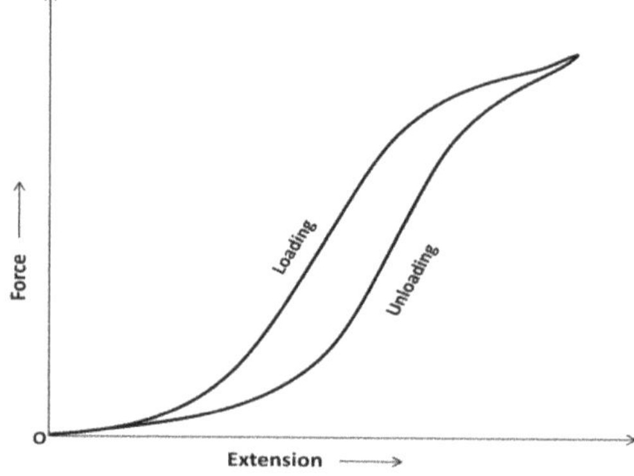

Figure 1.8: Elastic hysteresis.

1.8 TYPES OF ELASTICITY

In the stress-strain diagram (Figure 1.7), the region within the elastic limit (region OA) is of importance to structural and manufacturing sectors since it describes the maximum stress a particular material can take before being permanently deformed. The modulus of elasticity is simply the ratio between stress and strain. Elastic Moduli can be of three types,

Young's Modulus or Modulus of Elasticity: is defined as ratio of Normal Stress to Longitudinal Strain.

Shear Modulus or Rigidity Modulus: is defined as ratio of Shear stress to Shear Strain.

Bulk Modulus: is defined as, when a body is subject to three mutually perpendicular stresses, of equal intensity, the ratio of direct stress to the corresponding volumetric strain is known as Bulk Modulus.

1.8.1 Young's modulus

When a wire is acted upon by two equal and opposite forces in the direction of its length, the length of the body is changed. The change in length per unit length ($\Delta L/L$) is called the longitudinal strain and the restoring force (which is equal to the applied force in equilibrium) per unit area of cross-section of wire is called the longitudinal stress.

For small change in the length of the wire, the ratio of the longitudinal stress to the corresponding strain is called the **Young's modulus of elasticity (Y)** of the wire. Thus,

$$Y = \frac{\text{longitudinal stress}}{\text{longitudinal strain}} = \frac{F/A}{\Delta L/L}$$

$$\therefore Y = \frac{FL}{A\Delta L}$$

Let there be a wire of length 'L' and radius 'r'. It's one end is clamped to a rigid support and a mass M is attached at the other end. Then

$$F = Mg \text{ and } A = \pi r^2$$

Substituting in above equation, we have

$$\therefore Y = \frac{MgL}{\pi r^2 \Delta L}$$

1.8.2 Shear modulus

When a body is acted upon by an external force tangential to a surface of the body, the opposite surfaces being kept fixed, it suffers a change in shape of the body, its volume remains unchanged. Then the body is said to be sheared.

The ratio of the displacement of a layer in the direction of the tangential force and the distance of the layer from the fixed surface is called the 'shearing strain' and the tangential force acting per unit area of the surface is called the 'shearing stress'.

For small strain in the ratio of the shearing stress to the shearing strain is called the **Shear modulus (G)** of the material of the body.

$$G = \frac{\text{Shearing stress}}{\text{Shearing strain}} = \frac{F/A}{\theta}$$

1.8.3 Bulk Modulus

If a uniform pressure (normal force) is applied all over the surface of an object, then volume of object changes. The change in volume per unit volume of the body is called the 'volume strain' and the normal force acting per unit area of the surface (pressure) is called the normal stress or volume stress. For small strains, the ratio of the volume stress to the volume strain is called **Bulk modulus (K).**

$$K = \frac{\text{Volume stress}}{\text{Volume strain}} = \frac{F/A}{\Delta V/V} = \frac{PV}{\Delta V}$$

The reciprocal of the Bulk modulus of the material of a body is called the "compressibility' of that material.

1.9 CANTILEVER-DEPRESSION OF CANTILEVER

Bending of Beams

A beam is a rod or a bar of uniform cross-section of homogeneous, isotropic elastic material whose length is very large compared to its thickness.

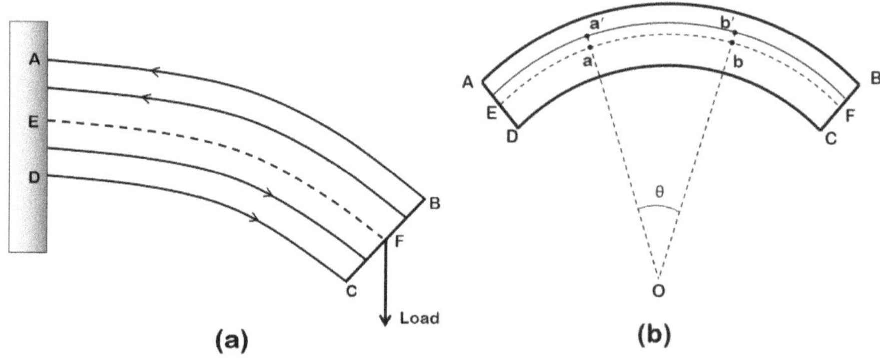

Figure 1.9: (a) Bending of beam, (b) Arc formation while bending of beam.

When a beam is fixed at one end and loaded at the other end as shown in figure 1.9(a) within the elastic limit, it will bend and couple will produced inside it. The upper surface of the beam gets stretched and becomes a convex shape and lower surface gets compressed and becomes a concave form.

All the longitudinal filaments in its upper half are extended and those in lower half are compressed. The extension is maximum in the uppermost filament and the compression is maximum in the lower most filaments. The amount of extension and compression decreases towards the axis of the beam. Thus filament 'EF' neither extended nor compressed. This surface is called Neutral surface. The plane in which all filaments are bent to form circular arcs is called the plane of bending. Thus in figure 1.9(a) plane 'ABCD' is the plane of bending.

Bending Moment

Let a small part of the beam bent in the form of a circular arc "ab" as shown in figure 1.9(b). This arc subtends an angle θ at 'O'. Let R be the radius of curvature of this part of the neutral axis. Let a'b' be an element at a distance 'z' from the neutral axis.

We know that arc = Radius x angle subtended

$\therefore a'b' = (R + z) \cdot \theta$ and $ab = R \cdot \theta$

$$\begin{aligned}\therefore \text{increase in length} &= a'b' - ab \\ &= (R + z) \cdot \theta - R \cdot \theta \\ &= z \cdot \theta \qquad (1.1)\end{aligned}$$

Now, strain = Change in length/Original length

$$= \frac{z \cdot \theta}{R \cdot \theta} = \frac{z}{R} \qquad (1.2)$$

Hence, the strain is proportional to the distance from the natural axis. Now, consider a small area δa at a distance 'z' from the natural axis.

$$\text{Young's modulus } Y = \frac{\text{Stress}}{\text{Strain}}$$

$$\therefore \text{Stress} = Y \cdot \text{Strain}$$

$$\therefore \frac{F}{\delta a} = Y \cdot \frac{z}{R}$$

$\therefore$ The force F on area δa is given by $F = Y \cdot \frac{z}{R} \cdot \delta a$

Then, the moment of this force = Force x distance

$$\therefore \text{moment of force} = Y \cdot \frac{z}{R} \cdot \delta a \cdot z$$

$$= Y \cdot \frac{z^2}{R} \cdot \delta a$$

Then, the total moment of forces acting on all the filament is given by

$$= \sum Y \cdot \frac{z^2}{R} \cdot \delta a$$

$$= \frac{Y}{R} \cdot \sum \delta a \cdot z^2$$

Here, $\sum \delta a \cdot z^2$ is called the geometrical moment of inertia I_g of the section.

$$I_g = \sum \delta a \cdot z^2 = aK^2$$

Where 'a' is the area of the surface and 'k' is the radius of gyration.

$$\therefore \text{The moment of forces} = \frac{Y}{R} \cdot I_g$$

This is actually the restoring couple 'M' of beam.

$$M = \frac{Y}{R} \cdot I_g \qquad (1.3)$$

1.9.1 Uniform Bending

In the case of uniform bending, a beam is loaded uniformly on its both ends; therefore beam forms an arc of a circle. The elevation is produced in the beam.

Let us consider a beam 'AB' of negligible mass, supported symmetrically on two knife edges 'C' and 'D'. It is loaded with equal weight W at each end. Let 'l' be the length between the two knife edges and 'a' be the length between the knife edge and the load. Due to the applied load the beam bends into an arc of circle and produces an elevation 'y'.

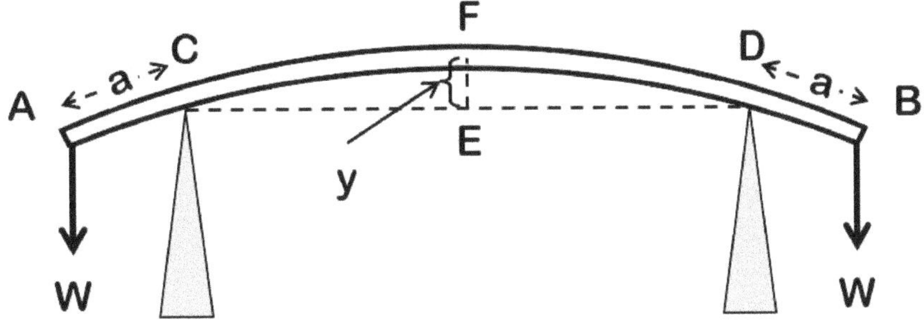

Figure 1.10: Uniform bending of beam.

Since, restoring couple 'M = Wa' is constant, 'R' is also constant. Therefore the beam bends into an arc of a circle of radius 'R'. Hence the bending in this case is said to be uniform.

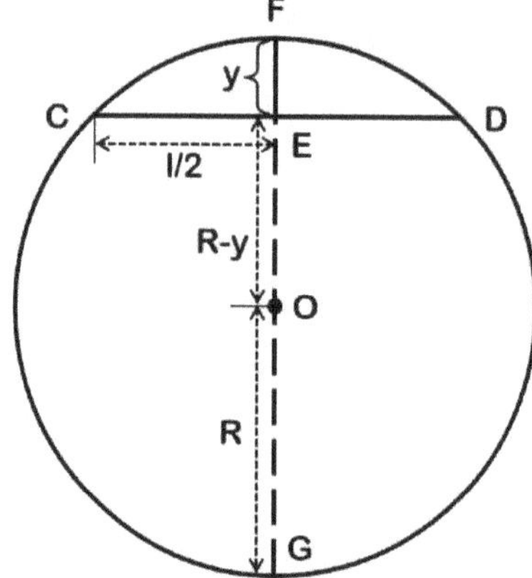

Figure 1.11: visualization of circular arc formed by uniform bending of beam.

Now, from the property of circle, we can write

$$(CE) \times (ED) = (EF) \times (EG)$$

$$\therefore \left(\frac{l}{2}\right) \times \left(\frac{l}{2}\right) = (y) \times (2R - y)$$

$$\therefore \frac{l^2}{4} = (2Ry - y^2) \qquad (1.4)$$

Here 'y' is the elevation produced in the beam. Since the elevation is very small compared to the radius of curvature of the circle, 'y^2' can be neglected.

$$\therefore \frac{l^2}{4} = 2Ry$$

$$\therefore R = \frac{l^2}{8y} \qquad (1.5)$$

Substituting equation (1.5) in equation (1.3) we get,

$$M = Wa = mga = \frac{YI_g}{\left(\frac{l^2}{8y}\right)}$$

$$\therefore Y = \frac{mgal^2}{8yI_g} \qquad (1.6)$$

Rectangular cross-section

If 'b' and 'd' are the breadth and thickness of the beam, then $I_g = \frac{bd^3}{12}$ and Young's modulus of the material of the beam by uniform bending can be calculated as

$$\therefore Y = \frac{3mgal^2}{2ybd^3} \qquad (1.7)$$

Circular cross-section

If 'r' be the radius of the beam, then $I_g = \frac{\pi r^4}{4}$ and Young's modulus of the material of the beam by uniform bending can be calculated as

$$\therefore Y = \frac{mgal^2}{2y\pi r^4} \quad (1.8)$$

1.9.2 Non-Uniform Bending

In the case of non-uniform bending, the beam is loaded at its midpoint, the depression produced will not form an arc of a circle.

Let us consider a beam 'AB' of negligible mass, supported symmetrically on two knife edges. It is loaded with weight W at centre of beam. Let 'l' be the length of beam. Due to the applied load the beam bends and produces a depression 'y'.

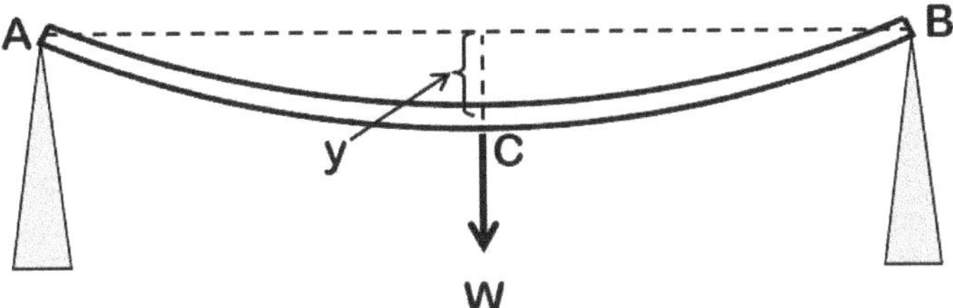

Figure 1.12: Non-Uniform bending of beam.

The cantilever

A beam fixed horizontally at one end and loaded at the other end is called cantilever.

Let 'AB' be the natural axis of the cantilever of length 'L' as shown in Figure 1.13. It is fixed at 'A' end and loaded at 'B' with a weight 'W'. Then the end 'B' is depressed into the position B′ and the natural axis takes up the position AB'. Consider a section 'P' of the beam at a distance 'x' from the fixed end 'A'.

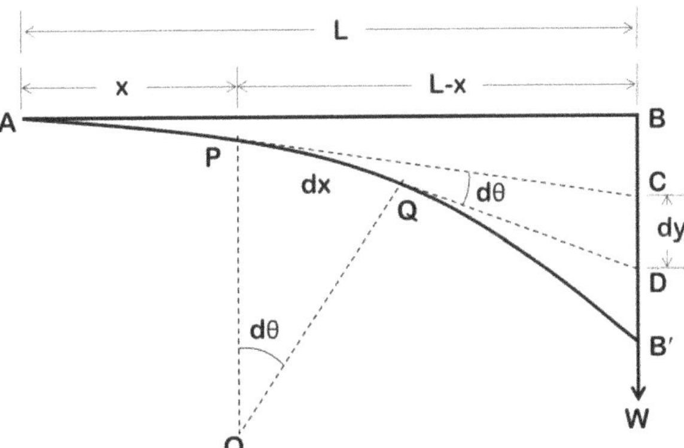

Figure 1.13: Schematic diagram of a cantilever.

$$\text{The bending moment} = W \times PB'$$
$$= W(L - x)$$

Since the beam is in equilibrium, we can write

$$W(L - x) = \frac{Y}{R} I_g \quad (1.9)$$

Where, R is the radius of curvature. Now consider a point 'Q' at a small distance 'dx' from 'P'. We have

$$PQ = Rd\theta$$

$$\therefore dx = Rd\theta$$

$$\therefore R = \frac{dx}{d\theta}$$

Now we can write eqn. 1.9 as,

$$W(L - x) = YI_g \frac{d\theta}{dx}$$

$$d\theta = \frac{W(L - x)dx}{YI_g}$$

Now, the depression of 'Q' below 'P' is equal to say 'dy', then

$$dy = (L - x)d\theta$$

$$dy = \frac{W(L - x)^2 dx}{YI_g}$$

Now, the total depression

$$y = \int_0^L dy = \int_0^L \frac{W(L - x)^2 dx}{YI_g}$$

$$\therefore y = \frac{W}{YI_g}\int_0^L (L - x)^2 dx$$

$$\therefore y = \frac{W}{YI_g}\int_0^L (L^2 - 2Lx + x^2)dx$$

$$\therefore y = \frac{W}{YI_g}\left[L^2x - Lx^2 + \frac{x^3}{3}\right]_0^L$$

$$\therefore y = \frac{W}{YI_g}\left[L^3 - L^3 + \frac{L^3}{3}\right]$$

$$\therefore Y = \frac{WL^3}{3yI_g} \qquad \textbf{(1.10)}$$

Here in our case the beam is loaded at the center. Let a beam be supported on two knife edges at its two ends 'A' and 'B', and let it be loaded in the middle at 'C' with weight 'W' as shown in figure 1.14.

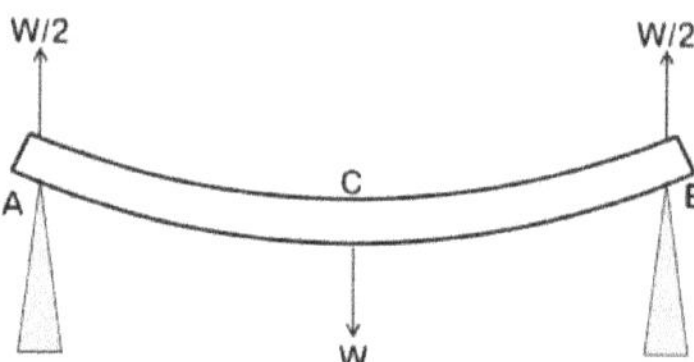

Figure 1.14: Beam loaded at the centre.

Since the middle part of the beam is horizontal, then the beam may be considered as equivalent to two inverted cantilevers, fixed at 'C' and loaded at ends 'A' and 'B' by weight 'W/2'. If 'L' is the length of the beam 'AB', then the length of each cantilever is 'L/2'.
Then the young's modulus of beam is given by

$$\therefore Y = \frac{\frac{W}{2}\left(\frac{L}{2}\right)^3}{3yI_g} \tag{1.11}$$

For rectangular cross section: $\Rightarrow I_g = \frac{bd^3}{12}$

Therefore young's modulus of rectangular beam can be given as

$$\therefore Y = \frac{4\left(\frac{W}{2}\left(\frac{L}{2}\right)^3\right)}{ybd^3} = \frac{mgL^3}{4ybd^3} \tag{1.12}$$

For circular cross section: $\Rightarrow a = \pi r^2$ and $I_g = \frac{\pi r^4}{4}$

Therefore young's modulus of circular beam can be given as

$$\therefore Y = \frac{4\left(\frac{W}{2}\left(\frac{L}{2}\right)^3\right)}{3y\pi r^4} = \frac{mgL^3}{12y\pi r^4} \tag{1.13}$$

1.10 I-SHAPE GIRDER

A girder is a support beam used in construction. It is the main horizontal support of a structure which supports smaller beams. The term "girder" is often used interchangeably with "beam" in reference to bridge design.

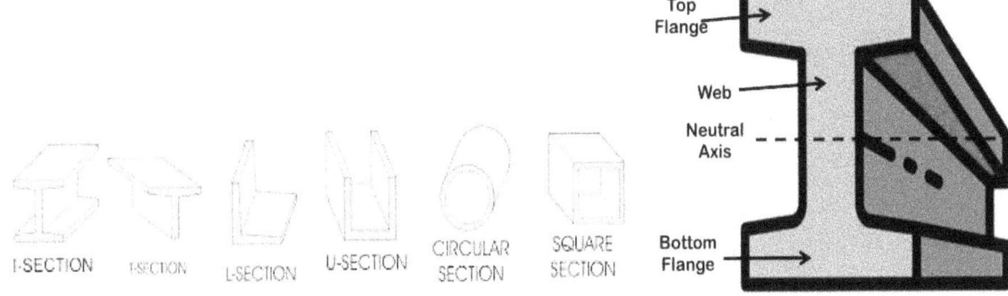

Figure 1.15: Girder shapes and designs.

I-shaped beams have very high moment of inertia for the same volume of the given material. So they have high stability in terms of bending moments. The two horizontal parts (called flanges) of the I-shaped beam can bear high bending and shearing stress. That means they do not get twisted and tilted easily. That is why they are used in girders, and as rails on the railway tracks.

Bridges should be constructed in such a way that it does not bend too much or break under the load of traffic or its own load.

From the theory of elasticity we know that when a load W = mg is placed at the midpoint of a bar of length L, breadth b and thickness d, then the bar bends at the midpoint by an amount given by:

$$y = \frac{mgL^3}{4Ybd^3}$$

Above expression mention that, to reduce the bending for a given load, we should use a material of large Young's modulus (y is inversely proportional to Y). For a given amount of material, we should increase the thickness of the bar rather than the breadth (as y is proportional to $1/d^3$ and only to $1/b$). But on increasing the thickness too much also the bar may bend. Thus a compromise between the breadth and thickness is made by using I-shaped beam having large load bearing surface for the construction of bridges.

I-shaped girders are commonly used in

→ Residential and commercial constructions

→ Framing in heavy duty automobiles

→ Machine bases

→ Construction of platforms
→ Support frames and columns for trolley ways and lifts

1.11 TWISTING COUPLE ON A CYLINDER OR WIRE-SHAFT

A pair of forces equal in magnitude, but oppositely directed, and displaced by perpendicular distance constitutes a couple. It can also be defined as a system of forces with a resultant moment but without any force acting on it. The resultant moment of a couple is called as torque.

Consider a cylindrical object of length "ℓ" radius "r" and shear modulus "G". Its upper end is fixed and a couple is applied in a plane perpendicular to its length at lower end as shown in Figure 1.16 (a). Consider this cylinder is consisting large number of co-axial hollow cylinders. Now, consider a one hollow cylinder of radius 'x' and radial thickness 'dx' as shown in Figure1.16 (b). Let 'θ' is the twisting angle. The displacement is greatest at the rim and decreases as the center is approached where it becomes zero.

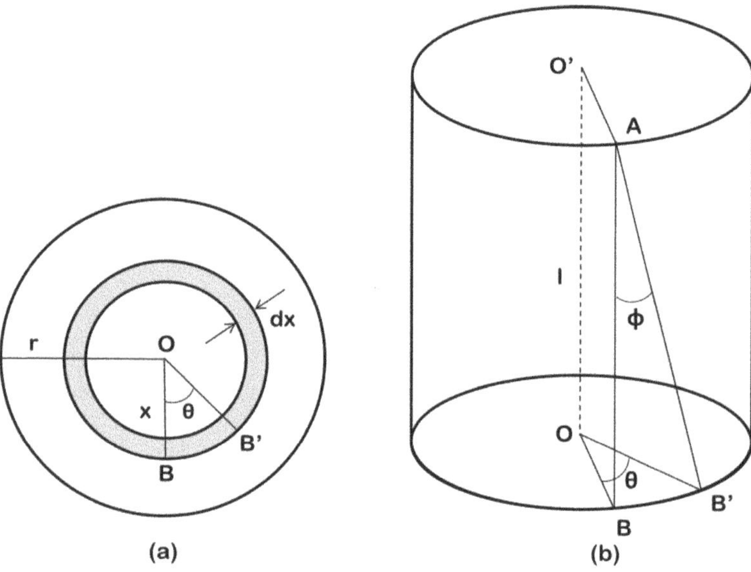

Figure 1.16: Twisting couple of a cylinder.

Now we can write

$$BB' = \ell\emptyset = x\theta$$

$$\therefore \emptyset = \frac{x\theta}{\ell} \qquad \textbf{(1.14)}$$

The shear modules can be given as

$$\text{Shear modulus (G)} = \frac{\text{Shear stress (T)}}{\text{Shear strain }(\emptyset)}$$

$$\therefore \text{Shear stress (T)} = G\emptyset = \frac{Gx\theta}{\ell} \qquad \textbf{(1.15)}$$

$$\text{But Shear stress (T)} = \frac{\text{Sheaing force}}{\text{Surface area over which force acts}}$$

Here in this case the surface area over which force acts can be given as 2πxdx.

$$\therefore \text{Sheaing force} = 2\pi x dx\ \frac{Gx\theta}{\ell}$$

$$\therefore \text{Sheaing force} = \frac{2\pi G\theta}{\ell} x^2 dx$$

The moment of this force can be given as

$$= \frac{2\pi G\theta}{\ell} x^2 dx \cdot x$$

$$= \frac{2\pi G\theta}{\ell} x^3 dx \qquad (1.16)$$

Integrating eqn.1.16 over a range from x = 0 to x = r we will get a total twisting couple on a cylinder

$$= \int_0^r \frac{2\pi G\theta}{\ell} x^3 dx$$

$$= \frac{2\pi G\theta}{\ell} \left[\frac{x^4}{4}\right]_0^r$$

$$\therefore \text{Total twisting couple} = \frac{\pi G\theta r^4}{2\ell}$$

Therefore twisting couple per unit twist (θ = 1) is

$$\therefore \mathbf{C} = \frac{\pi G r^4}{2\ell} \qquad (1.17)$$

This twisting couple per unit twist is also called the torsional rigidity of the cylinder or wire.

1.12 TORSIONAL PENDULUM

A heavy cylindrical rod or disc, suspended from the end of a fine wire, whose upper end is fixed, is called torsional pendulum.

If rod or disc is turned, the wire will twist and when released, it executes torsional vibrations about the axis. Let θ be the twisting angle.

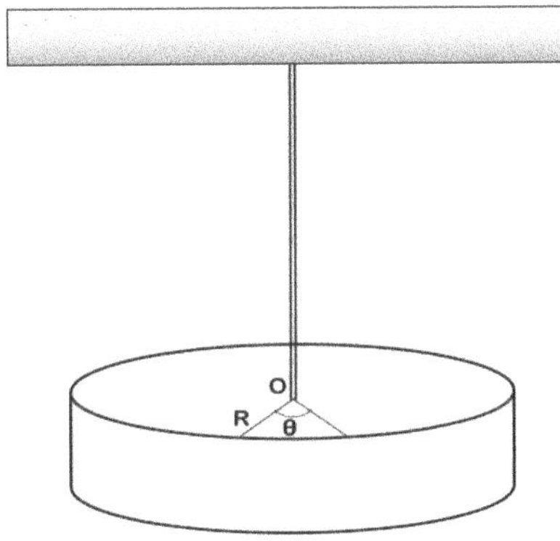

Figure 1.17: Torsional pendulum.

Then the restoring couple set up in it is.

$$\text{Total twisting couple } (C\theta) = \frac{\pi G\theta r^4}{2\ell}$$

This produces an angular acceleration

$$I\frac{d\omega}{dt} = -C\theta$$

Here 'I' is the momentum of inertia of cylindrical rod or disc. And negative sign indicates the restoring couple.

$$\therefore \frac{d\omega}{dt} = \frac{-C\theta}{I}$$

Now the motion of the rod or disc is simple harmonic. Its time period is given by

$$T = 2\pi\sqrt{\frac{\text{displacement}}{\text{angular acceleration}}}$$

$$\therefore T = 2\pi\sqrt{\frac{\theta}{C\theta/I}}$$

$$\therefore \mathbf{T = 2\pi\sqrt{\frac{I}{C}}} \qquad \mathbf{(1.18)}$$

This is called the equation of time period for torsional pendulum.

-: POINTS TO REMEMBER :-

→ Stress is the restoring force per unit area developed in the object to oppose the deformation of object under external force.

$$\textbf{Stress} = \frac{\text{restoring force}}{\text{area of cross-section}} \frac{\text{deforming force}}{\text{area of cross-section}} = \frac{F}{A}$$

Unit of stress are $N{\cdot}m^{-2}$ and Pa. It is denoted by the symbol "σ".

→ Strain in a material is defined as the ratio of change in dimension to the original dimension of object under external force.

Strain is a dimensionless quantity. It is denoted by the symbol "ε".

→ Hooke's Law states that Strain is Proportional to the Stress which produced it.

$$k = \frac{\text{Stress}}{\text{Strain}}$$

Here the constant 'k' is coefficient of elasticity and is known as modulus of elasticity. Its units are $N{\cdot}m^{-2}$ and Pa.

→ For small change in the length of the wire, the ratio of the longitudinal stress to the corresponding strain is called the Young's modulus of elasticity (Y) of the wire.

$$Y = \frac{\text{longitudinal stress}}{\text{longitudinal strain}} = \frac{F/A}{\Delta L/L} = \frac{FL}{A\Delta L} = \frac{MgL}{\pi r^2 \Delta L}$$

→ For small strain in the ratio of the shearing stress to the shearing strain is called the Shear modulus (G) of the material of the body.

$$G = \frac{\text{Shearing stress}}{\text{Shearing strain}} = \frac{F/A}{\theta}$$

→ For small strains, the ratio of the volume stress to the volume strain is called Bulk modulus (K).

$$K = \frac{\text{Volume stress}}{\text{Volume strain}} = \frac{F/A}{\Delta V/V} = \frac{PV}{\Delta V}$$

→ The reciprocal of the Bulk modulus of the material of a body is called the "compressibility' of that material.

→ The Young's modulus of rectangular beam can be given as

$$\textbf{in case of uniform bending of rectangular beam} \Rightarrow \therefore Y = \frac{3mgal^2}{2ybd^3}$$

$$\textbf{in case of uniform bending of circular beam} \Rightarrow \therefore Y = \frac{mgal^2}{2y\pi r^4}$$

$$\text{in case of non – uniform bending of rectangular beam} \Rightarrow \therefore Y = \frac{mgL^3}{4ybd^3}$$

$$\text{in case of non – uniform bending of circular beam} \Rightarrow \therefore Y = \frac{mgL^3}{12y\pi r^4}$$

→ Twisting couple per unit twist (θ=1) of a wire is given by

$$C = \frac{\pi G r^4}{2l}$$

This twisting couple per unit twist is also called the torsional rigidity of the cylinder or wire.

→ The equation of time period for torsional pendulum is given by.

$$T = 2\pi\sqrt{\frac{I}{C}}$$

-: SOLVED NUMERICALS :-

1) One end of a 1 m long wire having radius 1 mm is clamped to a rigid support and a mass 10 kg is attached at the other end. Due to this its length is increased by 10 mm then find the Young's modulus of this wire.

Given: M = 10 kg, L = 1m

r = 1 mm = 1x 10^{-3} m ΔL = 10 mm = 1x 10^{-2} m

Y = ?

Solution:

Young's modulus of a wire can be given as

$$Y = \frac{MgL}{\pi r^2 \Delta L}$$

$$\therefore Y = \frac{10 \times 9.8 \times 1}{\pi \times 1x\,10^{-6} \times 1x\,10^{-2}}$$

$$\therefore Y = \frac{98}{3.14x\,10^{-8}}$$

$$\therefore Y = \frac{98}{3.14x\,10^{-8}}$$

$$\boxed{\therefore Y = 3.12x\,10^9\ N \cdot m^{-2}}$$

2) Calculate the twisting couple on a solid shaft of length 1.5 m and diameter 120 mm when it is twisted through an angle 0.6°. The coefficient of rigidity for the material of the shaft may be taken to be 93X10^9 N/m^2.

Given: G = 93 x 10^9 N/m^2 θ = 0.6° = (0.6xπ)/180 rad

r = 60 mm = 6 x 10^{-2} m l = 1.5 mm

C = ?

Solution:

Twisting couple of a wire is given by

$$C = \frac{\pi G \theta r^4}{2l}$$

$$\therefore C = \frac{3.14\ x\ 93x10^9\ x\ 0.6x\pi\ x\ 1296x10^{-16}}{2\ x\ 1.5\ x\ 180}$$

$$\therefore C = \frac{7.14x10^{-2}}{540}$$

$\boxed{C = 1.32 x 10^4 \ N \cdot m}$

3) A sphere of mass 0.8 kg and radius 0.03 m is suspended from a wire of length 1 m and radius 5 x 10^{-4} m. If the period of torsional oscillations of this system is 1.23 sec. calculate the modulus of rigidity of the wire.

Given: m = 0.8 kg R= 0.03 m
r = 5 x 10^{-4} m l = 1 mm
T = 1.23 S G = ?

Solution:

→ Twisting couple per unit twist of a wire is given by $\mathbf{C = \frac{\pi G r^4}{2l}}$

→ Time period of a torsional pendulum is given by $\therefore \mathbf{T = 2\pi\sqrt{\frac{I}{C}}}$

→ Moment of inertia of a sphere is given by $\therefore \mathbf{I = \frac{2}{5}mR^2}$

Therefore we can write

$$T = 2\pi\sqrt{\frac{I}{C}} = 2\pi\sqrt{\frac{2}{5}mR^2 \times \frac{2l}{\pi \cdot G \cdot r^4}}$$

$$\boxed{\therefore G = 76517 \, X \, 10^6 \ N \cdot m}$$

4) A rectangular rod of 2 mm thickness and 25 mm breadth rests on two knife-edges 0.8 m apart and a load of 1 kg is suspended from its mid-point. Neglecting the weight of the rod, calculate the depression of the mid-point if Y for its material be 2.04x10^{11} N/m^2.

Given: Y = 2.04 x 10^{11} N/m^2 m = 1 kg
L = 0.8 m b = 0.025 m
d = 0.002 m y = ?

Solution:

The Young's modulus of a rectangular beam supported at two ends and loaded at center is given by

$$\mathbf{Y = \frac{mgL^3}{4ybd^3}}$$

$$\therefore 2.04 \times 10^{11} = \frac{1 \times 9.8 \times 0.8^3}{4 \times y \times 0.025 \times 0.002^3}$$

$$\therefore y = \frac{1 \times 9.8 \times 0.8^3}{4 \times 2.04 \times 10^{11} \times 0.025 \times 0.002^3}$$

$$\therefore y = \frac{5.02}{163.2}$$

$$\boxed{\therefore y = 0.031 \ m}$$

5) A solid rectangular metal sheet with dimensions are 2.51 X 37.95 cm and weighing 826 gm is suspended from the middle of its length by a wire of 37.85 cm length and 0.0501 cm radius. It is observed to make 50 compete swings in 335.7 sec. What is the rigidity coefficient of the wire?

Given: B = 2.51 x 10^{-3} m L = 37.95 x 10^{-3} m
m = 0.826 kg l = 37.85 x 10^{-2} m
r = 0.501 x 10^{-4} m T = 335.7/50 = 6.714 S
G = ?

Solution:

→ Moment of Inertia of a rectangular bar can be given as;

$$\mathbf{I = m\left(\frac{L^2+B^2}{12}\right)}$$

$$\therefore I = 0.826\left(\frac{(37.95\times10^{-2})^2+(2.51\times10^{-2})^2}{12}\right)$$

$$\therefore \mathbf{I = 99 \times 10^{-4}\ kg \cdot m^2}$$

→ Time period of a torsional pendulum is given by

$$\mathbf{T = 2\pi\sqrt{\frac{I}{C}}}$$

$$\therefore 6.714 = 2\pi\sqrt{\frac{99\times10^{-4}}{C}}$$

$$\therefore C = 86.61 \times 10^{-4}\ \frac{kg\cdot m^2}{S}$$

→ Now the twisting couple of a wire per unit twist is given by

$$\mathbf{C = \frac{\pi G r^4}{2l}}$$

$$\therefore 86.61 \times 10^{-4} = \frac{\pi \times G \times (0.501 \text{ x } 10^{-4})^4\cdot}{2 \times 37.85 \text{ x } 10^{-2}}$$

$$\therefore G = \frac{86.61\times10^{-4} \times 2\times37.85 \text{ x } 10^{-2}}{3.14\times (0.501 \text{ x } 10^{-2})^4}$$

$$\boxed{\therefore G = 3.314 \text{ x } 10^{10}\ N \cdot m^{-2}}$$

-: UNSOLVED NUMERICALS :-

1. Calculate the mass required to be suspended to stretch a steel wire of 4 m length and 2 mm diameter up to 1 mm? Young's modulus of steel is $2\text{x}10^{12}$ dyne·cm^{-2}. (Consider g=981 gm·cm^{-2})
   (Ans: 16.012 kg)
2. What is the percentage increase in length of a wire of 3 mm diameter, when stretched by a force of 200 kg. Young's modulus of the wire is $12.5\text{x}10^{11}$ dyne·cm^{-2}.
   (Ans: 0.055 %)
3. How much force is required to stretch a steel wire to double its length when its area of cross section is 2 cm^2 and Young's modulus is $2\text{x}10^{11}$ N·m^{-2}?
   (Ans: 4 x 10^7 N)
4. A uniform metal disc of diameter 0.1 m and mass 1.2 kg is fixed symmetrically to the lower end of a torsion wire of length 1 m and diameter 1.44 x 10^{-3} m whose upper end is fixed. The time period of torsional oscillations is 1.98 sec. Calculate the modulus of the rigidity of the material of the wire.
   (Ans. : 3.55 x 10^{10} N/m^2)
5. What couple must be applied to a wire, 1 meter long, 1 mm diameter, in order to twist one end of it through 90°, the other end remaining fixed? The rigidity modulus is 2.8 x 10^{11} dynes·cm^{-2}.
   (Ans. : 4.3 x 10^4 dyne·cm)

-: SHORT QUESTIONS :-

1. Define stress. What is the difference between normal, tensile, compressional and tangential/shearing stress?
2. Define strain. What is the difference between longitudinal/linear, shear and bulk/volumetric strain?
3. State Hooke's law. Give its equation and unit of elastic modulus.
4. What is Young's modulus? Give its equation.
5. What is Bulk modulus? Give its equation.
6. What is modulus of rigidity? Give its equation.
7. Define twisting couple.

8. What is torsional pendulum?
9. Define torsional pendulum and write the expression of its time period.
10. Write the expression of torsional rigidity of wire.
11. Define and explain bending moment.
12. Define: cantilever and bending of beam.
13. What is cantilever? Write expressions for depression of cantilever when the load is fixed at the center for rectangular and circular bar.
14. Define and differentiate between the terms (i) bending of a beam and (ii) Bending moment.
15. Write only the equations for the depression of the mid-point of rectangular and cylindrical beams loaded at the center and supported at ends.

-: DESCRIPTIVE QUESTIONS :-

1. Briefly discuss different types of stress.
2. Briefly discuss different types of strain.
3. Explain briefly the Stress-Strain diagram.
4. Draw the elastic hysteresis curve. Discuss briefly about Elastic after effect, elastic hysteresis and Elastic fatigue.
5. Derive the equation for the couple per unit twist produced in a cylindrical wire or shaft with the help of necessary figures.
6. Derive an expression for periodic time of a torsional pendulum. Discuss applications of torsional pendulum.
7. Derive the equation for the Young's modulus in case of uniform bending of beam having rectangular and circular cross-sections.
8. Derive the equation for the Young's modulus in case of non-uniform bending of beam having rectangular and circular cross-sections.
9. Write a short note on I-shaped girder.

* * * * *

CHAPTER-II WAVES, MOTION & ACOUSTICS

Learning goals:

At the end of this chapter reader will be able to

- ✓ Derive the equations of free, forced and damped equations.
- ✓ Explain different characteristics of Simple Harmonic Motion.
- ✓ Determine the value of gravitational acceleration using simple pendulum.
- ✓ Differentiate between transverse and longitudinal waves.
- ✓ Suggest the remedies for the better acoustics of building by identifying the affecting factors.
- ✓ Explain method for generation and detection of ultrasound.
- ✓ Explain how non-destructive testing are works.

PREREQUISITES:

In physics, mathematics, and related fields, a **wave** is a disturbance (change from equilibrium) of one or more fields such that the field values oscillate repeatedly about a stable equilibrium (resting) value.

Classification of Wave Motion

Based on the Medium of Propagation

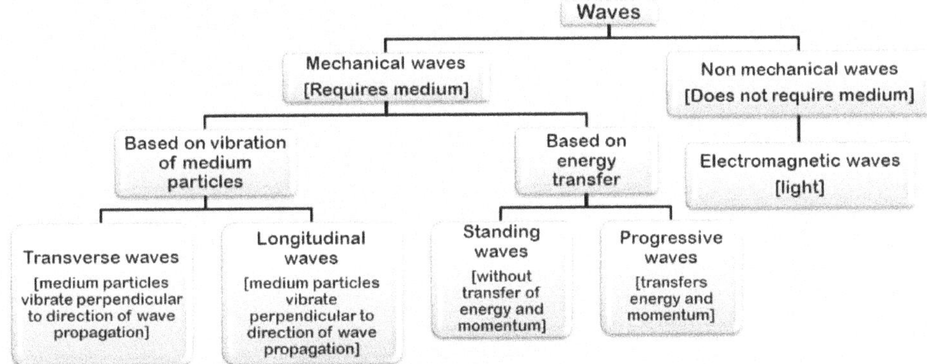

Based on the dimension of Propagation

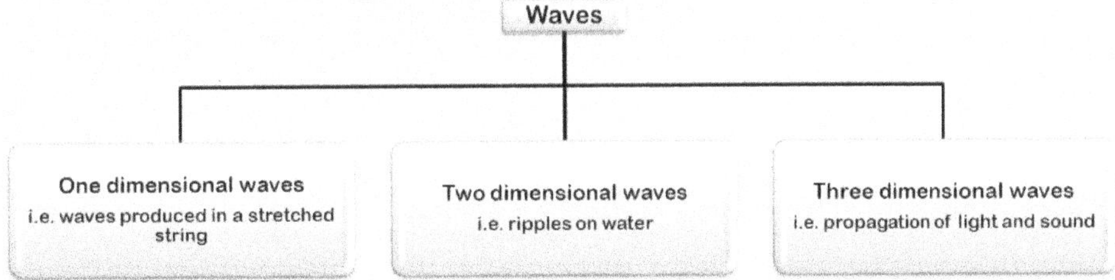

→ **Standing waves (or stationary waves)**

→ **Progressive wave**

If the relative amplitude of oscillation at different points in the field remains constant, the wave is said to be a standing wave. If the relative amplitude of oscillation at different points in the field, changes then wave is said to be a traveling wave or progressive wave.

Mechanical waves (Elastic waves)

Waves that require a medium for their propagation are called mechanical waves or elastic waves. The particles of the medium execute periodic motion about a mean position when the wave propagates through the medium. i.e. waves on a string. A mechanical wave is produced due to a disturbance at a point in a medium. The disturbed particle interacts with the neighbouring particle and its energy is handed over to the next particle (due to the inertia of the medium). The disturbed particles retune to the equilibrium position (due to the elasticity of medium).

Non-Mechanical Waves

Waves which do not require a medium for their propagation are called a non-mechanical wave. These types of waves can propagate through vacuum also. i.e. Electromagnetic waves and matter waves.

Motion

In physics, motion is the change in the position of an object over time. Motion is mathematically described in terms of displacement, distance, velocity, acceleration, speed, and time.

Oscillation/oscillatory motion

Oscillatory motion is a type of motion that can occur when a body is subjected to a force that varies with time.

Harmonic motion

Any motion that repeats itself at regular interval according to sinusoidal law is called harmonic motion.

Sound

In physics, sound is a vibration that propagates as an acoustic wave, through a transmission medium such as a gas, liquid or solid. In human physiology and psychology, sound is the reception of such waves and their perception by the brain. In a simple way sound is a vibration in an elastic medium with definite frequency & intensity which can be heard by the human ear.

Classification of sound

On the basis of frequency 'f' sound waves are classified into three types.

→ Infra sound - ($f < 20$ Hz)

→ Audible sound - ($20Hz < f < 20KHz$)

→ Ultra sound - ($f > 20KHz$)

Classification of audible sound

The audible sounds are generally classified into two categories.

1. Musical sound
2. Noise

Musical sound

The sound which produces pleasing effect on ear is called musical sound. e.g. Sounds produced by musical instruments like sitar, violin, flute, piano etc. The musical sound wave forms are regular in shape, have definite periodicity & they do not undergo a sudden change in amplitude as shown in figure below.

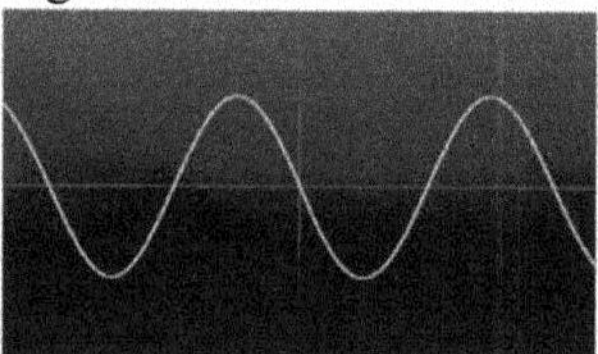

Noise

The sound that produces a jarring effect on the ear & unpleasant sound to ear is called Noise. e.g. Sound produced by aeroplane, road traffic, crackers, etc. The Noise wave form are irregular in shape, do not have definite periodicity & they undergo sudden change in amplitudes as shown in figure below.

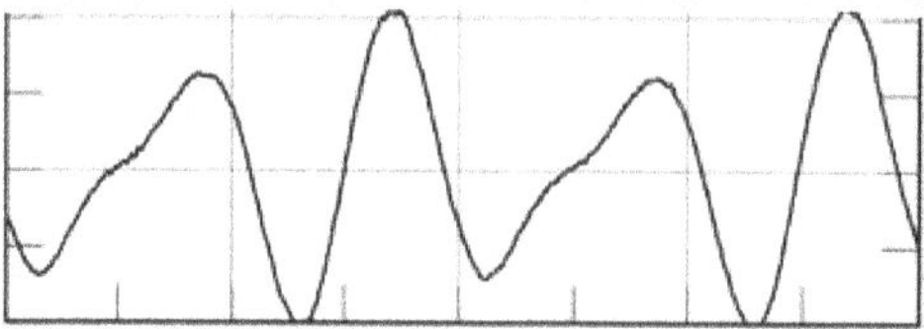

Characteristics of musical sound:

The characteristics of musical sounds are

→ Pitch – related to frequency of sound.

→ Loudness – related to intensity of sound.

→ Timbre – related to quality of sound.

Pitch

It is a sensation that depends upon the frequency. Pitch helps in distinguishing a note of high frequency & low frequency (i.e. it helps to distinguish a shrill sound from a flat sound.) sound of the same intensity produced by the same musical instrument. A shrill sound is produced by a sound of high frequency.

The voice produced by ladies & children are of high pitch type because, the frequency is high. Similarly, the sound produced by a bee or mosquito is of high pitch due to high frequency.

Thus, greater the frequency of a sound, the higher is the pitch & vice-versa. The pitch of sound changes due to doppler's principle when either the source or the observer or both are in motion.

Loudness

Loudness is a characteristic which is common to all sound whether classified as musical sound or noise. Loudness is a degree of sensation produced on ear. Thus, loudness varies from one listener to another. The loudness depends upon intensity & also upon the sensitiveness of the ear.

Loudness & intensity are related to each other by the relation.

$$\mathbf{L \propto \log_{10} I}$$
$$\mathbf{or\ L = K \log_{10} I}$$

Here K is a constant.

From this relation it is seen that, loudness is directly proportional to the logarithm of intensity, & is known as Weber-Fechner law.

From the above equation, dL/dI = K/I. Where, dL/dI is called as sensitiveness of ear. Therefore, sensitiveness decreases with increase of intensity. Loudness is a physiological quantity.

Timbre

It is the quality of sound which enables us to distinguish between two sounds having the same loudness & pitch. It depends on the presents of overtones. It helps us to distinguish between musical notes emitted by different musical instruments & voices of different person; even though, the sounds have same pitch & loudness.

Intensity

Intensity I of sound wave at a point is defined as the amount of sound energy Q flowing per unit area in unit time when the surface is held normal to the direction of the propagation of sound wave.

$$\mathbf{I = \frac{Q}{At}}$$

The intensity is a physical quantity which depend upon the factors like amplitude 'A', frequency 'f' & velocity 'v' of sound together with the density of the medium 'ρ'.

Therefore the Intensity I in a medium is given by

$$\mathbf{I = 2\pi^2 f^2 A^2 \rho v}$$

The unit of intensity is Wm^{-2}.

The minimum sound intensity which a human ear can sense is called the threshold intensity. Its value is 10^{-12} W/m^2. If the intensity is less than this value then our ear can't hear the sound.

This minimum intensity is also known as Zero or standard intensity. The intensity of a sound is measured with reference to the standard intensity.

Intensity level (relative intensity) I_L

The intensity level or relative intensity of a sound is defined as the logarithmic ratio of intensity I of a sound to the standard intensity I_0.

$$\mathbf{I_L = K \log_{10}\left(\frac{I}{I_0}\right)}$$

Let I & I_0 represents intensities of two sounds of a particular frequency; & L_1 & L_0 be their corresponding measures of loudness. Then, according to weber-fechner law,

$$\mathbf{L_1 = K \log_{10} I}$$
$$\mathbf{L_0 = K \log_{10} I_0}$$

Therefore, the intensity level or relative intensity is

$$\mathbf{I_L = L_1 - L_0}$$
$$\mathbf{\therefore I_L = K \log_{10} I - K \log_{10} I_0}$$
$$\mathbf{\therefore I_L = K \log_{10}\left(\frac{I}{I_0}\right)}$$

If K=1, then I_L is expressed in a unit called Bel.

From the above relation, it is seen that, 10 times larger intensity than standard intensity i.e. $I=10I_0$ corresponds to intensity level by 1 bel. Similarly, 100 times larger intensity than standard intensity, i.e. $I = 100I_0$ corresponds to 2 bel & 1000 times larger intensity than standard intensity, i.e. $I= 1000I_0$ corresponds to 3 bel & so on...

In practice, bel is the large unit. Hence, another unit known as decibel dB is more often used.

$$\mathbf{1Bel = 10dB}$$

$$\therefore I_L = 10 \log_{10}\left(\frac{I}{I_0}\right) \text{ dB}$$

Distinction between loudness & intensity:

Sr.	Loudness	Intensity
1.	It is a degree of sensation produced on the ear.	It is the quantity of sound energy flowing across unit area in unit time.
2.	It varies from listener to listener.	It is independent of listener.
3.	It is a physiological quantity.	It is physical quantity.
4.	Its unit is sone.	Its unit is $W{\cdot}m^{-2}$.

Echo

In audio signal processing and acoustics, **echo** is a reflection of sound that arrives at the listener with a delay after the direct sound. The delay is directly proportional to the distance of the reflecting surface from the source and the listener. Typical examples are the echo produced by the bottom of a well, by a building, or by the walls of an enclosed room and an empty room.

2.1 INTRODUCTION

Acoustics is the physics of sound, including all of the multiphysics disciplines concerned with the production, transmission, and detection of the sound signal. Sound means not only what is detected by the human ear but also infrasound and ultrasound; that is, wave propagation with frequencies below and above the human auditory range. The definition of sound also includes the propagation in media other than air. This could be elastic waves in solids (vibrations); pressure waves in liquids, like underwater acoustics; or the combined propagation in porous materials (poroelastic waves). For humans, sound is best understood as the sensation, as detected by the ear, of very small rapid changes in the acoustic pressure above and below a static value. This static value is the atmospheric pressure. This is hearing.

The purpose of this chapter is to give an introduction to fundamental acoustic concepts and to the physical principles of wave motion.

2.2 SIMPLE HARMONIC MOTION

A motion of a system in which acceleration of the system, and net force acting on the system, is proportional to the displacement and acts in the opposite direction of the displacement is called simple harmonic motion.

A good example of SHM is an object with mass 'm' attached to a spring on a frictionless surface, as shown in Figure 2.1. The object oscillates around the equilibrium position, and the net force on the object is equal to the force provided by the spring. This force obeys Hooke's law

$$F_s = -kx \tag{2.1}$$

If the net force can be described by Hooke's law and there is no damping (slowing down due to friction or other non-conservative forces), then a simple harmonic oscillator oscillates with equal displacement on either side of the equilibrium position. The maximum displacement from equilibrium is called the amplitude 'A'.

What is so significant about SHM? For one thing, the period 'T' and frequency 'f' of a simple harmonic oscillator are independent of amplitude. The string of a guitar, for example, oscillates with the same frequency whether plucked gently or hard.

Two important factors do affect the period of a simple harmonic oscillator. The period is related to how stiff the system is. A very stiff object has a large force constant 'k', which causes the system to have a smaller period. For example, you can adjust a diving board's stiffness, the stiffer it is, the faster it vibrates, and the shorter its period. Period also depends on the mass of the oscillating system. The more massive the system is, the longer the period. For example, a heavy person on a diving board bounces up and down more slowly than a light one. In fact, the mass 'm' and the force constant 'k' are the only factors that affect the period and frequency of SHM. To derive an equation for the period and the frequency, we must first define and analyze the equations of motion.

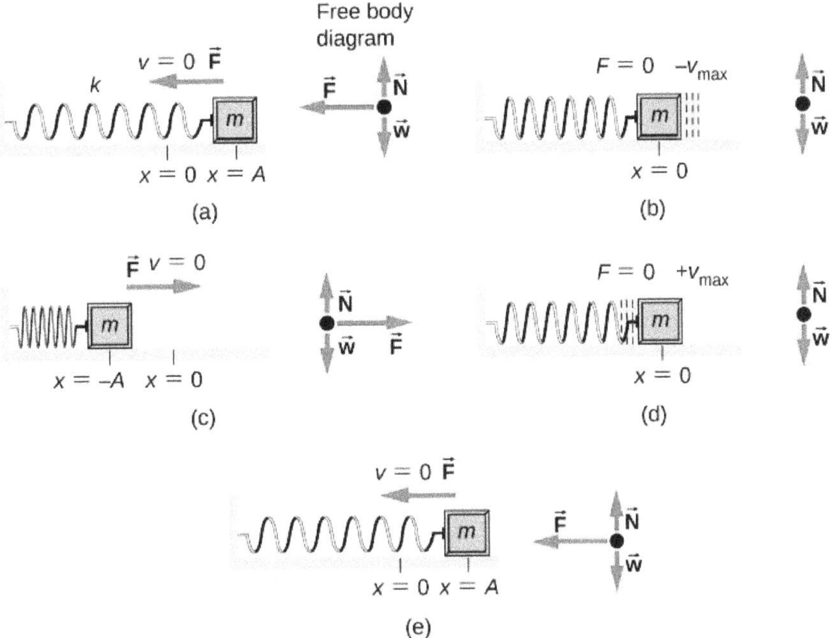

Figure 2.1: **An object attached to a spring sliding on a frictionless surface is an uncomplicated simple harmonic oscillator. In the above set of figures, a mass is attached to a spring and placed on a frictionless table. The other end of the spring is attached to the wall. The position of the mass, when the spring is neither stretched nor compressed, is marked as x=0 and is the equilibrium position.**

(a) The mass is displaced to a position x=A and released from rest.

(b) The mass accelerates as it moves in the negative x-direction, reaching a maximum negative velocity at x=0.

(c) The mass continues to move in the negative x-direction, slowing until it comes to a stop at x=-A.

(d) The mass now begins to accelerate in the positive x-direction, reaching a positive maximum velocity at x=0.

(e) The mass then continues to move in the positive direction until it stops at x=A. The mass continues in SHM that has an amplitude A and a period T. The object's maximum speed occurs as it passes through equilibrium. The stiffer the spring is, the smaller the period T. The greater the mass of the object is, the greater the period T.

2.2.1 EQUATIONS OF SHM

Consider a block attached to a spring on a frictionless table (Figure 2.2). The equilibrium position (the position where the spring is neither stretched nor compressed) is marked as x=0. At the equilibrium position, the net force is zero.

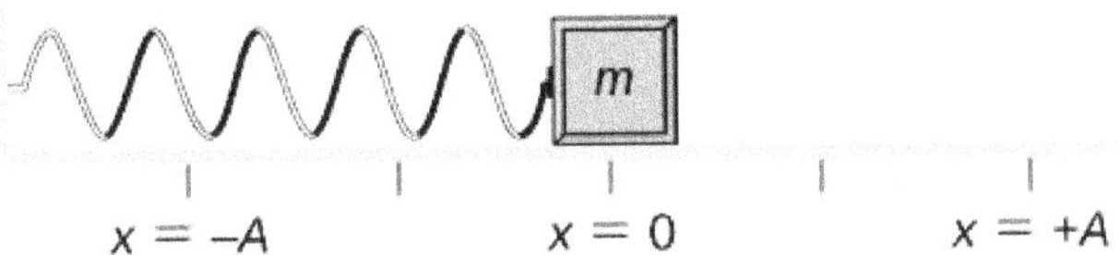

Figure 2.2: **A block is attached to a spring and placed on a frictionless table. The equilibrium position, where the spring is neither extended nor compressed, is marked asx=0.**

Work is done on the block to pull it out to a position of x=+A, and it is then released from rest. The maximum *x*-position 'A' is called the amplitude of the motion. The block begins to oscillate in SHM between x = +A and x = −A. Figure 2.3 shows the motion of the block as it completes one and a half oscillations after release.

The sinusoidal function is seen to repeat at every multiple of 2π, whereas the motion of the block repeats after every period 'T'. However, the function $\sin(\frac{2\pi}{T}t)$ repeats every integer multiple of the period, maximum of the sine function is one, so it is necessary to multiply the sine function by the amplitude 'A' to obtain the displacement at any time 't'.

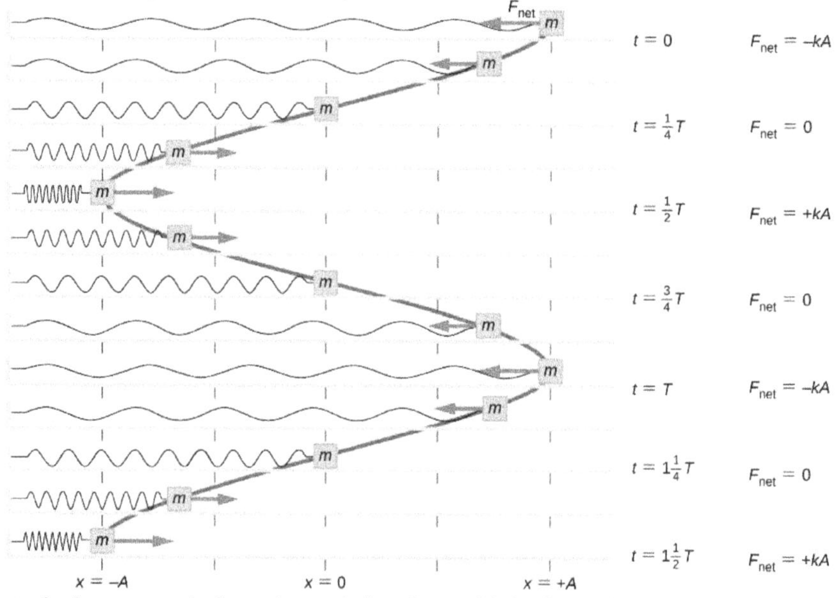

Figure 2.3: **A block is attached to one end of a spring and placed on a frictionless table. The other end of the spring is anchored to the wall. The equilibrium position, where the net force equals zero, is marked as x=0. Work is done on the block, while pulling it out to x=+A, and the block is released from rest. The block oscillates between x=+A and x=-A.**

$$x(t) = A\sin\left(\frac{2\pi}{T}t\right) \tag{2.2}$$

Since the restoring force is proportional to displacement from equilibrium, we can recall Eqn. (2.1) as

$$F = -kx$$
$$\therefore F = ma = -kx$$
$$\therefore m\frac{d^2x}{dt^2} = -kx.$$
$$\therefore m\frac{d^2x}{dt^2} + kx = 0$$

This equation is called the differential equation of simple harmonic motion. It can also be written as,

$$\therefore \frac{d^2x}{dt^2} + \omega^2 x = 0 \tag{2.3}$$

Here $\omega = \sqrt{\frac{k}{m}}$ is called the angular frequency. Time period of oscillation can be given as $T = 2\pi\sqrt{\frac{m}{k}}$.

2.2.2 CHARACTERISTICS OF SHM

Displacement

Simplified general solution of Eqn. (2.3) can be written as,

$$x(t) = A\sin(\omega t + \phi) \tag{2.4}$$

This equation gives the displacement of system from its equilibrium at any instant of time 't'.

Amplitude

Values of displacement obtained from Eqn. (2.4) varies periodically between '+A' and '-A'. Thus 'A' is the maximum value of displacement, called as amplitude of oscillation.

Velocity

By differentiating Eqn. (2.4) we can get the velocity of the system undergoing SHM.

$$v = \frac{dx}{dt} = \omega A\cos(\omega t + \phi) \tag{2.5}$$

Velocity varies between $+\omega A$ and $-\omega A$. When displacement is maximum, velocity is zero and when displacement is zero, velocity is maximum on either side. We can also write from Eqn. (2.5) as,

$$v = \omega A\sqrt{(1 - \sin^2(\omega t + \phi))}$$

$$\therefore v = \omega A\sqrt{\left(1 - \frac{x^2}{A^2}\right)}$$

$$\therefore v = \omega\sqrt{(A^2 - x^2)} \qquad (2.6)$$

$$\therefore v^2 = \omega^2(A^2 - x^2)$$

$$\therefore \frac{v^2}{\omega^2} = (A^2 - x^2)$$

$$\therefore \frac{v^2}{\omega^2 A^2} = \left(1 - \frac{x^2}{A^2}\right)$$

$$\therefore \frac{\mathbf{v^2}}{\boldsymbol{\omega^2 A^2}} + \frac{\mathbf{x^2}}{\mathbf{A^2}} = \mathbf{1} \qquad (2.7)$$

This is the equation of ellipse. It suggest that, the graph of velocity (v) → displacement (x) of a SHM will be ellipse as shown in Figure 2.4.

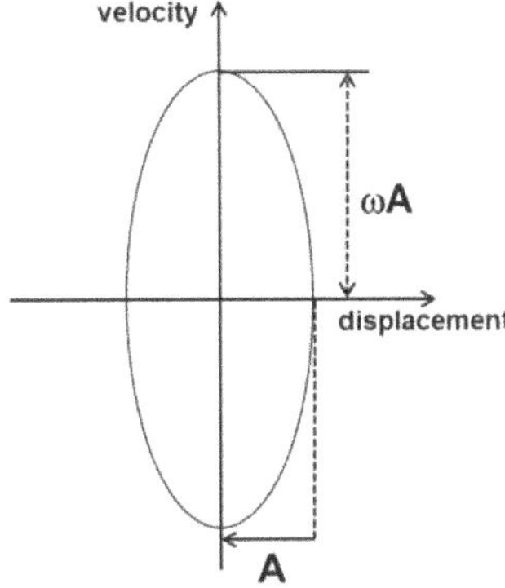

Figure 2.4: Graphical representation of relationship between velocity and displacement of a system undergoing SHM.

Acceleration

By differentiating Eqn. (2.5) we can get the acceleration of the system undergoing SHM.

$$\mathbf{a = \frac{dv}{dt} = -\omega^2 A\sin(\omega t + \phi) = -\omega^2 x} \qquad (2.8)$$

This equation suggest that the acceleration of a system undergoing SHM is proportional and in the opposite direction to the displacement.

Time Period

The time taken by a system to complete one oscillation is called the time period. Therefore time period of SHM is the least time after which the motion will repeat itself. Thus, the motion will repeat itself after nT. where n is an integer. Time period of SHM can be given as,

$$\mathbf{T = 2\pi\sqrt{\frac{m}{k}}}$$

Frequency

Frequency of SHM is the number of oscillations that a system performs per unit time. It is the reciprocal of time period.

$$\mathbf{f = \frac{1}{2\pi}\sqrt{\frac{k}{m}}}$$

Phase

Phase of SHM represents the state of motion of the system by specifying the position and direction of displacement of system. The angle $(\omega t+\Phi)$ is called the phase of oscillation. Φ is called phase constant. The phase constant and amplitude gives the value of displacement of system at time t=0.

Difference between Periodic and Simple Harmonic Motion

Periodic Motion	Simple Harmonic Motion
In the periodic motion, the displacement of the object may or may not be in the direction of the restoring force.	In the simple harmonic motion, the displacement of the object is always in the opposite direction of the restoring force.
The periodic motion may or may not be oscillatory.	Simple harmonic motion is always oscillatory.
Examples are the motion of the hands of a clock, the motion of the wheels of a car, etc.	Examples are the motion of a pendulum, motion of a mass suspended on spring, etc.

2.3 SIMPLE PENDULUM

Simple pendulum is the example of simple harmonic motion. Simple pendulum consists of a mass 'm', called the pendulum bob, attached to the end of a string. The length 'L' of the simple pendulum is measured from the point of suspension of the string to the center of the bob as shown in Figure 2.5.

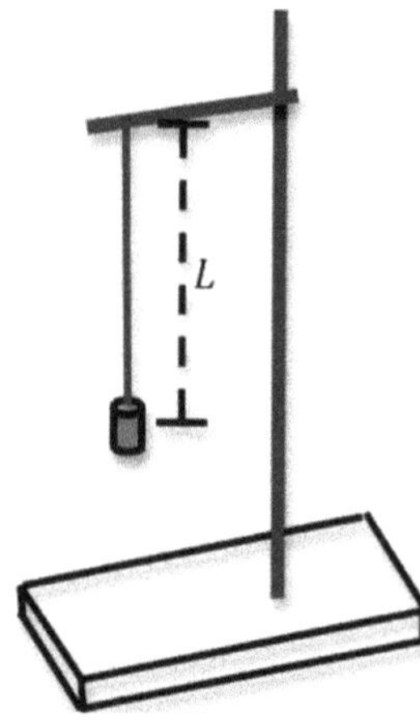

Figure 2.5: Schematic diagram for experimental set-up of a simple pendulum.

If the bob is moved away from the rest position through some angle of displacement 'θ' as shown in Figure 2.6, the restoring force will return the bob back to the equilibrium position. The forces acting on the bob are the force of gravity and the tension force of the string. The tension force of the string is balanced by the component of the gravitational force that is in line with the string (i.e. perpendicular to the motion of the bob). The restoring force here is the tangential component of the gravitational force.

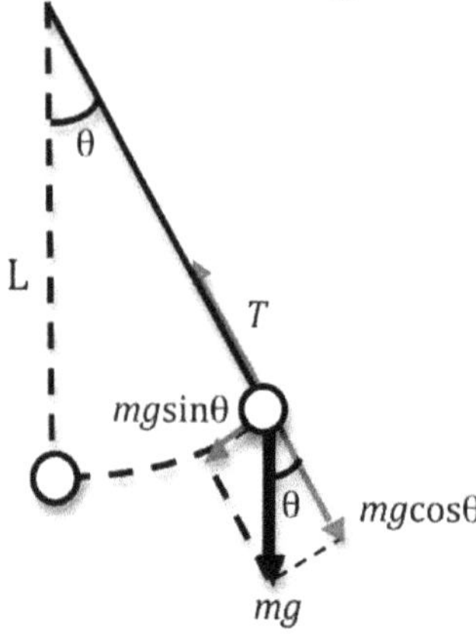

Figure 2.6: Free body diagram of simple pendulum.

When we apply trigonometry to the smaller triangle in Figure 8, we get the magnitude of the restoring force $|F| = \mathbf{mg\ sin\theta}$. This force depends on the mass of the bob, the acceleration due to gravity '**g**', and the sine of the angle through which the string has been pulled. Again Newton's second law must apply, so

$$\mathbf{F = -mg\,sin\theta}$$

where the negative sign implies that the restoring force acts opposite to the direction of motion of the bob. For a small value of 'θ' we can write sinθ≈θ.

$\therefore \mathbf{F = -mg\theta = -mg\frac{x}{L}}$

The force constant can be given as $\mathbf{k = \frac{mg}{L}}$. Therefore the angular frequency can be given as,

$$\omega = \sqrt{\frac{k}{m}} = \sqrt{\frac{g}{L}} \quad \text{(2.9)}$$

Therefore corresponding frequency and time period of a simple pendulum can be given as,

$$\mathbf{f = \frac{\omega}{2\pi} = \frac{1}{2\pi}\sqrt{\frac{g}{L}}} \quad \text{(2.10)}$$

$$\mathbf{T = \frac{1}{f} = 2\pi\sqrt{\frac{L}{g}}} \quad \text{(2.11)}$$

2.4 FREE, DAMPED AND FORCED OSCILLATIONS

Any object executing simple harmonic motion may be called as harmonic oscillator.

2.4.1 Free oscillations

A system is said to be executing free oscillation if it oscillate with its natural frequency. The natural frequency of oscillations of an oscillator depends upon its mass, dimensions and the restoring force. Further natural frequency is independent of the initial displacement or amplitude. A few examples of free oscillations are: (i) A tuning fork, when set into vibration executes free vibration. (ii) The spring of a Sonometer or a Sitar when plucked and released, execute free vibration.

Thus we can define free oscillations as the oscillations that appear in a system as a result of a single initial deviation of a system from its equilibrium state.

We can also define natural frequency as the frequency with which the system oscillates freely at its own.

Thus if no resistance is offered to the motion of any oscillating system by air friction or other forces, the system will continue to oscillate indefinitely at its natural frequency. Such an oscillator is called ideal oscillator. The period of oscillations of an ideal oscillator is independent of the amplitude and is a characteristic property of the oscillation. The ideal systems are frictionless and energy is not dissipated and hence the total mechanical energy and amplitude of the system remains constant. The equation for free oscillations is nothing but the differential equation of simple harmonic motion as described in Eqn. (2.3).

2.4.2 Damped oscillations

Eqn. (2.3) describes a periodic motion that will last forever. This is true if the only force acting on the mass is the restoring force spring 'F_s'. Most motions in nature do not have such simple "free" oscillations. It is more likely there will be some kind of friction or resistance to damp out the free motion. Thus the forces acting on a system executing damped oscillation can be given as follows:

1. A restoring force (F_1=-kx) proportional to and oppositely directed to the displacement.
2. A frictional force (F_2=-bv) proportional to and oppositely directed to the velocity.

Therefore the total force acting on the system can be given as,

$F = ma = F_1 + F_2 = -kx - bv$

$\therefore m\frac{d^2x}{dt^2} = -kx - b\frac{dx}{dt}$

$$\therefore m\frac{d^2x}{dt^2} + b\frac{dx}{dt} + kx = 0$$

$$\therefore \frac{d^2x}{dt^2} + \frac{b}{m}\frac{dx}{dt} + \frac{k}{m}x = 0$$

$$\therefore \frac{d^2x}{dt^2} + \gamma\frac{dx}{dt} + \omega_0^2 x = 0 \tag{2.12}$$

Here $\gamma = {}^{b}/_{m}$ is the damping coefficient of the system and $\omega_0 = \sqrt{{}^{k}/_{m}}$ is the natural frequency of the system. A simple sinusoid will not satisfy this equation. In fact, the form of the solution is strongly dependent upon the value of γ.

If $\gamma > 2\omega_0$, the system is "over damped" and the mass will not oscillate. The solution will be a sum of two decaying exponentials.

If $\gamma = 2\omega_0$, the system is "critically damped" and, again, no oscillations occur. The solution is a simple decaying exponential. Shock absorbers in cars are so constructed that the damping is nearly critical. One does not increase the damping beyond critical because the ride would feel too hard.

For sufficiently small damping $\gamma < 2\omega_0$, the solution is expressed as;

$$A_0 e^{\frac{-\gamma t}{2}} \cos(\omega_d t + \phi) \tag{2.13}$$

and the angular frequency is expressed as;

$$\omega_d = \sqrt{\omega_0^2 - \left(\frac{\gamma}{2}\right)^2} \tag{2.14}$$

Here ω_d is damping frequency. Note that damping frequency is smaller than the natural frequency. For small damping one may neglect the shift. Decay of amplitude with time in damped oscillation is shown in Figure 2.7.

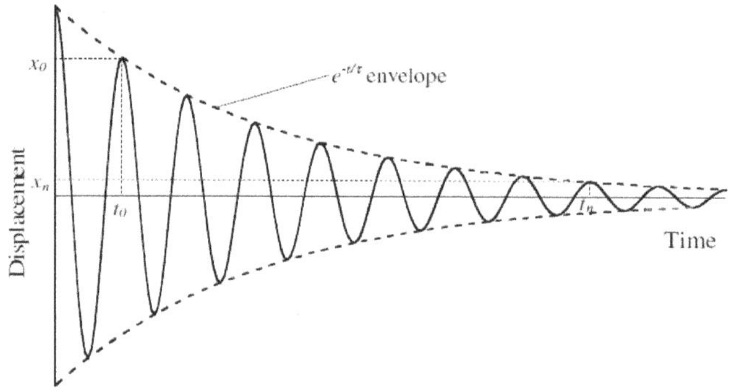

Figure 2.7: Amplitude behaviour with time in damped oscillation.

2.4.3 Forced oscillations

The oscillations produced by an oscillator under the effect of an external periodic force of frequency other than the natural frequency of the oscillator are called forced oscillations. Examples of forced oscillations are: (i) The sound box of a violin execute force oscillations, (ii) When the system of a vibrating tuning fork is passed against the table top, it starts vibrating with the frequency of vibration of tuning fork.

Thus the forces acting on a system executing forced oscillation can be given as follows:

1. A restoring force ($F_1 = -kx$) proportional to and oppositely directed to the displacement.
2. A frictional force ($F_2 = -bv$) proportional to and oppositely directed to the velocity.
3. A driving force (external periodic force) ($F_3 = F_0 \sin\omega_f t$).

Therefore the total force acting on the system can be given as,

$$F = ma = F_1 + F_2 + F_3 = -kx - bv + F_0 \sin\omega_f t$$

$$\therefore m\frac{d^2x}{dt^2} = -kx - b\frac{dx}{dt} + F_0 \sin\omega_f t$$

$$\therefore m\frac{d^2x}{dt^2} + b\frac{dx}{dt} + kx = F_0 \sin\omega_f t$$

$$\therefore \frac{d^2x}{dt^2} + \frac{b}{m}\frac{dx}{dt} + \frac{k}{m}x = \frac{F_0}{m}\sin\omega_f t$$

$$\therefore \frac{d^2x}{dt^2} + \gamma\frac{dx}{dt} + \omega_0^2 x = \frac{F_0}{m}\sin\omega_f t \qquad (2.15)$$

This equation differs from Eqn. (2.12) by the term on the right, which makes it inhomogeneous. The theory of linear differential equations tells us that any solution of the inhomogeneous equation added to any solution of the homogeneous equation will be the general solution.

Solution to the homogeneous equation is called transient solution since for all values of b, the solution damps out to zero rapidly. Solution of the inhomogeneous equation does not vanish and so it is call steady state solution. Solution to the inhomogeneous equation can be written as,

$$x = A\sin(\omega_f t + \delta) \qquad (2.16)$$

Plugging Eqn. (2.16) into Eqn. (2.15), we see that the amplitude of the steady state motion is given by,

$$A = \frac{F_0/m}{\sqrt{\left(\omega^2-\omega_f^2\right)^2+\left(\frac{\omega_f b}{m}\right)^2}} \qquad (2.17)$$

and the phase shift 'δ' is given by,

$$\delta = -\tan^{-1}\left(\frac{\omega_f b/m}{\omega^2-\omega_f^2}\right) \qquad (2.18)$$

Here 'ω' is the free oscillation frequency and 'ω_f' is the driving frequency.

Now consider that the driving frequency goes to zero. There will no phase shift (the displacement is in phase with the driving force) and the amplitude will remain constant. So putting $\omega_f = 0$ in Eqn. (2.17) we get,

$$A = A_0 = \frac{F_0}{m\omega^2} = \frac{F_0}{k} \qquad (2.19)$$

From Eqn. (2.17) and (2.19), we can write the amplitude in terms of the zero frequency extension as,

$$A = \frac{A_0\omega^2}{\sqrt{\left(\omega^2-\omega_f^2\right)^2+\left(\frac{\omega_f b}{m}\right)^2}} \qquad (2.20)$$

For low driving frequencies, the phase shift goes to zero. The displacement will vary as $\sin\omega_f t$ and be in phase with the driving force. The amplitude is close to the zero frequency limit:

$$A(\omega_f < \omega) \approx A_0$$

For very high driving frequencies, the phase shift goes to 180°. The displacement will again vary as $\sin\omega_f t$ but it will be 180° out of phase with the driving force. The amplitude drops off rapidly with increasing frequency.

$$A(\omega_f > \omega) \approx A_0\left(\omega/\omega_f\right)^2$$

At intermediate frequencies, the amplitude reaches a maximum where the denominator of Eqn. (2.17) reaches a minimum. The system is said to be at resonance at this situation. At resonance (actually at ω), the displacement is 90° out of phase with the driving force and the amplitude is given by;

$$A(\omega) = A_0\left(\frac{\omega m}{b}\right)$$

Thus the phenomenon of setting a system of large amplitude into oscillations by the influence of another system oscillating with the same natural frequency is called resonance.

The resonant amplification (also known as "Quality Factor") is defined to be the ratio of the amplitude at resonance to the amplitude in the limit of zero frequency. From Figure 2.8, it is clear that the amplitude is maximum when $\omega_f = \omega$ at all values of quality factor.

$$Q = \frac{A(\omega)}{A_0} = \left(\frac{\omega m}{b}\right)$$

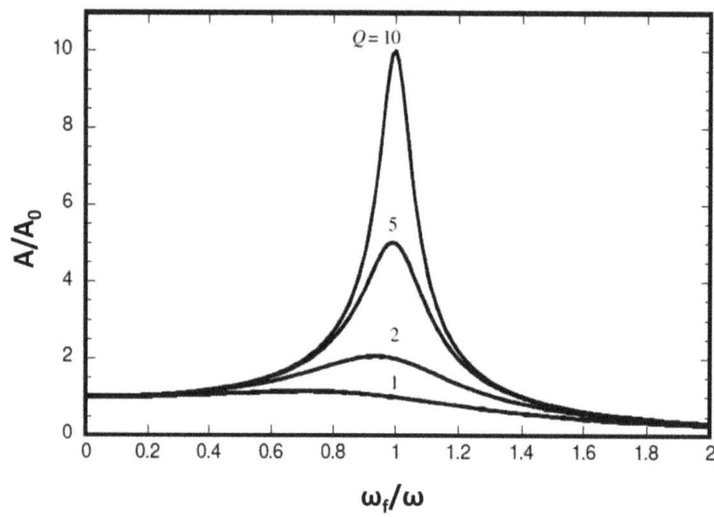

Figure 2.8: A/A_0 Vs ω_f/ω graph at different values of quality factor.

2.5 TRANSVERSE AND LONGITUDINAL WAVES

A wave motion in which particles of the medium oscillates in the direction perpendicular to the direction of propagation of wave is called transverse wave. For example when a rope is laid out horizontally in a room and a motion is introduced on the left end of the rope, then the energy that moves in the rope will move from left to right causing a simultaneous upward and downward movement in the rope. This type of wave created is a transverse wave [Figure 2.9 (b)].

A wave motion in which particles of the medium oscillates in the direction parallel to the direction of propagation of wave is called longitudinal wave [Figure 2.9 (a)]. If a tuning fork is hit against a hollow pipe, the air inside this pipe, which is the medium for the wave, will move in a parallel motion. Sound waves normally travel in longitudinal waves.

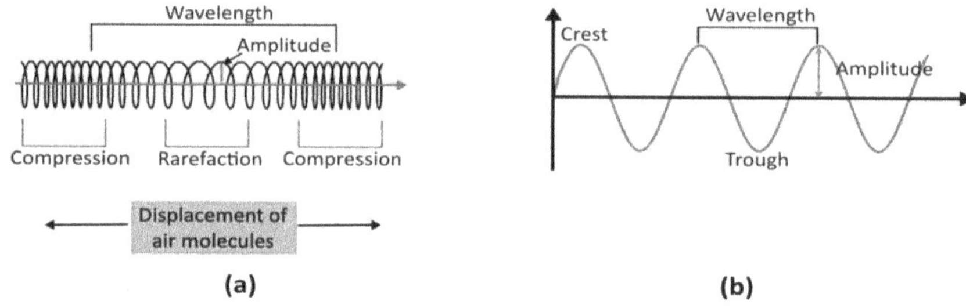

Figure 2.9: wave pattern of (a) Longitudinal wave, (b) Transverse wave.

2.6 SOUND ABSORPTION CO-EFFICIENT (a)

Definition-1: The sound absorption coefficient "a" of a material is defined as the ratio of the sound energy absorbed by it to the total sound energy incident on it.

$$\textbf{Absorption coefficient} = \frac{\textbf{Sound energy absorbed by the surface}}{\textbf{Total sound energy incident on the surface}}$$

A second form of definition for absorption coefficient is given by Sabine. In order to compare the relative efficiency of different sound absorbing material Sabine assumed a standard Sound absorbing material. Sabine chose an area of $1m^2$ open window to be the standard unit of absorption. Since, all the sound energy falling on it passes through & hence can be said to be completely absorbed. Thus, with this concept, the absorption coefficient of a material is defined as the ratio of sound energy absorbed by material to that absorbed by an equal area of an open window.

Definition-2: It is defined as reciprocal of the area of the sound absorbing material which absorb the same amount of sound energy as that of 1 m^2 of an open window. For example: If a sound absorbing material of $5m^2$ absorbs the same amount of sound energy as absorbed by $1m^2$ of open window; then, the absorption coefficient material is given by 1/5 = 0.20. The unit of absorption coefficient is Sabine or also called O.W.U (Open Window Unit).

2.7 REVERBERATION & REVERBERATION TIME

The persistence or prolongation of sound in a hall even though the source of sound is cut off is called Reverberation.

This is because, a sound produced in a room undergoes multiple reflections from the walls, floor, ceiling & any other reflecting materials before it become inaudible. Thus, a person in the room continues to receive the successive reflections of progressively diminishing intensity. Therefore the sound lasts for some time even after the source has stopped emitting the sound. This effect is called reverberation.

The time taken by the sound to fall below the minimum audibility level after the source stopped sounding is called reverberation time. The expression for reverberation time is derived based on Sabine's method.

Sabine's formula

Sabine defined the reverberation time as, the time taken by the sound intensity to fall to 1 millionth of its original intensity after the source stopped emitting sound. The reverberation time is given by

$$T = \frac{0.161\ V}{\sum aS}$$

Where, V is the volume of the hall.

a is the absorption coefficient.

S is the surface area.

2.8 FACTORS AFFECTING ACOUSTICS OF BUILDINGS

Until the beginning of twentieth century, people did not give any importance to the acoustic characteristics of buildings, lecture halls and auditoria. Hence many a times, the lectures, musical performances etc. given inside them were not that much clear. When Harvard University constructed an auditorium (Fogg Art Museum Hall) during the year 1900, many of the lecture programmes and orchestra performed inside the auditorium were miserably poor acoustically and nothing could be understood. Wallace C. Sabine, who was the professor of Physics in Harvard University, was requested to identify the cause of the problem and suggest a suitable remedy. It was at that time research towards acoustical characteristics of buildings started. The research work of Sabine provided good results. For any auditorium, lecture halls or buildings to be acoustically good.

Sabine suggested the following requirements:

1. The sound must be sufficiently loud everywhere inside the hall.
2. The quality of sound produced by a source of sound (like human beings and instruments) must remain unaltered.
3. The successive sounds of speech and music must remain distinct (i.e. must not overlap) and free from extraneous noises.
4. There should be no echoes more than necessary for the upkeep of continuity.
5. There should not be undesirable focusing of sound in any part of the hall and depletion in any other part.
6. There should not be unpleasant reinforcement of and articulation by objects inside the hall.

Depending on the purpose for which a hall or building is designed, some or all of the above conditions are to be satisfied to be acoustically good. To achieve the above requirements so as to make any hall or building to be acoustically good one have to consider the effects of the following parameters and make suitable efforts:

→ Reverberation
→ Loudness of sound
→ Focusing effects
→ Echelon effect
→ Noises
→ Resonance
→ Interference
→ Echoes

2.8.1 Reverberation

When a sound is produced inside a hall, it spreads out in all directions and is expected to be heard once by an audience inside the hall. But, inside the hall, the sound waves get reflected so many times and a series of waves of successively decreasing amplitudes pass through the listeners' ears until they die due to frictional forces in the air. As a result, even though the source of sound produced a particular sound and stopped, the sound is continuously heard for a short interval of time, until the intensity falls below the limit of audibility. It was found by Sabine, in his research that each sound wave undergoes 200 to 300 reflections inside a hall before it becomes inaudible. This phenomenon of persistence of sound inside a hall for some time even after the source of sound is stopped is called reverberation.

In order to have good acoustic effect, the reverberation time has to be maintained at optimum value. The reason is, if the reverberation time is too small, the loudness becomes inadequate. As a result, the sound may not reach the listener. Thus, this gives the hall a dead effect. On the other hand, if the reverberation time is too long, the greater will the confusion due to mixing of different syllables. This makes the sound unintelligible. Thus, reverberation time should neither be too large nor small. Hence, to maintain a good acoustic effect the reverberation time should be maintained at optimum value.

Remedies:

The reverberation time can be maintained at an optimum value by adopting the following ways,

1. By providing the windows & openings.
2. By having full capacity of audience in the hall or room.
3. By using heavy curtains with folds.
4. By covering the floor with carpets.
5. By decorating the walls with beautiful pictures, maps etc.
6. By covering the ceiling & walls with good sound absorbing materials like felt, fiber board, false roofing etc.

The reverberation time depends on the size of the hall & the quality of sound. Thus, the reverberation time can be controlled either by inserting or removing sound absorbing material in a room or hall.

2.8.2 Loudness

The uniform distribution of loudness in a hall or room is an important factor for satisfactory hearing. Sometimes, the loudness may get reduced due to the excess of sound absorbing materials used inside the hall or room.

Remedies:

If the loudness is not adequate, the loudness can be increased by adopting the following methods.

1. By using suitable absorbents at the places where we feel loudness to be high. As a result of this, the distribution of loudness may become uniform.
2. By constructing low ceilings for the reflection of sound towards the listener.

3. By using large sounding boards behind the speakers & facing the audience.
4. By using public address system like loudspeakers.

2.8.3 Focusing & Interference effects

The presence of any concave surface or any other curved surface in the hall or room may make the sound to be concentrated at this focus region. As a result, the sound may not be heard at all at other regions. These regions are recalled as dead space. Hence, such surfaces must be avoided.

In addition to focusing there should not be interference of direct & reflected waves. This is because, a constructive interference may produce a sound of a maximum intensity in some places & destructive interference may produce a sound of minimum intensity in other places. Thus, there will be an un even distribution of sound intensity.

Remedy:

Curved surfaces can be avoided. In case, if curved surfaces are present, they should be covered with suitable sound absorbing materials.

2.8.4 Echo

An echo is heard due to reflection of sound from a distant sound reflecting output. If the time interval between the direct sound & reflected sound is less than $1/15^{th}$ of a second, the reflected sound is helpful in increasing the loudness. But, those sound arriving later than this cause confusion.

Remedy:

An echo can be avoided by covering long distance walls & high ceiling with suitable sound absorbing material. This prevents the reflection of sound.

2.8.5 Echelon effect

It refers to the generation of a new separate sound due to multiple echoes. A set of railings or any regular reflecting surface is said to produce the echelon effect. This echelon effect affects the quality of the original sound.

Remedy:

The remedy to avoid echelon effect is to cover such surfaces with sound absorbing materials.

2.8.6 Resonance

Resonance occurs due to the matching of frequency. In case, if the window panels & sections of wooden portions have not been tightly fitted they may start vibrating creating an extra sound in addition to the sound produced in the hall or room.

Remedy:

The resonance may be avoided by fixing the window panels properly. Any other vibrating object which may produce resonance can be placed over a suitable sound absorbing material.

2.8.7 Noise

The hall or room should be properly insulated from external & internal noises. In general, there are three types of noises.

1. Air borne noise.
2. Structure borne noise.
3. Inside noise.

Air borne noise

Extraneous noises which are coming from outside through open windows, doors & ventilators are known as air borne noise. The air borne noise can be avoided by following the below remedies.

Remedies:

1. The hall or room can be made air conditioned.
2. By using doors & windows with separate frames having proper sound insulating material between them.

Structure borne noise

The noises which are conveyed through the structure of the building is called structure borne noise. The structural vibration may occur due to street traffic, operation of heavy machines etc.

Remedies:

1. This noise can be eliminated by using double walls with air space between them.
2. By using anti vibration mounts this type of noise can be reduced.
3. By covering the floor & walls with proper sound absorbing materials this noise can be eliminated.

Inside noise

The noises which are produced inside the hall or room is called as inside noise. The inside noise may be produced due to machineries like air conditioners, refrigerators, generators, fans, type writers etc. To avoid this inside noises the following remedies can be adopted.

Remedies:

1. The sound producing machineries can be placed over sound absorbing materials like carpet, pads, wood, felt etc.
2. By using curtains of sound absorbing materials.
3. By covering the floor, wall & ceiling with sound absorbing materials.

2.9 ULTRASONIC WAVES

The sound waves of frequency greater than 20 kHz are called ultrasonic sound waves. This sound is inaudible to human ear. The ultrasonic waves due to their shorter wave length have greater penetrating power.

Ultrasonic waves are widely used in medical diagnostics, marine applications, NDT etc. In this chapter, two different methods of producing ultrasonic sound waves, their velocity determination and their application in SONAR is explained.

2.10 PROPERTIES OF ULTRASONIC WAVES

1. The frequency of ultrasonic wave is greater than 20 kHz.
2. They have high energy content.
3. Due to smaller wavelength, they have a high penetrating power.
4. They can travel over a long distance as a highly directional beam.
5. Their speed of propagation increases with increase in frequency.
6. Just like ordinary sound waves, they get reflected and absorbed.
7. They produce heat when they pass through a substance.
8. If an arrangement is made in a liquid to form stationary ultrasonic waves, it acts as diffraction grating. It is called as acoustic grating.

2.11 PRODUCTION OF ULTRASONIC WAVES- PIEZOELECTRIC METHOD

Piezoelectric effect:

When pressure is applied to one pair of opposite faces of crystals like quartz, tourmaline, Rochelle salt etc, cut with their faces perpendicular to its optic axis, equal and opposite charges appear across its other faces as shown in Figure 2.10. This phenomenon is known as piezoelectric effect.

The sign of charges get reversed if the crystal is subjected to tension instead of pressure.

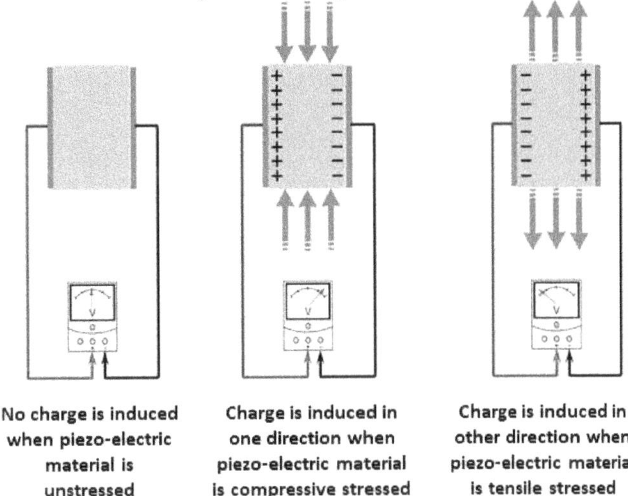

Figure 2.10: Schematic explanation of Piezoelectric effect.

The electricity produced by means of piezoelectric effect is called piezoelectricity. The materials which can undergo piezoelectric effect are called as piezoelectric materials or crystals. If dynamic stress is applied to the piezoelectric material, then frequency of developed emf is equal to the frequency of dynamical pressure.

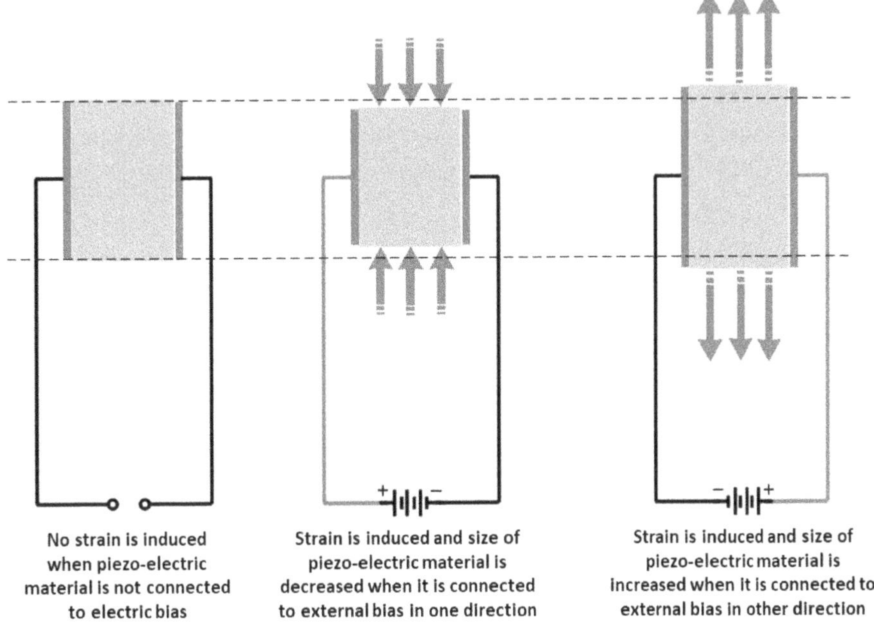

Figure 2.11: Schematic explanation of Inverse Piezoelectric effect.

Principle: inverse piezoelectric effect

If an alternating voltage is applied to one pair of opposite faces of the crystal, alternatively mechanical contraction and expansion are produced in the crystal and the crystal starts vibrating. This phenomenon is known as inverse piezoelectric effect or electrostriction effect as shown in Figure 2.11.

Construction:

The circuit diagram is shown in Figure 2.12. The Quartz crystal is placed between two metal plates. These plates are connected to the coil L_3. Coils L_1, L_2 and L_3 are inductively coupled to each other. Coil L_2 is connected to the emitter-collector junction of an NPN transistor through battery. Coil L_1 is connected with a variable capacitor C_1 forming the tank circuit which is connected to base-emitter junction of NPN transistor.

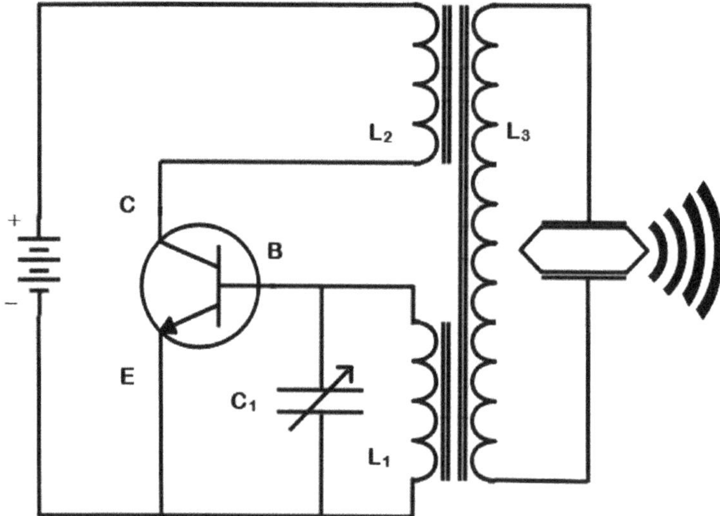

Figure 2.12: Circuit diagram for Piezoelectric oscillator.

Working:

When battery is switched on, the oscillator produces high frequency alternating voltages given by

$$f = \frac{1}{2\pi\sqrt{L_1 C_1}}$$

The frequency of oscillation can be controlled by variable capacitor C_1. Due to the transformer action an emf is induced in the secondary coil L_3. This emf excites the quartz crystal into vibrations. By adjusting a variable capacitor C_1, the crystal is set into one of the modes of resonant conditions. Thus, the vibrating crystal produces longitudinal ultrasonic waves in the surrounding air. The frequency of vibration is

$$f = \frac{p}{2l}\sqrt{\frac{E}{\rho}} \tag{2.21}$$

Where E is the young's modulus, ρ is the density of material and p=1, 2, 3… for fundamental, first overtone, second overtone….. respectively.

Merits:

1. It is more efficient than magnetostriction oscillator. Almost all the modern ultrasonic generators are of this type only.
2. Ultrasonic frequency as high as 5×10^8 Hz can be obtained with this arrangement.
3. Output of this oscillator is very high.
4. It is not affected by temperature and humidity.

Demerit:

1. Cost of piezoelectric quartz is very high and its cutting and shaping are very complex.

2.12 DETECTION OF ULTRASONIC WAVES

Kundt's tube method

Kundt's tube is basically a transparent horizontal pipe which contains a small amount of a fine powder such as cork dust, talc or Lycopodium. An ultrasound generator is connected at one end of this tube. Other end of the tube is blocked by a metallic reflector, which is movable and it can be used to adjust the length of the tube. Typical Kundt's tube is shown in Figure 2.13.

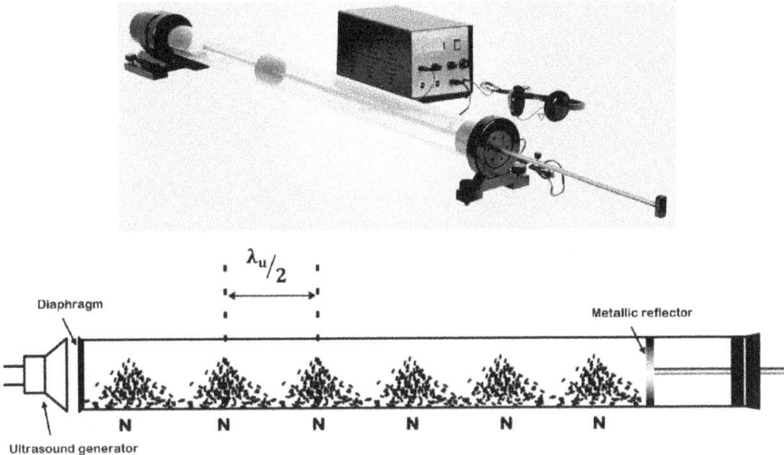

Figure 2.13: Experimental setup for determination of ultrasonic waves by Kundt's tube.

The sound generator is turned on and the piston is adjusted until the sound from the tube suddenly gets much louder. This indicates that the tube is at resonance. This happens because the ultrasound generated from the source travels through the tube and get reflected from the metallic reflector. The interference takes place between incident ultrasound from the source and reflected ultrasound from the reflector. Resonance occurs only when the path length of ultrasound, from source end of the tube to the reflector and back again, is a multiple of wavelength of ultrasound. Therefore the length of tube is a multiple of half a wavelength. At this point the sound waves in the tube are in the form of standing waves, and the amplitude of vibrations of air are zero at equally spaced intervals along the tube, called the nodes. The powder is caught up in the moving air and settles in little piles or lines at these nodes, because the air is still and quiet there. The distance between the piles is one half wavelength $\lambda/2$ of the sound. By measuring the distance between the piles, wavelength of ultrasound in air can be determined. The frequency f of the ultrasound is known, therefore speed of sound 'c' in air can be determined by:

$$c = f \times \lambda \tag{2.22}$$

2.13 NON-DESTRUCTIVE TESTING (NDT)

Non-destructive testing (NDT) is the process of inspecting, testing, or evaluating materials, components or assemblies for discontinuities, or differences in characteristics without destroying the serviceability of the part or system. In other words, when the inspection or test is completed the part can still be used. In contrast to NDT, other tests are destructive in nature and are therefore done on a limited number of samples ("lot sampling"), rather than on the materials, components or assemblies actually being put into service. These destructive tests are often used to determine the physical properties of materials such as impact resistance, ductility, yield and ultimate tensile strength, fracture toughness and fatigue strength, but discontinuities and differences in material characteristics are more effectively found by NDT. Most frequently used NDT methods are listed below:

1. Visual Testing (VT)
2. Liquid Penetrant Testing (PT),
3. Magnetic Particle Testing (MT),
4. Ultrasonic Testing (UT),
5. Radiographic Testing (RT) and
6. Electromagnetic Testing (ET).

2.13.1 Advantages of NDT

NDT offers several advantages over other destructive testing methods as following:

Less Waste: Since component is not destroyed during NDT, it can be used after testing. Thus NDT offers less waste of samples.

Less Downtime. Using some methods, materials can be tested even while they are in use, which eliminates the need to shut down operations during testing.

Accident Prevention. NDT can help to prevent accidents, which helps to reduce the costs associated with repairs, replacement, and equipment loss and business shut down.

Identify Areas of Concern Before Failure. Components that fail can be costly to repair or replace and may lead to an unexpected shutdown of the business or in some cases, disasters. NDT can identify these areas of concern before they become a problem.

Comprehensive Testing. Since this type of testing does not alter substances, every component or product can be tested. There is no need for selective sampling, which tests only a portion of the components. NDT techniques can also be applied at multiple stages of development and construction, allowing manufacturers to identify and repair or replace problem pieces before construction is complete, as well as after the product has been put to use.

Increased Product Reliability. Advanced and more comprehensive testing ensures better products. Problems can be identified and fixed before the product goes to market, and products that are already in use can be tested more frequently to ensure they continue to perform as expected.

2.13.2 NDT through ultrasound

NDT through ultrasound is also popular as ultrasonic testing, ultrasonic pulse-echo method or ultrasonic flaw detection. Ultrasonic testing uses the same principle as is used in SONAR. Using ultrasonic probe (which contains both ultrasonic transmitter and receiver) an ultrasound is introduced into the object being inspected. Presence of any crack, flaw, defect or impurity in the object will have a different density and acoustic velocity different from the object. Therefore if ultrasound hits a material with a different acoustic impedance (density and acoustic velocity), some of the sound will reflect back to the ultrasonic probe and can be presented on a visual display. By knowing the speed of ultrasound through the object (the acoustic velocity) and time required for ultrasound to return to the ultrasonic probe, depth of defect from the surface of object can be determined. In many cases, an experienced operator can determine the type of discontinuity (like slag, porosity or cracks in a weld) that caused the reflector. NDT through ultrasound can be done in several different ways as explained below.

Straight Beam inspection

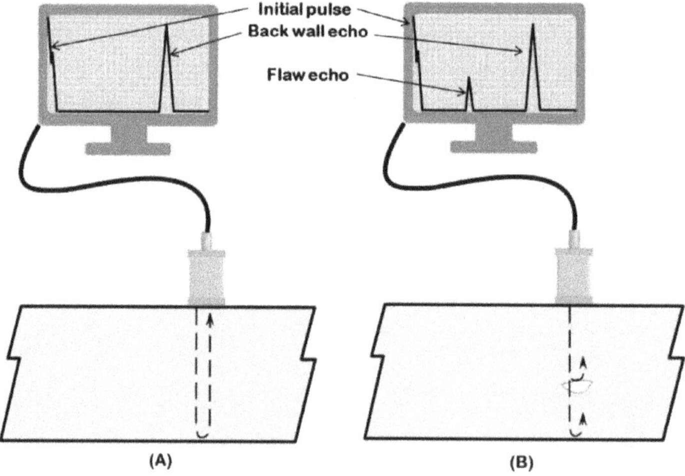

Figure 2.14 : Ultrasonic flaw detection using straight beam inspection.

Straight beam inspection uses longitudinal waves to interrogate the test piece as shown in Figure 2.14. If there is no defect present in the path of ultrasound then ultrasound will get reflected from the back wall of the test piece and return to the transducer. Therefore the screen will display two peaks from which first one corresponds to starting pulse and other corresponds to the back wall echo as shown in Figure 2.14 (A). But if a defect is present in the path of ultrasound then ultrasound will hit a defect, and get reflected to the transducer faster than the ultrasound reflected from the back-wall of the test piece due to the shorter distance from the transducer. This results in additional peak corresponding to flaw echo as shown in Figure 2.14 (B).

Angle Beam inspection

Angle beam inspection uses the same type of transducer but it is mounted at some angle on the surface of test piece. Figure 2.15 demonstrate the ultrasonic flaw detection using angle beam inspection. Most commonly used inspection angles are 45°, 60° and 70° with the angle being calculated up from a line drawn through the thickness of the part (not the part surface). Ultrasonic transducer and wedge combination (also referred to as a "probe") is moved back and forth towards the weld so that the ultrasound beam passes through the full volume of the weld. If a defect is present in the weld it will reflect the ultrasound back to the transducer. This will result in the flaw echo displayed on the screen. In the absence of defect only initial pulse will be displayed on the screen.

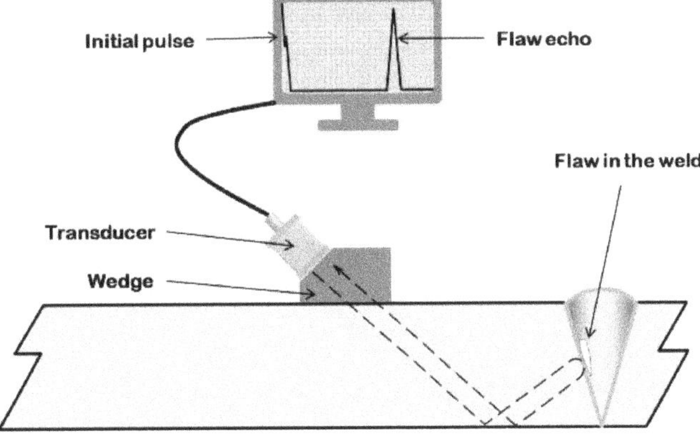

Figure 2.15: Ultrasonic flaw detection using angle beam inspection.

Immersion Testing

Immersion Testing is a technique where the part is immersed in a tank of water with the water being used as the coupling medium to allow the sound beam to travel between the transducer and the part. The UT machine is mounted on a movable platform (a "bridge") on the side of the tank so it can travel down the length of the tank. The transducer is swivel-mounted on at the bottom of a waterproof tube that can be raised, lowered and moved across the tank. The bridge and tube movement permits the transducer to be moved on the X-, Y- and Z-axes. All directions of travel are gear driven so the transducer can be moved in accurate increments in all directions, and the swivel allows the transducer to be oriented so the sound beam enters the part at the required angle. Round test parts are often mounted on powered rollers so that the part can be rotated as the transducer travels down its length, allowing the full circumference to be tested. Multiple transducers can be used at the same time so that multiple scans can be performed.

Through Transmission

Through transmission inspections are performed using two transducers, one on each side of the part as shown in Figure 2.16. The transmitting transducer sends ultrasound through the part and the receiving transducer receives it. Reflectors in the part will cause a reduction in the amount of sound reaching the receiver so that the screen presentation will show a signal with a lower amplitude (screen height).

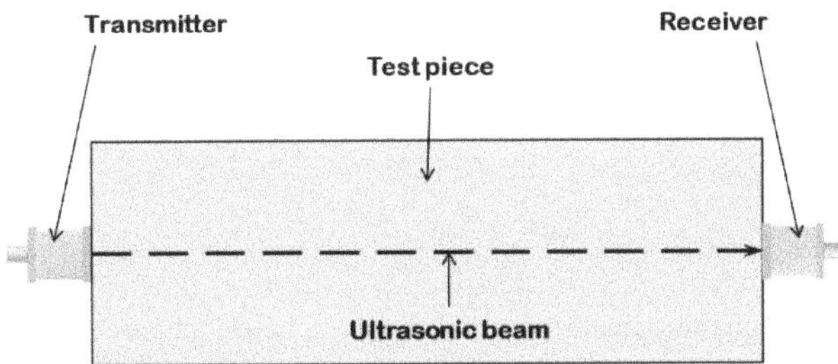

Figure 2.16: Ultrasonic flaw detection using through transmission inspection.

Phased Array

Phased array inspections are done using a probe with multiple elements that can be individually activated. By varying the time when each element is activated, the resulting sound beam can be "steered", and the resulting data can be combined to form a visual image representing a slice through the part being inspected.

Time of Flight Diffraction

Time of Flight Diffraction (TOFD) uses two transducers located on opposite sides of a weld with the transducers set at a specified distance from each other. One transducer transmits sound waves and the other transducer acting as a receiver. Unlike other angle beam inspections, the transducers are not manipulated back and forth towards the weld, but travel along the length of the weld with the transducers remaining at the same distance from the weld. Two sound waves are generated, one travelling along the test piece between the transducers, and the other travelling down through the weld at an angle then back up to the receiver. When a crack is encountered, some of the sound is diffracted from the tips of the crack, generating a low strength sound wave that can be picked up by the receiving unit. By amplifying and running these signals through a computer, defect size and location can be determined with much greater accuracy than by conventional UT methods.

-:POINTS TO REMEMBER:-

→ The differential equation of simple harmonic motion can be written as, $m\frac{d^2x}{dt^2} + kx = 0$ **or** $\frac{d^2x}{dt^2} + \omega^2 x = 0$

Here $\omega = \sqrt{\frac{k}{m}}$ is called the angular frequency.

→ Time period of oscillation can be given as $T = 2\pi\sqrt{\frac{m}{k}}$.

→ Simplified general solution of differential equation for simple harmonic motion can be written as, $x(t) = A\sin(\omega t + \phi)$.

→ Velocity of the system undergoing SHM can be given as, $v = \frac{dx}{dt} = \omega A\cos(\omega t + \phi)$.

→ Acceleration of the system undergoing SHM can be given as, $a = \frac{dv}{dt} = -\omega^2 A\sin(\omega t + \phi) = -\omega^2 x$. This equation suggest that the acceleration of a system undergoing SHM is proportional and in the opposite direction to the displacement.

→ Time period of SHM can be given as, $T = 2\pi\sqrt{\frac{m}{k}}$.

→ Frequency of SHM is the number of oscillations that a system performs per unit time. It is the reciprocal of time period. $f = \frac{1}{2\pi}\sqrt{\frac{k}{m}}$

→ Frequency and time period of a simple pendulum can be given as, $f = \frac{\omega}{2\pi} = \frac{1}{2\pi}\sqrt{\frac{g}{L}}$ and $T = \frac{1}{f} = 2\pi\sqrt{\frac{L}{g}}$

→ Differential equation for damped harmonic motion can be given as, $\frac{d^2x}{dt^2} + \gamma\frac{dx}{dt} + \omega_0^2 x = 0$ Here $\gamma = {}^{b}/_{m}$ is the damping coefficient of the system and $\omega_0 = \sqrt{{}^{k}/_{m}}$ is the natural frequency of the system.

If $\gamma > 2\omega_0$, the system is "over damped" and the mass will not oscillate.

If $\gamma = 2\omega_0$, the system is "critically damped" and, again, no oscillations occur.

For sufficiently small damping $\gamma < 2\omega_0$, the solution is given by, $A_0 e^{\frac{-\gamma t}{2}}\cos(\omega_d t + \phi)$ and the angular frequency is given by $\omega_d = \sqrt{\omega_0^2 - \left(\frac{\gamma}{2}\right)^2}$ Here ω_d is damping frequency.

→ Differential equation for damped harmonic motion can be given as, $\frac{d^2x}{dt^2} + \gamma\frac{dx}{dt} + \omega_0^2 x = \frac{F_0}{m}\sin\omega_f t$

→ The sound absorption coefficient "a" of a material is defined as the ratio of the sound energy absorbed by it to the total sound energy incident on it.

→ The sound lasts for some time even after the source has stopped emitting the sound. This effect is called reverberation.

→ The time taken by the sound to fall below the minimum audibility level after the source stopped sounding is called reverberation time.

→ Sabine defined the reverberation time as, the time taken by the sound intensity to fall to 1 millionth of its original intensity after the source stopped emitting sound. The reverberation time is given by $\mathbf{T = \frac{0.161\ V}{\sum aS}}$
Where, **V** is the volume of the hall, **a** is the absorption coefficient and **S** is the surface area.

→ **Piezoelectric effect:** When pressure is applied to one pair of opposite faces of crystals like quartz, tourmaline, Rochelle salt etc, cut with their faces perpendicular to its optic axis, equal and opposite charges appear across its other faces. This phenomenon is known as piezoelectric effect.

→ **Inverse piezoelectric effect:** If an alternating voltage is applied to one pair of opposite faces of the crystal, alternatively mechanical contraction and expansion are produced in the crystal and the crystal starts vibrating. This phenomenon is known as inverse piezoelectric effect or electrostriction effect.

→ Frequency of the ultrasonic waves produced by piezoelectric method depends upon length 'l', density 'ρ' and young's modulus 'E' of the rod as, $\mathbf{f = \frac{p}{2l}\sqrt{\frac{E}{\rho}}}$

-: SOLVED NUMERICALS :-

1) To make a pendulum making oscillations with time period of 1 second, what should be the length of a pendulum?

Given: T=1 sec, g=9.8 m/s^2, L=?

Solution:

Time period of a simple pendulum can be given as,

$$\mathbf{T = 2\pi\sqrt{\frac{L}{g}}}$$

$$\therefore T^2 = 4\pi^2\frac{L}{g}$$

$$\therefore L = \frac{T^2 g}{4\pi^2}$$

$$\therefore L = \frac{1\times 9.8}{4\pi^2}$$

$$\therefore L = \frac{T^2 g}{4\pi^2}$$

$$\therefore L = 0.248\ \text{m}$$

$$\boxed{\therefore L = 24.8\ \text{cm}}$$

2) A hall has volume of 7500 m^3 and total surface area of 5600 m^2. What should be the total absorption coefficient in the hall if the reverberation time of 1.5 sec is to be maintained?

Given: V = 7500 m^3, s = 5600 m^2, T = 1.5 sec Σa =?

Solution:

According to Sabine formula, the reverberation time can be given as,

$$\mathbf{T = \frac{0.161\ V}{\sum as}}$$

$$\therefore \sum a = \frac{0.161\ V}{T\sum s}$$

$$\therefore \sum a = \frac{0.161\times 7500}{1.5\times 5600}$$

$$\boxed{\therefore \sum a = 0.144}$$

3) The volume of room is 700 m^3. The wall area of the room is 270m^2, the floor area is 140m^2 and the ceiling area is 140 m^2 .The average sound absorption coefficient for wall is 0.03, for the ceiling is 0.8 and for the floor is 0.06. Calculate the average absorption coefficient and the reverberation time.

Given: $V = 700\ m^3$, $S_w = 270\ m^2$, $S_f = 140\ m^2$, $S_c = 140\ m^2$,
$a_w = 0.03$, $a_f = 0.06$, $a_c = 0.8$, $\Sigma as/\Sigma s = ?$, $T = ?$

Solution:

$$\sum as = (a_w \cdot s_w) + (a_f \cdot s_f) + (a_c \cdot s_c)$$
$$\therefore \sum as = (0.03 \times 270) + (0.06 \times 140) + (0.8 \times 140)$$
$$\therefore \sum as = 128.5$$

And $\sum s = s_w + s_f + s_c$
$$\therefore \sum s = 270 + 140 + 140$$
$$\therefore \sum s = 550$$
Now $\frac{\sum as}{\sum s} = \frac{128.5}{550}$
$$\boxed{\therefore \frac{\sum as}{\sum s} = 0.23}$$

Now, according to Sabine formula, the reverberation time can be given as,
$$T = \frac{0.161\ V}{\sum as}$$
$$\therefore T = \frac{0.161 \times 700}{128.5}$$
$$\boxed{\therefore T = 0.88\ sec}$$

(4) Calculate the frequency at which piezoelectric oscillator circuit should be tuned so that a piezoelectric crystal of thickness 0.1 cm vibrates in its fundamental mode to generate ultrasonic waves. Given, Young's modulus = 80GPa and density of crystal material = 2654 kg·m^{-3}.

Given: $p = 1$, $Y = 80 \times 10^9\ N/m^2$, $\rho = 2654\ kg/m^3$
$l = 1 \times 10^{-3}$ m, $f = ?$

Solution:

Frequency of a piezoelectric device can be calculated as;
$$\mathbf{f} = \frac{p}{2l}\sqrt{\frac{Y}{\rho}}$$

$$\therefore f = \frac{1}{2\times 10^{-3}}\sqrt{\frac{80\times 10^9}{2654}}$$

$$\therefore f = 2.74 \times 10^6\ \text{Hz}$$

$$\boxed{\therefore \mathbf{f = 2.74\ MHz}}$$

-: UNSOLVED NUMERICALS :-

1. A hall of volume 1000 m^3 has a sound absorbing surface of 400m^2. If the average absorption coefficient of the hall is 0.2, what is the reverberation time of the hall?
   (Ans: T = 2.01 Sec)
2. Volume of an auditorium is 12,000 m^3. Its reverberation time is 1.5 second. If average absorption coefficient of interior surface is 0.4, find the area of interior surfaces.
   (Ans: s = 3220 m^2)
3. Calculate the thickness of a quartz plate needed to produce ultrasonic waves of frequencies (i) 2MHz (ii) 30KHz.

(Given $\rho = 2650 Kg/m^3$ and Young's Modulus = $8 X 10^{10} N/m^2$).

(Ans: (i) l = 1.37 mm, (ii) l = 91.6 mm

-: SHORT QUESTIONS :-

1. Define periodic motion.
2. Define simple harmonic motion.
3. What is the difference between free vibrations and damped vibrations?
4. Define resonance.
5. What is the difference between transverse and longitudinal wave?
6. Define sound absorption coefficient.
7. Define reverberation time.
8. List out the factors affecting acoustics of building.
9. Define Ultrasonic waves.
10. Give the properties of ultrasonic wave.
11. Define piezoelectric effect.
12. What is inverse piezoelectric effect?
13. Write down the principle of piezo-electric ultrasound generator.
14. What is NDT? List out names of few NDT methods.

-: DESCRIPTIVE QUESTIONS :-

1. Write down the equation of restoring force acting on a particle executing SHM. Derive a differential equation of motion from it.
2. Discuss in detail about characteristics of a simple harmonic motion.
3. Differentiate between periodic motion and simple harmonic motion.
4. Write a short note on simple pendulum and derive an equation for the time period of a simple pendulum.
5. Write down the differential equation for a damped harmonic oscillation. Prove that the ratio of external force to the mass of particle experiencing damped harmonic motion must be less than the angular frequency, to keep the motion oscillatory.
6. Write a short note on free, damped and forced oscillations.
7. What is the reverberation and reverberation time? Write down its equation. Explain why it is necessary to maintain the reverberation time within a certain limit.
8. Discuss various factors affecting the acoustics of buildings and give their remedies.
9. What are ultrasonic waves? List out the properties of ultrasound.
10. Explain with required circuit diagram the generation of ultrasonic waves with piezoelectric effect.
11. Briefly discuss the applications of ultrasound.
12. Explain in detail how NDT is used to determine the internal defects in a material without damaging the material?
13. Differentiate Destructive and Non-destructive testing methods.
14. Write down various advantage and disadvantage of NDT.

* * * * *

CHAPTER-III OPTICS

Learning goals:

At the end of this chapter reader will be able to

- ✓ Explain Huygens' Principle: Fundamental principle for wave propagation.
- ✓ Differentiate between interference and diffraction.
- ✓ Differentiate between constructive and destructive interference.
- ✓ Analyze result of thin film interference, such as soap bubbles and oil films.
- ✓ Explain the arrangement of Young's double slit experiment, Newton's rings experiment and Michelson Interferometer.
- ✓ Explain the phenomena behind Anti-reflection coating.
- ✓ Differentiate between Fresnel and Fraunhofer diffraction– diffraction due to 'n' slits- plane transmission grating.
- ✓ Explain Rayleigh criterion for limit of resolution - resolving power of grating.

3.1 Huygen's Principle: Fundamental principle for wave propagation

When we create any kind of wave whether it is light wave or sound wave; there will be a source of these waves. From the source, the wave travels spherically and when it travels away, it becomes plane wave as radius of curvature of the wavefront increases and becomes almost parallel. Huygen proposed a fundamental understanding and concept of wave theory in 1678.Wavefront is a collection of points on which the propagating wave reaches at the same instant of time.Huygen's principle states that all points on a wavefront serve as point sources of spherical secondary wavelets. After a time t, the new position of the wavefront will be that of a surface tangent to theses secondary wavelets. Every point of the secondary wavefront becomes the source of a new wavefront and then then each point of this new wavefront again becomes a source of another new wavefront and this is how the wave propagates as shown in Figure 3.1. Light travels in straight line but when the light waves faces the sharp edge obstacles or slits whose dimensions are comparable with the wavelength of incident light, then the light diffracts and this phenomenon of diffraction of light can be understood with the help of Huygen's wavelet theory.

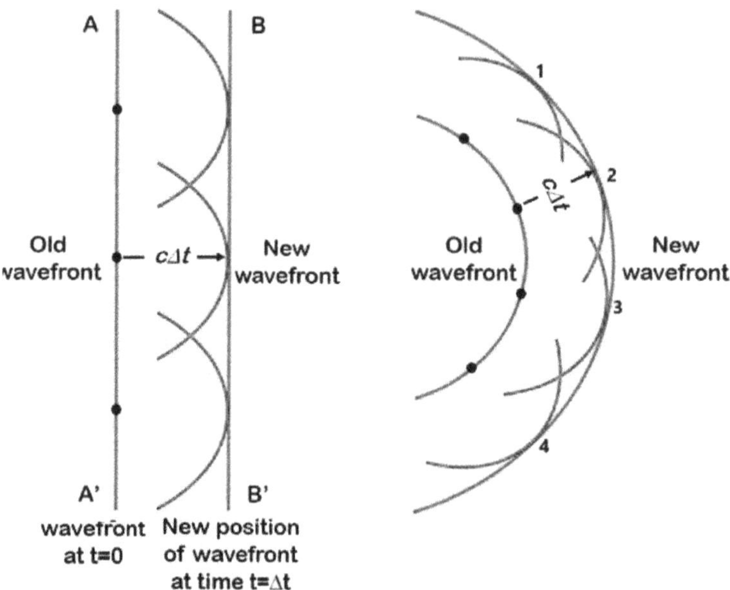

Figure 3.1: The propagation of plane wave

3.2 Superposition of Waves: Basic principle for understanding interference and diffraction

When the waves of different amplitude and different frequency meets at certain points in space, their result will be interference in general. When two or more waves of almost same amplitude and same frequency travelling in same direction meets in space, then at these points in space, certain points or regions may get brighter while certain points or region may get darker. This brightness or darknes is because of redistribution of energy. The regions which get brighter are due to constructive interference and the regions which gets darker are due to destructive interference.

Constructive interference:

When two light waves of same frequency and almost same amplitude meets in space with a phase difference of 0, 2π, 4π….., 2mπ (where m = 0, ±1, ±2,…) or with the path difference of 0, λ, 2λ, 3λ……………….mλ ((where m = 0, ±1, ±2,…) then constructive interference happens and the regions in which this phenomenon happens become brighter and we see bright fringes or bright points. Figure 3.2 shows constructive interference of two waves.

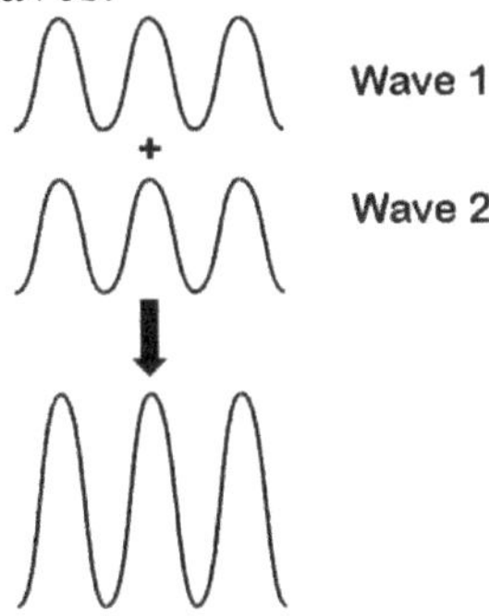

Figure 3.2: Constructive (Waves meeting in phase) Interference

Destructive interference:

When two light waves of same frequency and almost same amplitude meets in space with a phase difference of π, 3π, 5π , ….., (2m+1) π (where m = 0, ±1, ±2,…) or with the path difference of 0, λ/2, 3λ/2……………….(m+1/2)λ ((where m = 0, ±1, ±2,…), then destructive interference happens and the regions in which this phenomenon happens become dark and we see dark fringes or dark points. Figure 3.3 shows destructive interference of two waves.

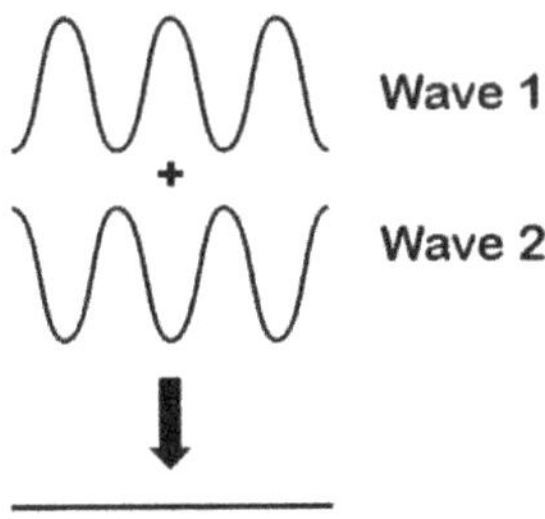

Figure 3.3: Destructive (Waves meeting out of phase) Interference

3.3 Coherence

When we switch on an ordinary light bulb, the atom in tungsten filament of the bulb goes to higher excited state and stay there for just 10^{-8} s and comes back to normal state. Many atoms go to excited state and come to ground state but the phase difference between the transition of an atom to ground state and the transition of another atom into ground state is not constant. This variation is very fast and the eye is not sensitive to it. So, we see normal illumination. But when all the atoms come to ground state at the same time, then there is a constant or zero phase difference among the photons then the appeared light will be coherent light. We can produce coherent sound waves also by connecting two loudspeakers by one audio oscillator. We can produce coherent waves by connecting two antennas by same radio oscillator. Constant phase difference in between the interfering waves is very important for getting constructive and destructive interference. Constant phase difference in between interfering waves can be achieved by division of wavefront and by division of amplitude. When we derive two sources of light from a single source by dividing the wavefront, then these two sources will be coherent as the phase difference in between them will be constant as happens in case of Young's double slit experiment. When we derive two sources of light from a single source by dividing the amplitude then these two sources will be coherent as the phase difference in between them will be constant as happens in case of interference from thin films.

3.4 Young's double slit experiment

In this experiment, light is incident on a slit whose dimension are comparable with the wavelength of incident light. The emerging light from S_0, diffracts and is incident on the two equidistant slits S_1 and S_2, having a separation of distance d. The light coming out of S_1 and S_2 interferes in between the space of screen and on the screen as well. Alternative bright fringes with maximum intensity called Maxima and dark fringes with minimum intensity called minima are obtained on the screen. When the waves interfere constructively, a bright fringe is obtained but when the waves interfere destructive light a dark fringe is obtained on the screen. Thus, we get alternative bright and dark fringes on screen as shown in following Figure 3.4.

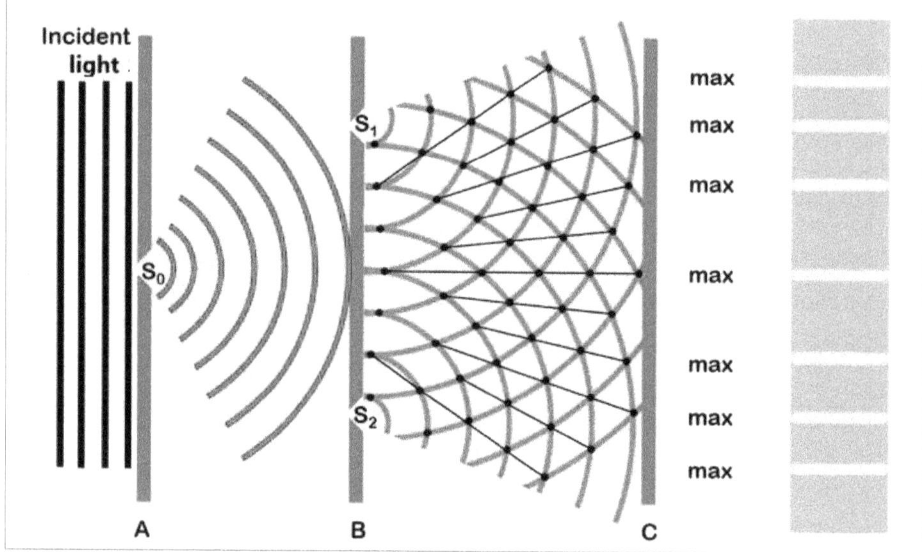

Figure 3.4: Young's double slit experiment and Bright and dark fringes obtained for monochromatic Na light source

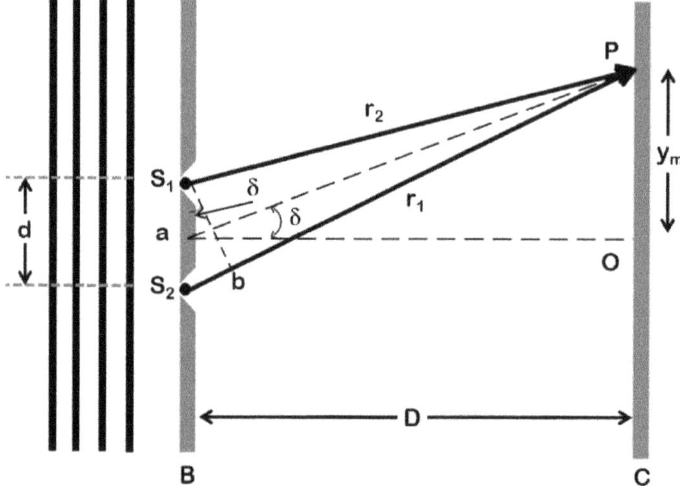

Figure 3.5: Light ray diagram of Young's double slit experiment

As shown in above Figure 3.5, the distance between slits and the screen is D. The distance between equidistant sources S_1 and S_2 is d. Two light sources are generated from a single source S. The two waves travelling from S_1 and S_2 meet at point P on the screen C.The interference fringes are obtained on the screen. The fringes on the screen will be bright or dark, will depend on the intensity of light at that point. In order to find the path difference between interfering waves at P, a perpendicular from S_2 is drawn on S_1P. The point of intersection of the perpendicular is b. After the point b on S_1P, the distance travelled by both the interfering waves S_2P and bP become equal. Therefore, the path difference between these two interfering waves is S_1b.

Path difference = S_1b

From triangle S_2bS_1,

$$\text{Path difference} = S_1b = d\sin\delta \quad \left(\because \text{ from } \triangle S_1bS_2 \ \sin\delta = \frac{Perpendicular}{Hypotenuse} = \frac{S_1b}{d}\right) \tag{3.1}$$

Here, δ is the angle of diffraction.

The relation between path difference and phase difference is given as

$$\frac{\text{Path Difference}}{\lambda} = \frac{\text{Phase Difference}}{2\pi}$$

Or

$$\text{Path Difference} = \frac{\lambda}{2\pi}\text{ Phase Difference} \tag{3.2}$$

Therefore, for constructive interference

$$\text{Path Difference} = \frac{\lambda}{2\pi}2m\pi = m\lambda \ \ (\text{where } m = 0, \pm1, \pm2, \ldots) \tag{3.3}$$

So, from equation (3.1) and (3.3)

$$d\sin\delta = m\lambda \tag{3.4}$$

Similarly,

Also, for Destructive interference,

$$\text{path difference } d\sin\delta = (m + 1/2)\lambda \tag{3.5}$$

From triangle AOP;

$$\tan\delta = \frac{y_m}{D} \tag{3.6}$$

As θ is very small for large value of D and small value of y_m, so that $\sqrt{(D^2 + {y_m}^2)} \sim D$

So,

$$\tan\delta \sim \sin\delta \tag{3.7}$$

Therefore from (3.6) and (3.7); $\text{Sin}\delta = \frac{y_m}{D}$ (3.8)

Therefore from (3.4) and (3.8) ; For Constructive interference;

$$\frac{m\lambda}{d} = \frac{y_m}{D} \tag{3.9}$$

For m[th] bright fringe

$$y_m = D\frac{m\lambda}{d} \tag{3.10}$$

And for (m+1)[th] bright fringe

$$y_{m+1} = D\frac{(m+1)\lambda}{d} \tag{3.11}$$

Therefore, the fringe width can be defined as the width between any two consecutive interference Maximas or minimas and can be written as;,

$$\text{Fringe width} = y_{m+1} - y_m = \Delta y = D\frac{(m+1)\lambda}{d} - D\frac{m\lambda}{d} = \frac{D\lambda}{d} \tag{3.12}$$

If the source of light is monochromatic, like Na lamp, then alternative bright and dark fringes of uniform width will be obtained on screen. But if the source of light is white like Xe-Arch lamp, then coloured fringes of varying fringe width will be obtained on the screen.

Intensity in Double slit Experiment (Young's double slit experiment);

In a light wave or electromagnetic wave, there are two oscillating electric and magnetic fields and the propagation of light wave is perpendicular to these oscillating fields. The intensity of electric field in an electromagnetic wave is much higher in comparison to magnetic field. Therefore, while taking phasor diagram, Wave vector of electric field is taken always. We want to derive an expression for intensity of light due to two interfering light waves at point P.

Electric field component of first light wave vary with time t and can be given as as;

$$E_1 = E_0 \sin\omega t \qquad (3.13)$$

Electric field wave vector of a sinusoidal wave disturbance can be represented graphically also by using a rotating phasor diagram fow wave 1, as shown in Figure3.6 ;

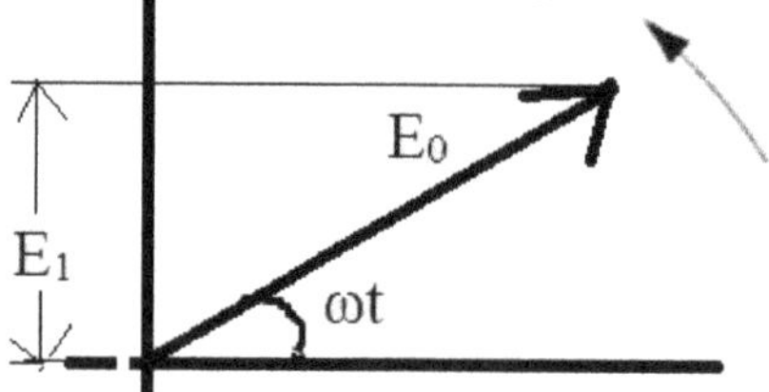

Figure 3.6: Rotating phasor of wave 1

Similarly, electric field wave vector of second interfering wave (2) is given as;

$$E_2 = E_0 \sin(\omega t + \theta) \qquad (3.14)$$

Where θ = phase difference between wave 1 and wave 2

Also, Electric field wave vector of a sinusoidal wave disturbance can be represented graphically also by using a rotating phasor diagram for wave 2, having a phase difference of θ wrt wave (1), as shown in Figure 3.7;

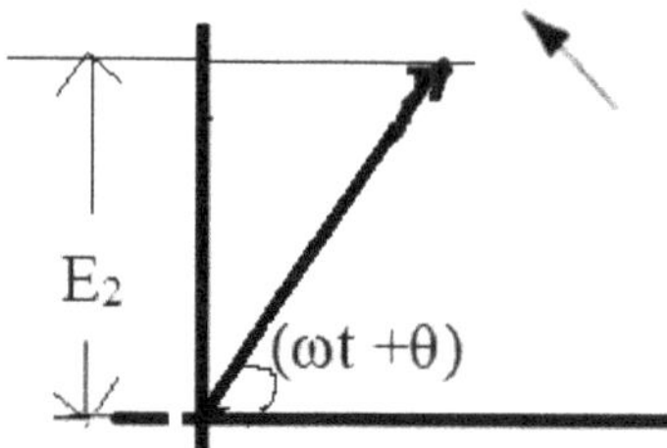

Figure 3.7 Rotating phasor of wave 2

The Interference of these two waves will give

$$E = E_1 + E_2 \qquad (3.15)$$

When these two waves are superimposed;

$$E = E_0 \sin\omega t + E_0 \sin(\omega t + \theta) \qquad (3.16)$$

$$E = E_0 (\sin\omega t + \sin(\omega t + \theta))$$

$$E = 2\,E_0 (\sin(\omega t + \theta/2)\cos(-\theta/2))$$

$$= 2\,E_0 (\sin(\omega t + \theta/2)\cos(\theta/2)) \qquad (3.17)$$

$$= 2\,E_0 (\sin(\omega t + \beta)\cos(\beta))$$

$$= 2\,E_0 \cos(\beta)\sin(\omega t + \beta) \qquad (3.18)$$

$$E = E_\varphi (\sin(\omega t + \beta) \qquad (3.19)$$

Equation (3.7) can we obtained by following phasor diagram, as given in Figure 3.8, also;

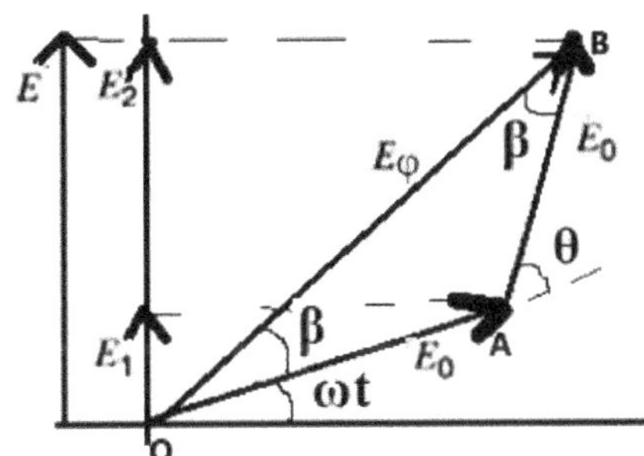

Fig. 3.8: Phasor diagram

Figure 3.8 shows isosceles △ AOB as two sides, OA and AB are congruent to each other
∴ ∠AOB (β) =∠ABO (β) and β + β = θ (external angle) or β = θ/2
In, △ AOB, OB = E_φ
∴ $E_\varphi = 2\ E_0 \cos(\beta)$ **(3.20)**

$$\frac{I_\varnothing}{I_0} = \frac{{E_\varnothing}^2}{{E_0}^2} = 4\cos^2\beta \quad \textbf{(3.21)}$$

For maximum intensity,

$\cos^2\beta = 1$ or $\cos\beta = \pm 1$ **(3.22)**

Or $\cos\beta = \cos 0, \cos 2\pi, \cos 3\pi, \ldots\ldots\ldots = \cos m\pi$, where, m = 0,1,2…

Or $\beta = m\pi$ or $\theta = 2m\pi$ **(3.23)**

The relation between path difference and phase difference is given as

$$\frac{\text{Path Difference}}{\lambda} = \frac{\text{Phase Difference}}{2\pi}$$

Or Path Difference $= \frac{\lambda}{2\pi}$ Phase Difference

$\Delta = \frac{\lambda}{2\pi}(2m\pi) = m\lambda$ **(3.24)**

Or $d \sin\delta = m\lambda$ ($\because \Delta = d \sin\delta$) **(3.25)**

Similarly, for minimum intensity,

$\cos^2\beta = 0$

Or $\cos\beta = 0$ **(3.26)**

Or $\cos\beta = \cos \pi/2, \cos 3\pi/2, \ldots\ldots\ldots$
$= \cos (m+1/2)\pi$ where, m = 0,1,2…

Or $\beta = \left(m + \frac{1}{2}\right)\pi$ or $\theta = (2m + 1)\pi$ **(3.27)**

Relation between path difference and phase difference between two interfering waves is given as

$$\frac{\text{Path Difference}}{2\lambda} = \frac{\text{Path Difference}}{2\pi}$$

$$\text{Path Difference} = \frac{\lambda}{2\pi}\text{ Phase Difference}$$

$\Delta = \frac{\lambda}{2\pi}(2m + 1)\pi) = (m + 1/2)\lambda$

Or $d\sin\delta = (m + 1/2)\lambda$ ($\because \Delta = d \sin\delta$) **(3.28)**

So, we can draw the following intensity pattern for double slit experiment;

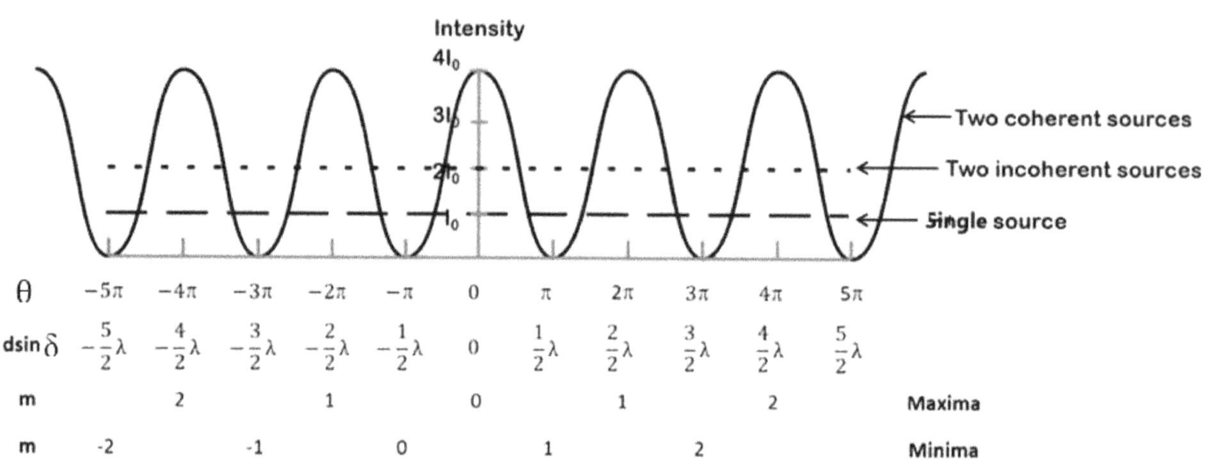

Figure 3.9: Intensity pattern for double slit experiment.

3.5 Interference from Thin Films:

Interference effects are commonly observed in thin films. Examples are the beautiful colors appearing from the feathers of a bird, soap bubbles and oil on water.

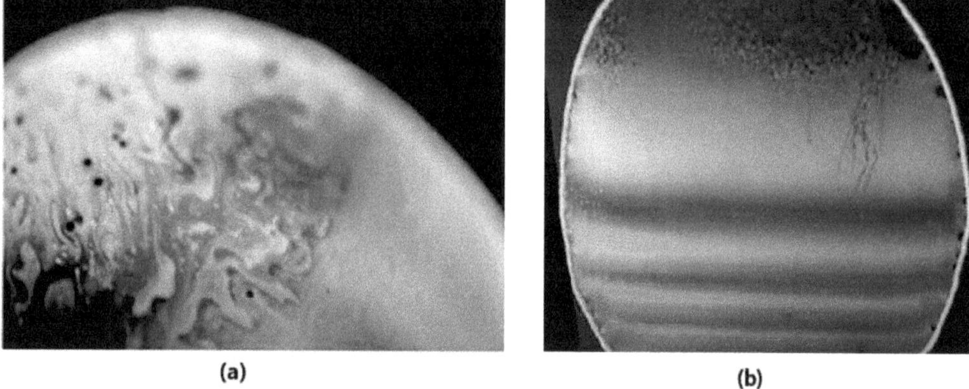

Figure 3.10(a) Amazing colors appearing from the surface of soap bubbles (b) Wonderful colors appear when a ring is dipped in a soap solution and held vertically

The amazing colors shown in above figure 3.10, are appearing because of the interference of the light waves reflected from both surfaces of the thin films. Interference from thin films is obtained when light waves interfere because of division of amplitude of the same light wave. In order to understand it, we take two mediums, one having lower index of refraction for example air (n_1~1) and another medium having higher index of refraction (n_2) for example glass, which are separated at the interface.

An electromagnetic wave such as light wave undergoes a phase change of π (or180°) upon reflection from a medium of higher index of refraction than the one in which it was traveling. This is analogous to a reflected pulse on a string as shown in Figure 3.11.

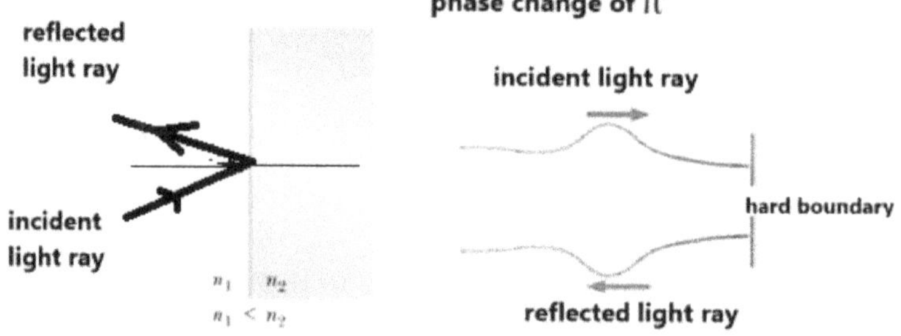

Figure 3.11: Reflection of wave from hard boundary.

There is no phase change when the wave is reflected from a boundary leading to a medium of lower index of refraction which is analogous to a pulse in a string reflecting from a free support as shown in Fig. 3.12

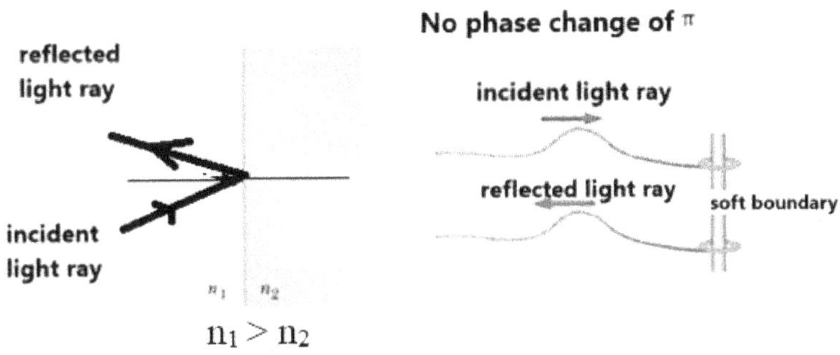

Figure 3.12: Reflection of wave from soft boundary

Light travelling from air is incident on the interface then there will be reflection and refraction of the light wave at the interface. The reflected waves from the interface of higher index of refraction (n_2) and getting back into the air will get a change of phase by π while the light wave travelling from reflected from higher index of refraction (n_2) and incident on the interface separating glass and air will not get any phase change. So, reflected wave from first boundary of thin film, refracted into the 2nd medium as well as reflected from another boundary of the film and again refracted wave from first boundary of the thin film meets in 1st medium such as air, then the phenomenon of interference occurs. Therefore, we get interference because of the reflected wave and transmitted wave emerging due to division of amplitude. This phenomenon of interference in thin fills can be understood from the following Figure 3.13.

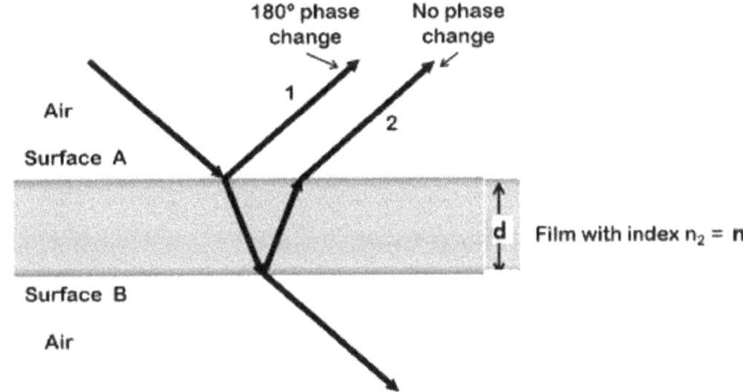

Figure 3.13: Reflection and Refraction (or Transmission) of waves

For normal incidence; when angle of incidence with the normal, $\theta_i = 0$,
The optical path difference between the two interfering waves;

$$\Delta = 2d + \frac{\lambda_n}{2} \quad (3.26)$$

Where t is the uniform thickness of the film and $\boldsymbol{\lambda_n}$ is the wavelength of light inside the medium

and $\boldsymbol{\lambda_n} = \frac{\lambda}{n_2} = \frac{\lambda}{n}$ $\quad (\because \; n_2 = n)$

For constructive interference;

Path difference between interfering light rays, $\Delta = m\lambda_n$ **(3.27)**

$$2d + \frac{\lambda_n}{2} = m\lambda_n \qquad \text{Or} \qquad 2d = (m - 1/2)\,\lambda_n \quad (3.28)$$

For destructive interference;

Path difference between interfering light rays, $\Delta = (m + \frac{1}{2})\lambda_n$ **(3.29)**

$2d + \frac{\lambda_n}{2} = (m + 1/2)\lambda_n$ Or $2d = m\,\lambda_n$ **(3.30)**

3.6 Newton's Rings:

It's the method for viewing interference of light rays by the light rays coming from a wedge-shaped air film which can be simply formed by putting a planoconvex lens on top of a flat glass surface. The air film between the glass surfaces varies in thickness from zero at the point of contact to some thickness t. A pattern of bright and dark concentric circular rings/fringes are observed as show in following Figure. These rings are called Newton's Rings as shown in Figure 3.14. The particle model of light could not explain the origin of the rings. Newton's Rings can be used to test optical lenses.

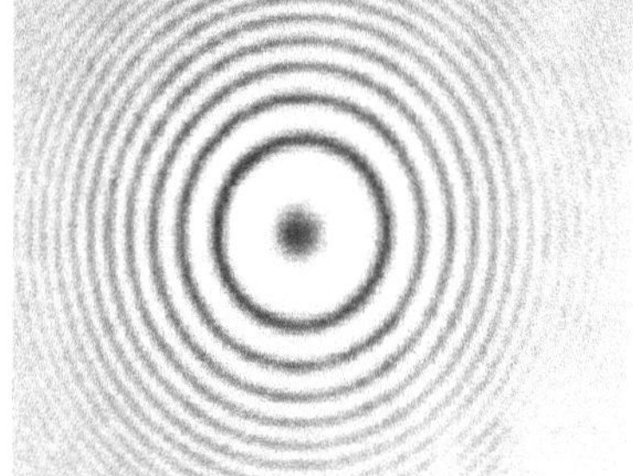

Figure 3.14: Newton's rings obtained from the wedge-shaped air film of varying thickness

Radius of the ring formed in Newton's ring experiment

In this experiment, a plano-convex lens is put on a plane glass plate as shown in following Figure 3.15. The radius of plano-convex lens is R, d is the thickness of wedge-shaped air film at a particular point P. The horizontal distance of the point P is r, which is the radius of any of the Newton's rings. The air film of varying thickness (from 0 to d) will be there between glass plate and the lens. Concentric bright and dark fringes or rings of varying diameter can be seen through the telescope or the naked eye.

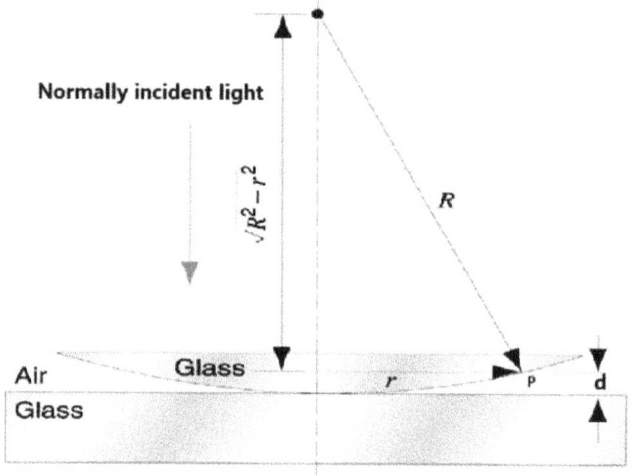

Figure 3.15: Plano Convex Lens on glass plate and formation of air film

The formation of fringes of varying diameter can be understood as follows;

$$d = R - r = R - \sqrt{(R^2 - r^2)} = R(1 - \sqrt{\left(1 - \frac{r^2}{R^2}\right)}\ ) = R\left(\left(1 - \left(1 - \frac{r^2}{R^2}\right)^{\frac{1}{2}}\right)\right)$$

$$d = R\left(1 - \left(1 - \frac{1}{2}\frac{r^2}{R^2}\right)\right) \quad \text{(Higher terms are neglected as } r << R\text{)}$$

$$d = \frac{r^2}{2R} \tag{3.31}$$

By considering normal incidence, we can write,

the geometrical path difference $= 2d$

For constructive interference;

total path difference (geometrical +optical) between interfering rays,

$$\Delta = 2d + (\lambda_n/2) = m\,\lambda_n \qquad (\because \lambda_n = \lambda, \text{ for air film}) \tag{3.32}$$

Therefore, $2d = (m - 1/2)\,\lambda$ **(3.33)**

$$2\frac{r^2}{2R} = (m - 1/2)\,\lambda$$

$$r = \sqrt{((m - 1/2)\,\lambda R} \tag{3.34}$$

where, m = 1, 2................. Here, the value of m can't be 0 because the radius will become negative, which is not possible. Here r gives the radius of mth bright fringe.

Similarly, For destructive interference;

total path difference (geometrical +optical) between interfering rays

$$\Delta = 2d + (\lambda_n/2) = (m + 1/2)\,\lambda_n \qquad (\because \lambda_n = \lambda, \text{ for air film}) \tag{3.35}$$

Therefore, $2d = m\,\lambda$

$$2\frac{r^2}{2R} = \;= m\,\lambda$$

$$r = \sqrt{m\,\lambda R} \tag{3.36}$$

where, m=0,1, 2.................

r from equation (3.36) gives the radius of dark fringes. For m=0, r =0. Therefore, the central point observed by the telescope will be dark.

3.7 Michelson Interferometer

Michelson interferometer is an instrument with the help of which we can measure very small changes in length with great precision and accuracy by using interference phenomenon for fringes pattern.

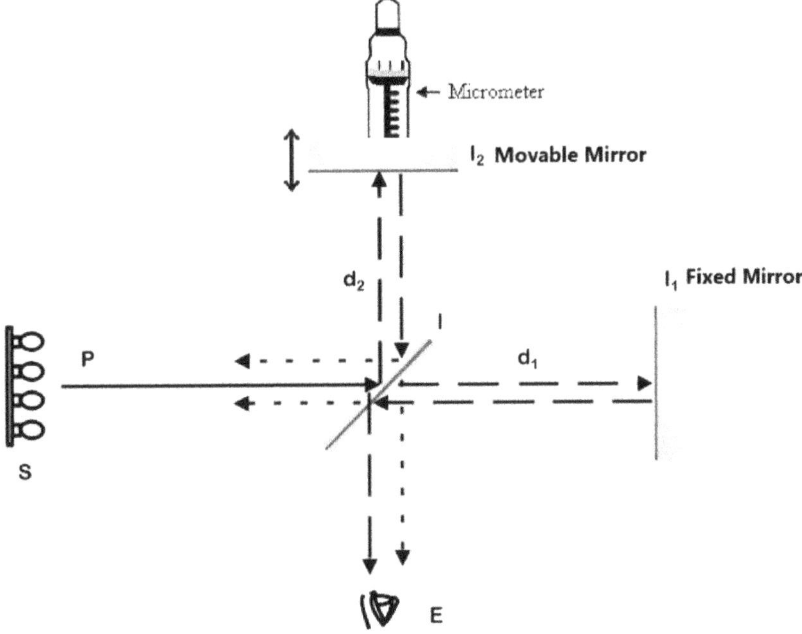

Figure 3.16: Experimental setup for Michelson Interferometer.

In this experiment, monochromatic light from an extended source is incident on a half polished very thin mirror I, the light is reflected and refracted from I. The refracted light is incident on another full polished mirror I_2 and the reflected light is incident on another fully polished mirror I_1, which has been kept perpendicular to mirror I_2. Both the reflected and refracted rays combine at I and then enters into the eye through the telescope as shown in Figure3.16. The reflected and transmitted light rays interfere at I after travelling a distance of $2d_2$ and $2d_1$ respectively. Therefore, the path difference between the light rays will be $2(d_2-d_1)$. This path difference can be changed by fine-tuned by the adjustable mirror. As the mirror I_2 is moved, the circular fringes seem to shrink or grow with new circular fringes viewed at the centre. For the centre of the fringe pattern to change from bright to bright or from dark to dark, the path difference between two interfering waves, would change by λ, which means that mirror moved a distance of $\lambda/2$ as the light ray travelled twice from I to I_2 and then I_2 to I. Therefore, by counting the number of fringes at the centre in the field of view of eye of telescope, we can measure the accurate change in length. The length of a 'standard meter' was measured by Michelson and he got noble prize for this discovery. The 'standard meter' was redefined as equivalent to 1553163.5 wavelengths of red light coming out of Cd light source. This definition of 'standard meter' was again revised in 1983 to be more precise.

3.8 Anti-reflection coating:

A ray of light travelling in a medium of refractive index n_1 (for example air) to another medium of refractive index n_2 (for example glass). If I is the intensity of incident light and I_r is the intensity of reflected light from the interface, then according to Fresnel's equations as obtained from the solution of plane wave equations of light for normally incident light;

$$\frac{I_r}{I_0} = \left(\frac{(n_2-n_1)}{(n_2+n_1)}\right)^2 \tag{3.37}$$

For air- glass surface ($n_1 \sim 1.0$ and $n_2 = 1.5$) then $\frac{I_r}{I_0} = 4\%$, which indicated that only 96% of incident light on the interface of air- glass surface is transmitted. In optics, instruments like telescope, lenses of camera and a combination of lenses used generally. When the light is entered on the interface of air and glass, light is lost by 4% in single reflection. So, in case of optical instruments in which the objective itself has 4 lenses, a significant portion of light is lost, which is highly undesirable, particularly when the intensity of incident light is very low. In order to reduce reflection losses, a transparent antireflective coating is deposited on the surface of glass as shown in Figure 3.17. This anti reflecting coating is also known as non-reflecting film, which was discovered by German Physicist Alexender Smakula. The best material for this is Magnesium Fluoride MgF_2. The refractive index of MgF_2 is 1.38 which is in between the refractive index of air and refractive index of glass.

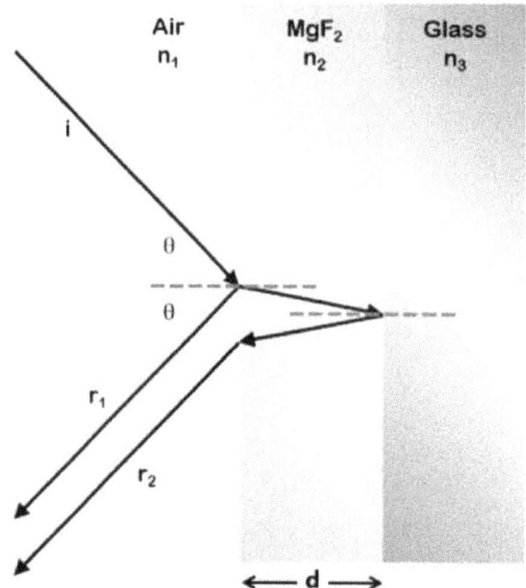

Figure 3.17: Reflection and Transmission of waves from different interfaces

We want complete destructive interfere in between light rays r_1 ad r_2.
Therefore, for destructive interference;
total path difference (geometrical +optical) between interfering rays

$$\Delta = 2d + (\lambda_n/2) + (\lambda_n/2) = (m + 1/2)\,\lambda_n \tag{3.38}$$

$$2d + \lambda_n = (m + 1/2)\,\lambda_n$$

$$2d = \left(m - \tfrac{1}{2}\right)\lambda_n \tag{3.39}$$

For minimum thickness of film; m =1 ,

$$d = \frac{\lambda_n}{4} \quad \text{or} \quad d = \frac{\lambda}{4n} \qquad \left(\because\ \lambda_n = \frac{\lambda}{n}\right) \tag{3.40}$$

So, the minimum thickness of the film must be $\frac{\lambda}{4n}$. For Na light of wavelength 5890 Å, the thickness of MgF_2 will be $\left[\frac{5890\times10^{-8}}{4\times1.38}\text{cm} = 1067.02 \times 10^{-8}\text{ cm} = 1.067 \times 10^{-5}\text{ cm}\right]$. Thus there will be destructive interference and intensity of reflected light will be be minimum if we coat MgF_2 film of thickness 1.067×10^{-5} cm (or 0.1067μm or 106.7 nm) on glass. The energy saved in reflection, will be available with transmitted light.

For absolute destructive interference, the intensities of the two reflected light waves r_1 and r_2 must be equal. So,

$$\left(\frac{n_2-n_1}{n_2+n_1}\right)^2 = \left(\frac{n_3-n_2}{n_3+n_2}\right)^2 \tag{3.41}$$

For air, n1 ~1.0, so,

$$\left(\frac{n_2-1}{n_2+1}\right)^2 = \left(\frac{n_3-n_2}{n_3+n_2}\right)^2 \quad \text{or} \quad \left(\frac{n_2-1}{n_2+1}\right) = \left(\frac{n_3-n_2}{n_3+n_2}\right)$$

By applying componendo-dividendo theorem;

If (a / b) = (c / d) then [(a + b) / (a – b)] = [(c + d) / (c – d)].
So,

$$\left(\frac{n_2-1+n_2+1}{n_2-1-n_2-1}\right) = \left(\frac{n_3-n_2+n_3+n_2}{n_3-n_2-n_3-n_2}\right) \tag{3.42}$$

$$\left(\frac{2n_2}{-2}\right) = \left(\frac{2n_3}{-2n_2}\right) \quad \text{or} \quad n_3 = n_2^{\,2} \tag{3.43}$$

Therefore, from equation (3.43), we can conclude that the refractive index of coating material must be approximately equal to square root of the refractive index of glass.

1.8.1 Non-Reflective Coatings for Solar Cell

Semiconductors like Si are used to fabricate solar cells-devices that generate electrical energy when solar cells are exposed to sunlight. Generally, silicon solar cells (n=3.5) are coated with thin film of silicon monooxide (SiO, n=1.45) in order to minimize reflection losses. Assuming normal incidence of light, we can determine the minimum thickness of the film that will produce the minimum reflection at a wavelength of 552nm.From equation 3.30 for destructive interference; $2d+\lambda_n/2+\lambda_n/2 = (m+1/2)$

$\lambda_n/2$ is added in equation 3.30, because the reflection is happening two times from the hard boundary as shown in Figure 3.18

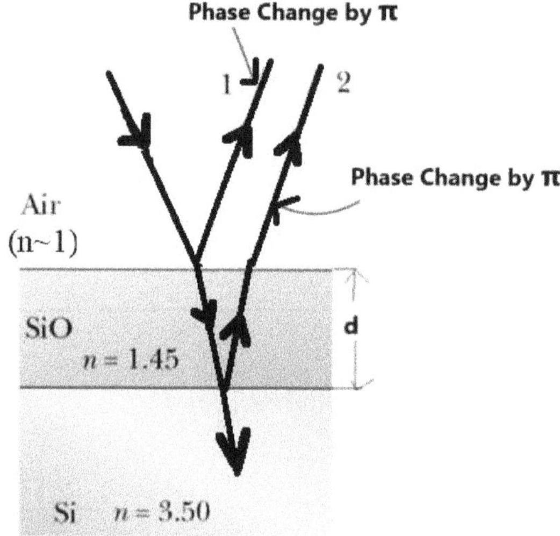

Figure 3.18: Non -reflective Coating of SiO on Si Solar Cells

2d = (m-1/2) , So, d = $\lambda/4n$ (*for m*=1)

$$d = \frac{1 \times 552 \text{ nm}}{4 \times 1.45} = 95.2 \text{ nm}$$

Therefore, a film of SiO of 95.2 nm thickness will produce destructive interference in reflected light for an incident light ray of 552 nm wavelength and therefore this saved energy will go in transmission and will be collected by the solar Cell. Thus, the efficiency of solar cell can be enhanced as more light will be absorbed.

3.9 Fresnel and Fraunhofer diffraction

3.9.1 Fresnel Diffraction:

When the screen is at any distance from the slits or aperture. The light rays entering the slits or aperture are not parallel. Also, the light rays leaving the slits or aperture are not parallel. Such type of general diffraction is called Fresnel Diffraction as shown in figure 3.19 Fraunhofer diffraction can be considered as a limiting case of Fresnel Diffraction.

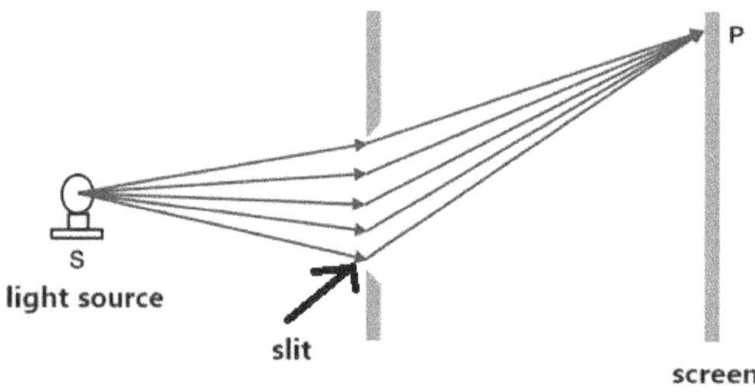

Figure 3.19: Fresnel Diffraction (the source S and the screen C, can be placed at any distance)

3.9.2 Fraunhofer diffraction

When the screen is very far from the slits or aperture and the light rays interfering on the screen can be considered as plane waves. Also, the source of light is far away from the slits or aperture and the wavefronts of light rays incident on it are also plane waves. This condition is called as Fraunhofer diffraction as shown in following Figure 3.20.

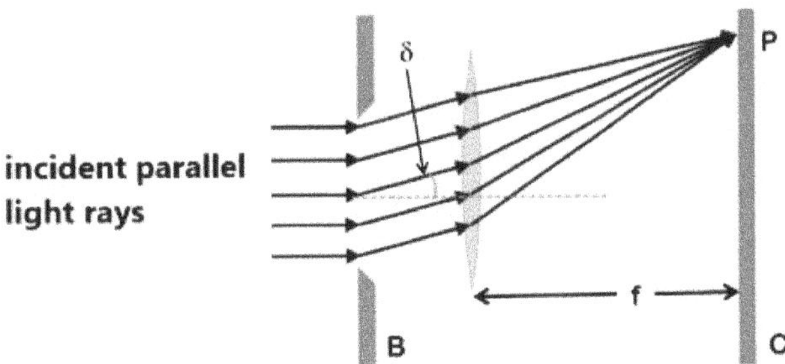

Figure 3.20: Fraunhofer diffraction (the source S being far away from the slits, therefore incident parallel light rays enter into the slits)

3.10 Diffraction by multiple Slits (Diffraction Grating):

Thomas Young used his double slit experiment to measure the wavelength of light for the first time. A variety of experiments based on interference are used these days to precisely measure the wavelength of light. When the number of parallel slits is increased in Young's double slit experiment, the bright fringes will get narrower. More the number of slits, narrower will be the bright fringe and precise would be the measurement of wavelength of light. When the number of slits are increased to 10^4 within 1 cm, then this kind of system is called diffraction grating. When the number of slits are increased, the number of secondary maxima become more but their intensities become lesser. Light ray diagram of diffraction grating is shown in following figure 3.21;

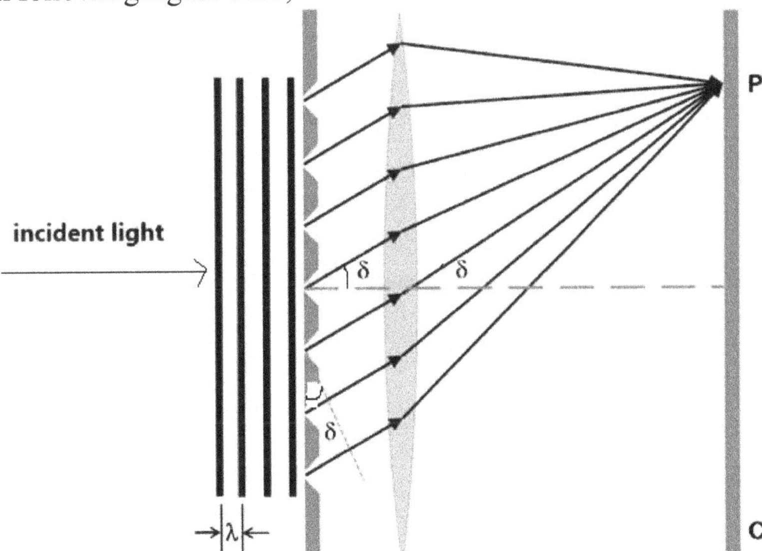

Figure 3.21: Diffraction from Grating.

Width of Central Principal Maxima

A principal maxima (maximum Intensity) will appear on the screen when the path difference between any two adjacent light rays from adjacent slits is an integer number of wavelength.

For Principal Maxima;

path difference between any two adjacent light rays,

$$d \sin d\delta_0 = m\lambda \quad \text{...where, } m = 0, \pm 1, \pm 2$$

for central principal maxima m = 0, therefore δ = 0

Means that all the phasors would be added at angle of 0^0 as shown in following Figure 3.22;

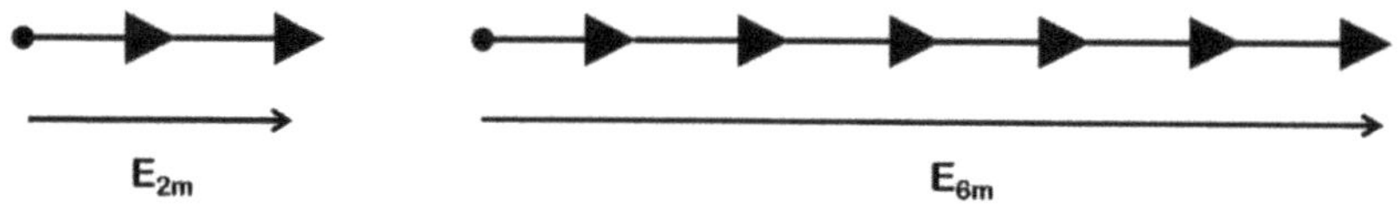

Figure 3.22: Two phasors and six phasors of waves meeting at 0^0 and their resultants leading to maximum resultant amplitudes

On either side of central principal maxima, there would be a minima of 0 intensity, which lies at an angle of $d\delta_0$, off the central axis as shown in following Figure 3.23. Also, on either side of any general principal maxima, there would be a minima of 0 intensity, which lies at an angle of $d\delta$, off the central axis as shown in Figure 3.23;

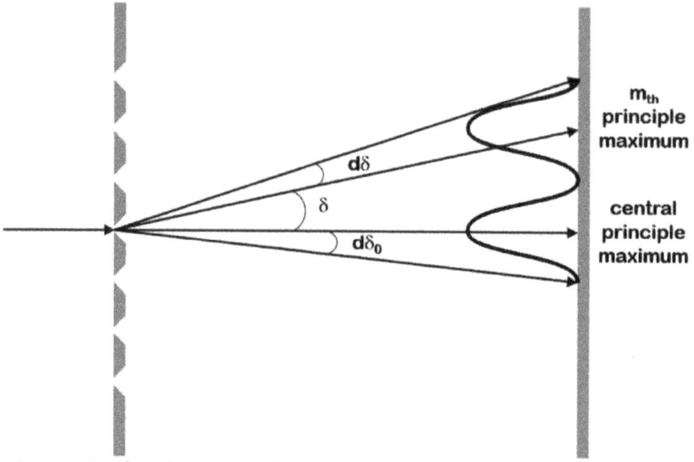

Figure 3.23: Central principal maxima and m^{th} order principal maxima

The meeting of two phasors(waves) and five phasors(waves) at angle of 0^0 for constructive interference are given in following figure a and b respectively while meeting of two phasors(waves) and five phasors(waves)for destructive interference at angle of 180^0 and $2\pi/6$ are given in following Figure 3.24;

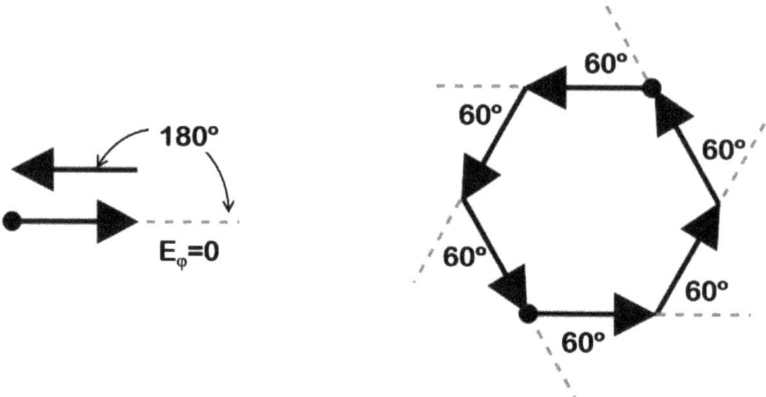

Figure 3.24: Two phasors and six phasors of waves meeting at 180^0 and 60^0 and their resultants leading resultant amplitude 0

In general, for N phasors, the phase difference is given by $2\pi/N$ for destructive interference.

$$\frac{\text{Path Difference}}{\lambda} = \frac{\text{Phase Difference}}{2\pi}$$

$$\text{path difference} = \frac{\lambda}{2\pi}\text{Phase Difference} = \frac{\lambda}{2\pi} \times \frac{2\pi}{N} \quad \text{(for destructive interference)}$$

$$= \frac{\lambda}{N} \tag{3.44}$$

From the following figure, the path difference at first minima = $d\sin(d\delta_0)$

Therefore,

$$d\sin(d\delta_0) = \frac{\lambda}{N} \tag{3.45}$$

$$\sin(d\delta_0) = \frac{\lambda}{Nd} \tag{3.46}$$

When N is very large then $\sin(d\delta_0) \to d\delta_0$

$$d\delta_0 = \frac{\lambda}{Nd} \tag{3.47}$$

Width of Principal Maxima of mth Order

Above equation tells us that if we increase N for a given λ and d then $d\delta_0$ decreases, which means that the central principal maxima become sharper.

For any other general principal minima of order m on the screen from above figure , we can write,

$$d \sin(\delta + d\delta) = m\lambda + \frac{\lambda}{N} \tag{3.48}$$

$$d \sin\delta \cos(d\delta) + d \cos\delta \sin(d\delta) = m\lambda + \frac{\lambda}{N} \quad (\because \sin(A+B) = \sin A \cos B + \cos A \sin B) \tag{3.49}$$

Further $\because d\delta \to 0$, then $\cos(d\delta) = 1$ and $\sin(d\delta) = d\delta$ **(3.50)**

Therefore.

$$d \sin\delta + d \cos\delta\,(d\delta) = m\lambda + \frac{\lambda}{N} \tag{3.51}$$

$$m\lambda + d \cos\delta\,(d\delta) = m\lambda + \frac{\lambda}{N} \quad (\because d \sin\delta = m\lambda) \tag{3.52}$$

Therefore, $d \cos\delta\,(d\delta) = \frac{\lambda}{N}$

$$d\delta = \frac{\lambda}{N d \cos\delta} \tag{3.53}$$

3.10.1 Resolving power of Grating

$\because d \sin\delta = m\lambda$

Differentiating above equation

$$d \cos\delta\,(d\delta) = m\, d\lambda \tag{3.54}$$

$$d\delta = \frac{m\, d\lambda}{d \cos\delta}$$

$$\frac{\lambda}{N d \cos\delta} = \frac{m\, d\lambda}{d \cos\delta} \quad \left(\because d\delta = \frac{\lambda}{N d \cos\delta}\right) \tag{3.55}$$

Therefore,

$$\frac{\lambda}{d\lambda} = mN \tag{3.56}$$

But $\frac{\lambda}{d\lambda}$ = R Resolving Power of Diffraction Grating

$$R = mN \tag{3.57}$$

3.10.2 Experimental Setup of Diffraction Grating;

Following Figure 3.25 shows a sample grating spectroscope, which can used to view the spectrum of a white light source. The light from source is focused on L_1 on slit S_1, which is placed on the focal length of L_2. The parallel light rays emerging from collimator are incident on diffraction grating. Parallel light rays associated with a particular interference maximum occurring at an angle δ falls on lens L_3, and are brought to focus in plane FF'. The image formed is examined by using an eyepiece. The full spectrum of light source can be seen by rotating telescope T at various angles.

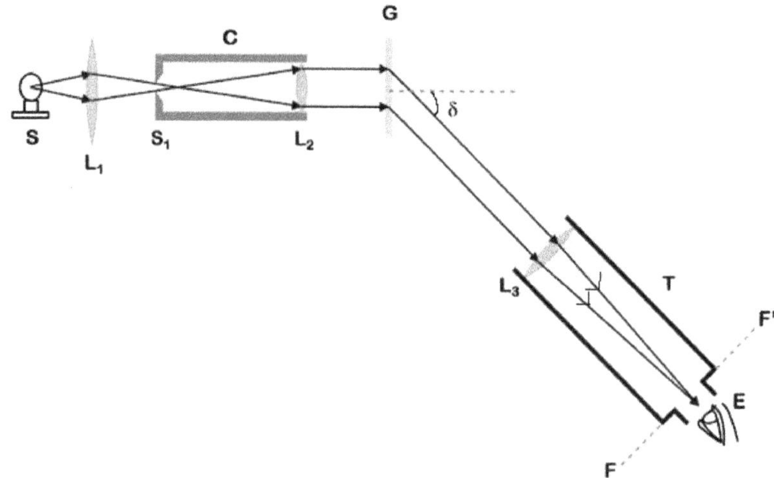

Figure 3.25: Spectroscope for viewing the spectrum of light source S

3.11 Rayleigh criterion for limit of resolution

When the angular separation of two-point sources is such that the central maxima of the diffraction pattern of one source falls on the first minima of the diffraction pattern of the another and vice versa. This is called Rayleigh's criterion of resolving images. Following figure shows, the images of two distant stars. When the stars are closer, then their images can hardly be identified as shown in Figure 3.24(a). When the stars are farther apart and separation among stars satisfy the Rayleigh's criteria of resolution as shown in Figure 3.24(b)., when the stars are much farther apart and their images are perfectly resolved s shown in Figure 3.24(c)

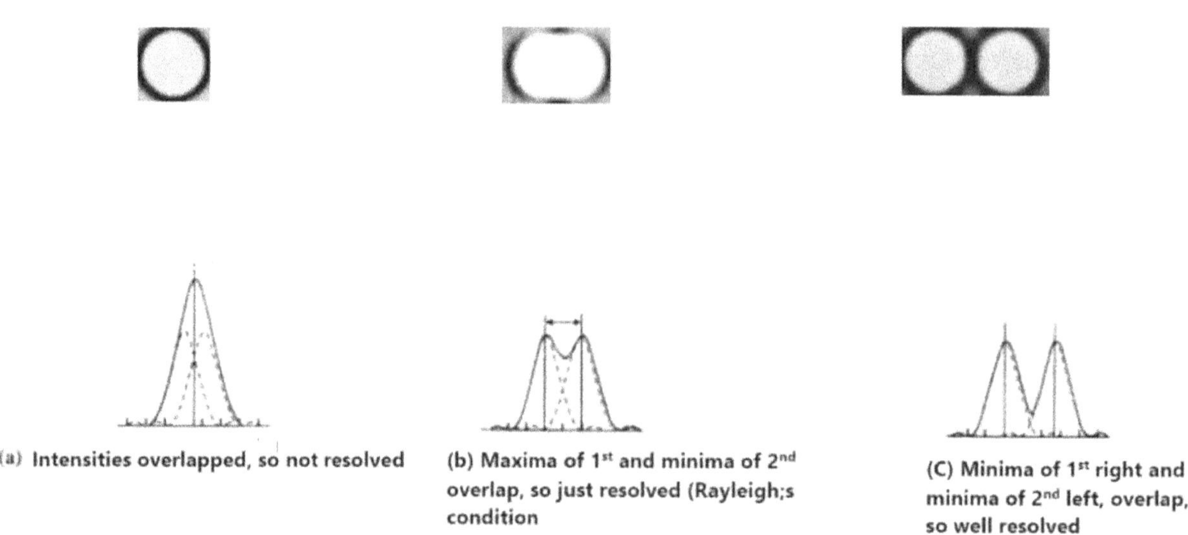

(a) Intensities overlapped, so not resolved

(b) Maxima of 1st and minima of 2nd overlap, so just resolved (Rayleigh;s condition

(C) Minima of 1st right and minima of 2nd left, overlap, so well resolved

Figure 3.26: Distant stars in different situations and their intensity pattern.

-: POINTS TO REMEMBER :-

→ Huygen's Principle: It states that all points on a wavefront which is a collection of points on which the propagating wave reaches at the same instant, serves as point sources of spherical secondary wavelets. After a time t, the new position of the wavefront will be that of a surface tangent to theses secondary wavelets and every point of the secondary wavefront becomes the source of a new wavefront and then then each point of this new wavefront again becomes a source of another new wavefront and this is how the wave propagates.

- → Superposition of Waves: When the waves of different amplitude and different frequency meets at certain points in space, their result will be interference in general and they are called to be superimposed.
- → Constructive Interference: When two light waves of same frequency and same amplitude meets in space with a phase difference of 0, 2π, 4π….., 2mπ (where m = 0, ±1, ±2,…) or with the path difference of 0, λ, 2λ, 3λ……………….mλ ((where m = 0, ±1, ±2,…) then constructive interference happens and the regions in which this phenomenon happens become brighter and we see bright fringes or bright points.
- → Destructive Interference: When two light waves of same frequency and same amplitude meets in space with a phase difference of π, 3π, 5π , ….., (2m+1) π (where m = 0, ±1, ±2,…) or with the path difference of 0, λ/2, 3λ/2……………….(m+1/2)λ ((where m = 0, ±1, ±2,…), then destructive interference happens and the regions in which this phenomenon happens become dark and we see dark fringes or dark points.
- → Formula for fringe width in Young's double slit experiment $y_{m+1} - y_m = \Delta y = \frac{D\lambda}{d}$

  Where D = distance between slits and the screen, d = distance between slits, λ = wavelength of light used
- → Formula for the intensity of light in Young's double slit experiment $\frac{I_\phi}{I_0} = \frac{E_\phi^2}{E_0^2} = 4\cos^2\beta$

  Where β = θ/2 (half of the phase difference between the two interfering light rays), Iφ= intensity of resultant wave and I0 = maximum intensity of each single wave.
- → Interference from thin films; A light wave undergoes a phase change of 180° upon reflection from a medium of higher index of refraction than the one in which it was traveling, which is analogous to a reflected pulse on a string. There is no phase change when the light wave is reflected from a boundary leading to a medium of lower index of refraction which is analogous to a pulse in a string reflecting from a free support.
- → Radius of mth bright Newton's rings, $r = \sqrt{((m - 1/2)\,\lambda R}$ and radius of dark Newton's rings, $r = \sqrt{m\,\lambda R}$
- → Anti-reflection coating: refractive index of coating material (n_2) must be approximately equal to square root of the refractive index of glass(n_3).
- → Michelson interferometer: It is an instrument which can measure very small changes in length with great precision and accuracy by using interference phenomenon for fringes pattern.
- → Fresnel Diffraction: When the screen is at any distance from the slits or aperture. The light rays entering the slits or aperture are not parallel.
- → Fraunhofer diffraction: When the screen is very far from the slits or aperture and the light rays interfering on the screen can be considered as plane waves. The light rays entering the slits or aperture are not parallel.
- → Diffraction by multiple Slits (Diffraction Grating: When the number of parallel slits is increased in Young's double slit experiment, the bright fringes will get narrower. More the number of slits, narrower will be the bright fringe and precise would be the measurement of wavelength of light. When the number of slits is increased to 10^4 within 1 cm, then this kind of system is called diffraction grating.
- → Rayleigh criterion for limit of resolution: When the angular separation of two-point sources is such that the central maxima of the diffraction pattern of one source falls on the first minima of the diffraction pattern of the another and vice versa.

-: SOLVED NUMERICALS :-

1). If the 2nd order bright fringe in Young's double-slit experiment occurs at an angle of 45.0°, then find out the relationship between the wavelength λ and the distance between slits, d?

Given: δ = 45.0°, m = 2

We know that for constructive interference in Young's double slit experiment, d sinδ = mλ

d sin45 = 2λ

So, **d = 2.83λ**

2). A screen is separated from doble slit sources by 2 m. The distance between the two slits is 0.040 mm. The 3rd order bright fringe on the screen is measured to be 6.0 cm from the central line. Determine the (a) wavelength of the light and the (b) distance between adjacent bright fringes.

Given: D = 2 m, d = 0.040 mm, y_m = 6.0 cm

we know that for m^th order bright fringe

$$y_m = D\frac{m\lambda}{d}$$

Or $\lambda = \frac{y_m d}{mD} = \frac{6.0\times10^{-2}\times0.040\times10^{-3}}{3\times2} = 4\times10^{-7}$ m = **400 nm.**

we know that the formula for fringe width in double slit experiment,

$$\Delta y = y_{m+1} - y_m = D\frac{(m+1)\lambda}{d} - D\frac{m\lambda}{d} = \frac{D\lambda}{d}$$

$$= \frac{2.0\times4\times10^{-7}}{0.040\times10^{-3}} = 2\times10\text{-}2 \text{ m} = \mathbf{2.0\ cm}$$

3). Calculate the minimum thickness of a soap bubble film (n =1.30) that will result in constructive interference in the reflected light if the film is illuminated by light with a wavelength of 600 nm.

We know that for constructive interference in thin film;

Or $2d = (m - 1/2)\,\lambda_n$.........

$2d = (m - 1/2)\,\lambda_n$.........$= \lambda_n/2$ (for minimum thickness, m=1)

Or $d = \lambda_n/4 = \lambda/4n$ ($\because \lambda_n = \lambda/n$)

$\therefore d = \frac{1\times600nm}{4\times1.30} =$ **115.38 nm**

4). A soap film (n=1.3) in air is 300 nm thick, which is illuminated at normal incidence of white light. What colours will appear in reflected light from this thin film.

We know that for constructive interference from thin film;

Or $2d = (m - 1/2)\,\lambda_n$

$2d = (m - 1/2)\,\lambda_n = \frac{(m-\frac{1}{2})\lambda}{n}$ ($\because \lambda_n = \lambda/n$)

Therefore;

$\lambda = \frac{2d\times n}{(m-\frac{1}{2})} = 4d\times n = 4\times300nm\times1.3 = 1560$ nm (for m = 1)

$\lambda = \frac{2d\times n}{(m-\frac{1}{2})} = \frac{4\times d\times n}{3} = \frac{4\times300nm\times1.3}{3} = 520$ nm (for m = 2)

$\lambda = \frac{2d\times n}{(m-\frac{1}{2})} = \frac{4\times d\times n}{5} = \frac{4\times300nm\times1.3}{5} = 312$ nm (for m = 3)

Therefore, only green colour with the wavelength of 520 nm corresponding to m = 2 will be seen in reflected light as other wavelengths appearing for m = 1 and m = 3 lie beyond visible range

5). Red light (λ = 630 nm) is incident in Michelson's interferometer experiment. Find the number of bright fringes when the mirror M2 is moved through 0.50 cm.

Each fringe corresponds to a movement of the mirror through half wavelength. Thus the number of fringes will be equal to the number of half wavelengths in 0.50 cm

the number of fringes $= \frac{0.50\times10^{-2}}{\frac{1}{2}\times630\times10^{-9}} = 0.0015873\times10^{7} = \mathbf{15873\ fringes}$

6). A parallel beam of Sodium light is allowed to be incident normally on a plane diffraction grating having 4000 lines per cm and a second order spectral line is observed at angle of 300. Calculate the wavelength of spectral line.

Given: Grating element $d = \frac{1}{4000}$ cm = 0.00025 cm , m = 2 , $\delta = 300$

We know the grating equation as; $\because d \sin\delta = m\lambda$

$$\therefore \lambda = \frac{d \sin\delta}{m} = \frac{d \sin\delta}{m} = \frac{0.00025 \sin30}{2} = \mathbf{6250\times10^{-8}\ cm}$$

-: SHORT QUESTIONS :-

1. Huygens' construction can be used only: (A) for light (B) for an electromagnetic wave (C) if one of the media is vacuum (or air) D) for transverse waves (E) for all of these and other situations **(Ans. E)**
2. What do you understand by the phenomenon of interference of light.
3. Explain Huygen's Principle.
4. What are coherent sources?
5. Write down the formula for the fringe width in Young's double slit experiment. Explain each term in it.
6. Write down the formula for the intensity of light in Young's double slit experiment. Explain each term in it.
7. If white light is used in Young's double slit experiment rather than monochromatic light, how does the interference pattern change.
8. Discuss the formation of Newton's rings. Why the centre of the fringes is dark, when used monochromatic light source of Sodium light Newton's rings experiment.
9. Discuss the formation of colures in thin film when white light or sunlight is incident on it.
10. Discuss the formation of fringes in Michelson Interferometer. We can do through Michelson Interferometer.
11. What is the necessary condition on path difference between two waves that interfere (a) constructively (b) destructively?

-: DESCRIPTIVE QUESTIONS :-

1. Derive the formula for the fringe width in Young's double slit experiment.
2. Derive the formula for the intensity of light in Young's double slit experiment.
3. Derive the formula for the diameter of a bright ring of nth order in Newton's rings Experiment.
4. What is plane diffraction grating? How would you use it to determine the wavelength of incident light?
5. Discuss about the Rayleigh Criterion of resolution. Derive an expression for the resolving power of grating.
6. Explain Fresnel and Fraunhofer diffraction with proper diagrams.
7. Explain anti-reflective coating and how it can be used to enhance efficiency of solar cells.
8. Yellow light is viewed by reflection from a thin vertical soap film. Let λ be the wavelength of the light within the film. Why is there a large dark space at the top of the film?

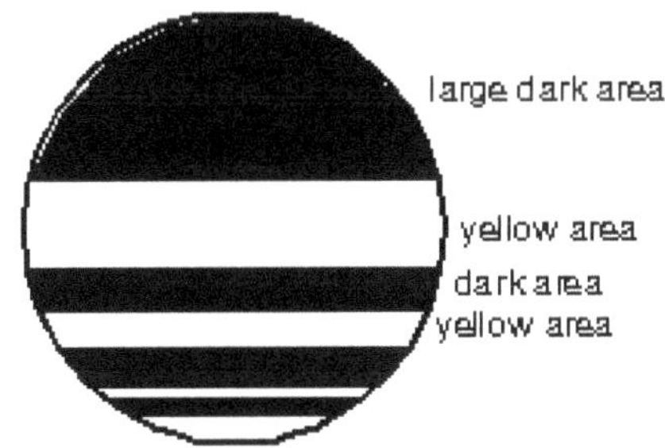

9. A glass (n = 1.6) lens is coated with a thin film (n = 1.3) to reduce reflection of certain incident light. If λ is the wavelength of the light in the film, what will be the least film thickness? **(Ans. λ/4)**
10. A grating has 400 slits per mm. How many orders of the entire visible spectrum (400 – 700nm) can be produced. **(Ans. m =3.57)**

* * * * *

CHAPTER-IV QUANTUM PHYSICS

Learning goals

At the end of this chapter reader will be able to

- ✓ Understand black body and its radiation. Explain and derive the Planck's law.
- ✓ Explain wave-particle duality. State and derive de Broglie's hypothesis. Calculate particle wavelengths using de Broglie's relation.
- ✓ Explain about concept of the wave function and its physical significance. State and explain Heisenberg's uncertainty principle and understand its implications in quantum mechanics.
- ✓ Derive the time-independent and time-dependent Schrödinger equations.
- ✓ Solve the particle in a box problem using Schrödinger equation.
- ✓ Explain quantum tunneling qualitatively. Describe the working principle of scanning tunneling microscope (STM).

PREREQUISITES:

- Laws of classical mechanics (Newton's laws of motion), Concepts of energy, momentum, and force
- Concepts of temperature, energy and electromagnetic waves
- Knowledge of basic differential equations
- Understanding of early quantum experiments (e.g., photoelectric effect, double-slit experiment)
- Basic knowledge of atomic structure and electron behavior

4.1 INTRODUCTION

By 1880, most of physics problems were being resolved with the use of Newtonian mechanics, thermodynamics and Maxwell's theory of electromagnetic. But these classical theories fail to explain phenomena like photoelectric effect (1905), black body radiation (1901), emission of light spectra (1913), Compton effect (1924). The theories of classical physics were not working successfully in describing the events of the microscopic world (at atomic level). The phenomenon of microscopic objects can be explained with laws of wave mechanics or quantum mechanics. Dual nature of light (particle and wave nature) can be explained with the help of wave mechanics and the dual nature of matter (particle and wave nature) can be explained with the help of quantum mechanics.

4.2 Black body radiation

4.2.1 Concept of Black body:

A body/entity which emits or absorbs all kinds of radiation is called black body. Ideally none of the matter in the universe is considered as a perfect black body. We can consider stars and the sun as ideal examples of black body as it emits all kinds of radiation when heated by nuclear fusion.

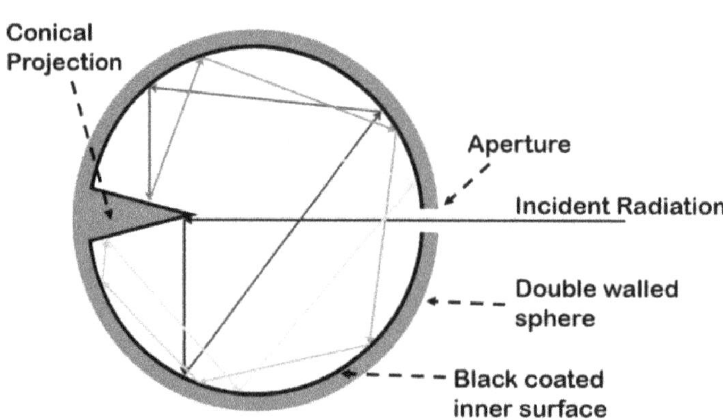

Figure 4.1: Schematic diagram for the black body

A spherical cavity blacked inside and completely closed except a narrow aperture serves as an ideal black body as shown in Figure 4.1. Light entering the cavity is trapped inside by multiple reflections from the walls. When heated, the black body would emit more from a unit area than any other body at a given temperature.

It is a matter of common experience that when a body is heated it emits radiation. The radiation emitted by hot bodies is called thermal radiation. Even at ordinary temperatures a body emits radiation over a range of frequencies. The relative brightness of the different frequencies depends on the temperature of the body. As the temperature of the body increases, the maximum intensity peak shifts to a lower and lower wavelength side. For example, an iron rod appears dark at ordinary temperatures and when heated it appears faint crimson at around 500 °C, then turns red, orange gradually and yellow at 800 °C, finally it emits white light above 1000 °C. The thermal radiation emitted by an idealized body called a black body is thoroughly analyzed using spectrographs and bolometers. The experimental results, illustrated in Figure 4.2 showed that at a given temperature the radiation energy density initially increases with lowering wavelength, the peaks at around a particular frequency and after that decreases at lower wavelength. Various efforts were made to calculate theoretically the frequency distribution of thermal radiation using Maxwell's theory and thermodynamics.

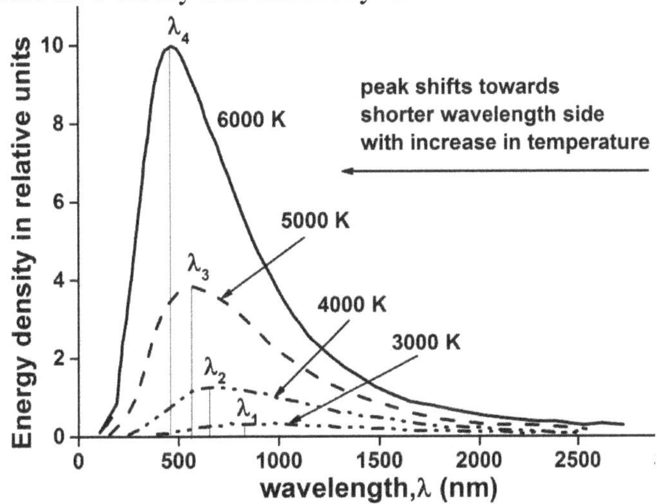

Figure 4.2 Energy density Vs wavelength curve for the black body under different temperature

4.2.2 Wien's displacement law for black body radiation:

Wien proposed an expression for the rate of emission of energy per unit area per unit wavelength interval at wavelength λ, Eλ as

$$E_\lambda = \frac{c_1 \cdot e^{\frac{-c_2}{\lambda T}}}{\lambda^5} \qquad (4.1)$$

where λ is the wavelength and T is the absolute temperature. Wien's law holds good for lower wavelengths.

4.2.3 Rayleigh-Jeans law for black body radiation:

The Rayleigh and Jeans derived formula for rate of emission of energy per unit area per unit wavelength interval at wavelength λ, Eλ as

$$E_\lambda = \frac{8\pi kT}{\lambda^4} \qquad (4.2)$$

According to this law, the intensity of thermal radiation should be increased with decreasing λ as the fourth power of λ. The theory agrees with experimental results at higher wavelengths but leads to absurd results at the lower wavelength side. The theory implies that radiation emitted by a hot body should have a large portion of UV rays. This is contrary to our observation and clearly violates the law of conservation of energy. This contradiction is called *ultraviolet catastrophe*. Thus classical theory fails to explain the distribution of thermal radiation emitted by solid bodies.

4.2.4 Plank's theory of black body radiation:

The radiation laws of Wein's and Rayleigh-Jeans were based on the principles of classical mechanics. Their failures to explain the spectral energy curves of black body radiation indicated that the fundamental assumptions of classical theory required suitable modifications. The correct law of radiation was finally discovered by a German physicist, Max Plank in 1901 by introducing a novel and revolutionary concept known as quantum mechanics. According to Plank, matter is composed of a large number of oscillating particles which vibrate with different frequencies. As far as the classical theory is concerned these oscillating particles may have any value of frequency and have any amount of vibration energy. However, according to quantum theory an oscillating particle in a body cannot have any arbitrary amount of energy. They could have discrete values of energy given by

$$E = nh\nu \tag{4.3}$$

where n is any positive integer (n = 0, 1, 2, 3 ....), ν is the frequency of oscillation and h is a constant known as a Planck's constant ($h = 6.62 \times 10^{-34}$ J·s), Further, Planck's assumption was that the vibrating particle does not radiate energy continuously but only in terms of discrete quanta which is known as photons. These quanta of energies are emitted when an oscillating particle changes from its one quantized state of vibration to another. So long as an oscillator remains in one of its quantized state it neither emits nor absorbs any energy. In the field of heat radiation, the black body is universally chosen as the standard radiator. A *black body* is defined to be a body which absorbs completely all radiations which falls on it and which reflects, transmits and scatters none. Black body radiation is assumed to consist of energy emitted by infinite number of atomic oscillators. If N_0 is the number of such oscillators in the state of lowest or zero point energy, then according to Maxwell's distribution law, the number of oscillators having energy E in access of the zero point energy E_0 will be $N_0e^{-E/kT}$, where T is the absolute temperature and k is Boltzmann's constant. If N is the total number of oscillator possessing different amounts of energy E_1, E_2 ...., etc., we have

$$N = N_0e^{-E_0/kT} + N_0e^{-E_1/kT} + N_0e^{-E_2/kT} + \dots \tag{4.4}$$

According to Planck's quantum theory, E can take only integer values of hν and so possible values of E are 0, hν, 2hν, 3hν etc., Eq. (4.4) becomes

$$N = N_0 + N_0e^{-h\nu/kT} + N_0e^{-2h\nu/kT} + \dots$$

$$= N_0 \sum_{n=0}^{\infty} e^{-nh\nu/kT} \tag{4.5}$$

The total energy E of the oscillator is

$$E = E_0N_0 + E_1N_0e^{-E_1/kT} + E_2N_0e^{-E_2/kT} + \dots$$

$$= 0 + h\nu\, N_0e^{-h\nu/kT} + 2h\nu\, N_0e^{-2h\nu/kT} + \dots$$

$$= \sum_{n=0}^{\infty} nh\nu\, N_0e^{-nh\nu/kT} \tag{4.6}$$

The mean energy $\bar{E}$ of an oscillator is given by

$$\bar{E} = \frac{E}{N} = \frac{\sum_{n=0}^{\infty} nh\nu\, N_0 e^{-nh\nu/kT}}{N_0 \sum_{n=0}^{\infty} e^{-nh\nu/kT}} \qquad (4.7)$$

Since n is integer, Eq. (4.7) becomes

$$\bar{E} = \frac{0 + h\nu\, e^{-h\nu/kT} + 2h\nu\, e^{-2h\nu/kT} + 3h\nu\, e^{-3h\nu/kT} + \ldots}{1 + e^{-h\nu/kT} + e^{-2h\nu/kT} + e^{-3h\nu/kT} + \ldots} \qquad (4.8)$$

Let $x = e^{-h\nu/kT}$, then Eq. (4.8) can be written as

$$\bar{E} = h\nu x \left[\frac{1 + 2x + 3x^2 + \ldots}{1 + x + x^2 + \ldots}\right] \qquad (4.9)$$

The limits of these convergent series can be found by the usual methods (note that $x < 1$). The convergent limit of the series in the numerator is $\frac{1}{(1-x)^2}$.

This can be checked by expanding $(1 - x)^{-2}$ according to the binomial theorem. The denominator is a simple geometric progression converging to $1/(1 - x)$. Substitution these limits in Eq. (4.9), we have

$$\bar{E} = h\nu x \frac{1/(1-x)^2}{1/(1-x)}$$

$$= \frac{h\nu x}{1 - x}$$

$$= \frac{h\nu}{\left(\frac{1}{x} - 1\right)} \qquad (4.10)$$

When x is replaced by its equivalent, the result is

$$\bar{E} = \frac{h\nu}{e^{h\nu/kT} - 1} \qquad (4.11)$$

Thus we see that the average energy of an oscillator given by Eq. (4.11) is different from the energy kT of a classical oscillator.

We know that the number of oscillators per unit volume in frequency interval of ν and ν + dν is given by

$$N = \frac{8\pi\nu^2}{c^3} d\nu \qquad (4.12)$$

Multiplying Eq. (4.12) with the average energy of oscillators given by Eq. (4.11), we get the total energy per unit volume belonging to the range of dν or the energy density belonging to the range dν as

$$E_\nu\, d\nu = \frac{8\pi\nu^2}{c^3} d\nu \times \frac{h\nu}{e^{h\nu/kT} - 1}$$

$$= \frac{8\pi h\nu^3}{c^3} \cdot \frac{1}{e^{h\nu/kT} - 1} d\nu \qquad (4.13)$$

This is known as the Planck's radiation law.

This law can also be expressed in terms of wavelength as

$$\nu = \frac{c}{\lambda} \quad \text{or} \quad d\nu = \frac{-c}{\lambda^2} d\lambda$$

Since an increase in frequency corresponds to a decrease in wavelength $E_\lambda\, d\lambda = -E_\nu\, d\nu$. Eq. (4.13) can now be expressed as

$$E_\lambda\, d\lambda = \frac{8\pi h}{c^3}\left(\frac{c^3}{\lambda^3}\right) \cdot \frac{1}{(e^{hc/\lambda kT} - 1)} \left(\frac{c}{\lambda^2} d\lambda\right)$$

$$E_\lambda\, d\lambda = \frac{8\pi hc}{\lambda^5} \cdot \frac{1}{(e^{hc/\lambda kT} - 1)}\, d\lambda \qquad (4.14)$$

This formula agrees well with experimental curves throughout the whole range of wavelengths. It is shown in Figure 4.3.

From Planck's radiation law, Wien's law and Rayleigh-Jeans law can be deduced as follows.

Case I: Wien's law from Plank's law

For low temperatures, λT is small. Now $e^{h\nu/kT} \gg 1$ and 1 can be neglected in the denominator of Eq. (4.14). Thus,

$$E_\lambda\, d\lambda = \frac{8\pi hc}{\lambda^5} \cdot e^{-hc/\lambda kT}\, d\lambda$$

Putting $8\pi hc = c_1$ and, $\frac{hc}{k} = c_2$, we have

$$E_\lambda = \frac{c_1 \cdot e^{\frac{-c_2}{\lambda T}}}{\lambda^5} \qquad (4.15)$$

This is Wien's law which agrees with experiment at short wavelength.

Case II: Rayleigh-Jeans law from Plank's law

For higher temperatures, λT is large.
Now,

$$e^{hc/\lambda kT} = 1 + \frac{hc}{\lambda kT} + \frac{1}{2}\left(\frac{hc}{\lambda kT}\right)^2 + \ldots$$
$$= 1 + \frac{hc}{\lambda kT}, \text{ neglecting higher powers}$$

Eq. (4.14) becomes

$$E_\lambda\, d\lambda = \frac{8\pi hc}{\lambda^5} \cdot \frac{1}{1 + \frac{hc}{\lambda kT} - 1}$$
$$= \frac{8\pi hc}{\lambda^5} \cdot \frac{\lambda kT}{hc}\, d\lambda$$
$$= \frac{8\pi kT}{\lambda^4}\, d\lambda \qquad (4.16)$$

This is Rayleigh-Jeans law which agrees with experiment at longer wavelength. One the basis of assumption can plotted graph as shown in Figure 4.3.

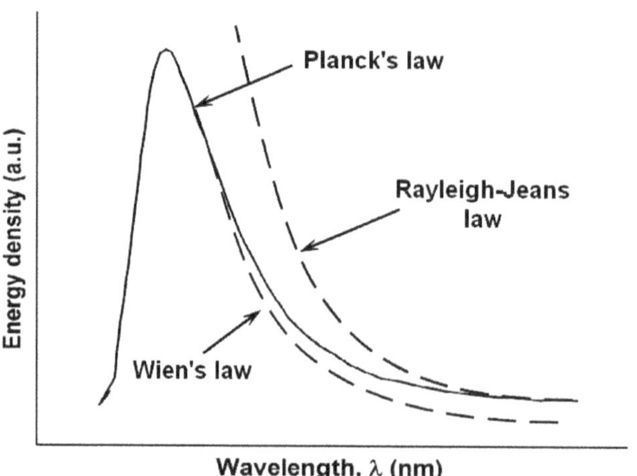

Figure 4.3: Graphs for radiation laws

4.2.5 Properties of photons

The following are some of the important properties of photons.

→ **Mass and momentum of a photon:**

Using Einstein's theory $E = mc^2$, the mass of the photon is

$$m = \frac{E}{c^2} = \frac{h\nu}{c^2} = \frac{hc}{\lambda c^2} = \frac{h}{c\lambda} \quad (4.17)$$

Similarly the momentum

$$p = mc = \frac{h}{c\lambda} \cdot c = \frac{h}{\lambda} \quad (4.18)$$

→ **Energy of a photon:**

The energy content of a photon is E=hν. This quantum value is not same for all kinds of radiations. It differs for different radiations as ν is different in each case.

→ **Non-electrical nature of photon:**

Photons are electrically neutral. Both electric and magnetic fields have no influence on photons. Further they do not ionize.

4.3 Wave-particle duality of matter - de Broglie matter waves

The suggestion that matter may have wave-like properties was first put forward in 1924-25 by Louis de Broglie. He argued that if light (which consists of waves according to classical picture) can sometimes behave like particles, then it should be possible for matter (which consists of particles, classically) to exhibit wave-like behavior under suitable circumstances. He made the hypothesis that the relation between the energy E of a particle and the frequency ν of the associated wave is exactly the same as that between the energy of a photon and the frequency of light radiation.

$$E = h\nu = \hbar\omega \quad (4.19)$$

where, $\omega = 2\pi\nu$ is the angular frequency.

The dual nature of light possessing both wave and particle properties is clearly illustrated by combining Plank's expression for the energy of a photon E = hν with Einstein's mass-energy relation $E=mc^2$ (where c is the velocity of light), to give

$$h\nu = mc^2$$

Introducing $\nu = c/\lambda$, we get

$$\therefore \lambda = \frac{h}{mc} = \frac{h}{p} \quad (4.20)$$

where λ is the wavelength of photon.

It was by analogy with this equation associating momentum with a photon that de Broglie proposed the concept of matter waves, according to which a material particle of mass m moving with velocity v should have an associated wavelength λ, called the de Broglie wavelength, given by

$$\therefore \lambda = \frac{h}{\text{momentum}} = \frac{h}{mv} = \frac{h}{p} \quad (4.21)$$

where h is Planck's Constant. Eq. (4.21) is known as the *de Broglie wave equation*. From Eq. (4.21), we find that if the particles, say, electrons are associated to various velocities, we can produce waves of various wavelengths. The higher the electron velocity, the smaller the de Broglie wavelength. Also, the wavelength associated with a moving particle is independent of any charge associated with it. The de Broglie wavelength of particle in terms of kinetic energy can be written by considering kinetic energy equation of particle with velocity v, therefore

$$KE = E = \frac{1}{2}mv^2$$

$$\therefore 2mE = m^2v^2$$

From Eq. (4.21)

$$\therefore \lambda = \frac{h}{mv} = \frac{1}{\sqrt{2mE}} \tag{4.22}$$

If the velocity v is given to an electron by accelerating it through a potential difference V, then the work done on the electron is 'eV'. This work done is converted into the kinetic energy of the electron, thus

$$\frac{1}{2}mv^2 = eV$$

$$v = \left[\frac{2eV}{m}\right]^{1/2}$$

$$\therefore \; mv = \sqrt{2meV}$$

Substituting this value in de Broglie equation, we have

$$\lambda = \frac{h}{\sqrt{2meV}} \tag{4.23}$$

Ignoring relativistic consideration m = m_0, the rest mass of the electron

$$\lambda = \frac{h}{\sqrt{2m_0eV}}$$

$$\lambda = \frac{6.62 \times 10^{-34}}{\sqrt{2 \times 9.1 \times 10^{-31} \times 1.6 \times 10^{-19} \times V}}$$

$$\lambda = \frac{12.27}{\sqrt{V}} \times 10^{-10} \; m$$

$$\lambda = \frac{1.227}{\sqrt{V}} \; nm \tag{4.24}$$

Suppose that the accelerating voltage V = 120 volt, then we get λ = 1.119 Å. Thus, the wavelength of electron wave at 120 volt is 1.119 Å – an order approximately equal to the successive distance between the planes of a crystal which gave an idea that a crystal may be used as diffraction grating (as used in X-rays) to detect the electron waves.

4.3.1 Characteristics of matter waves

→ From Eq. (4.21), $\lambda \propto \frac{1}{m}$

Thus the wavelength of matter wave is inversely proportional to the mass of the particle. The larger the mass of the particle, the shorter will be the wavelength and vice versa.

→ From Eq. (4.21), $\lambda \propto \frac{1}{v}$

Thus, the matter wavelength varies inversely with the velocity of particle. The greater the velocity of the particle, the smaller will be the matter wavelength and vice versa.

→ This is totally a new wave and cannot be equated to electromagnetic wave.

→ The velocity of matter wave depends on velocity of matter particle; hence its velocity is not a constant whereas the velocity of electromagnetic wave is.

→ Matter wave can travel with a velocity greater than the velocity of light

We know

$$E = mc^2 \text{ and } E = h\nu$$

$$\nu = \frac{mc^2}{h} \tag{4.25}$$

∴ Wave velocity of matter wave, $w = \nu \cdot \lambda$

$$= \frac{mc^2}{h} \times \frac{h}{mv} \quad \left(\because \lambda = \frac{h}{mv}\right)$$

$$w = \frac{c^2}{v} \tag{4.26}$$

Since the particle velocity v cannot exceed c, it suggests that the velocity of matter wave *w* is greater than the velocity of light.

4.3.2 Application of de Broglie matter waves

The de Broglie's matter wave concept finds its application in:

→ Explanation of confirmation of Bohr's postulates by Schrödinger in 1925.

→ In the construction of electron microscope.

→ In the study of crystal structure.

4.4 Concept of the wave function and its physical significance – Heisenberg's uncertainty principle

4.4.1 Concept of wave packet:

According to de Broglie hypothesis, a particle is represented by matter wave which is nothing but wave with wavelength λ. This assumption brings out two questions: (1) how can a wave which spread out over a large region of space represent a highly localized particle? and (2) if somehow a wave represents a particle, what exactly is that is waving in the particle wave?

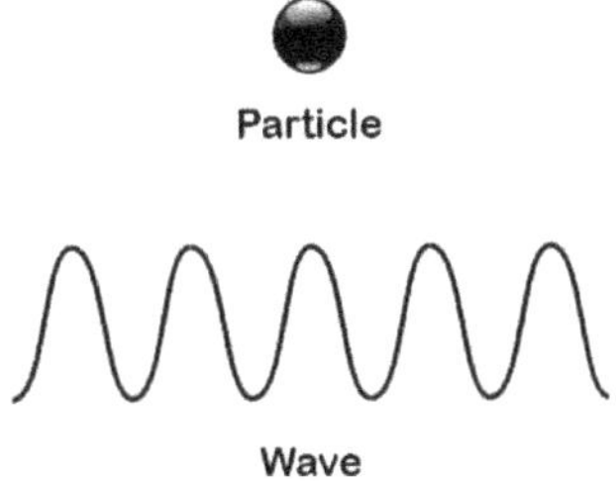

Figure 4.4: Localized particle at a point in space and its wave spread over a large volume

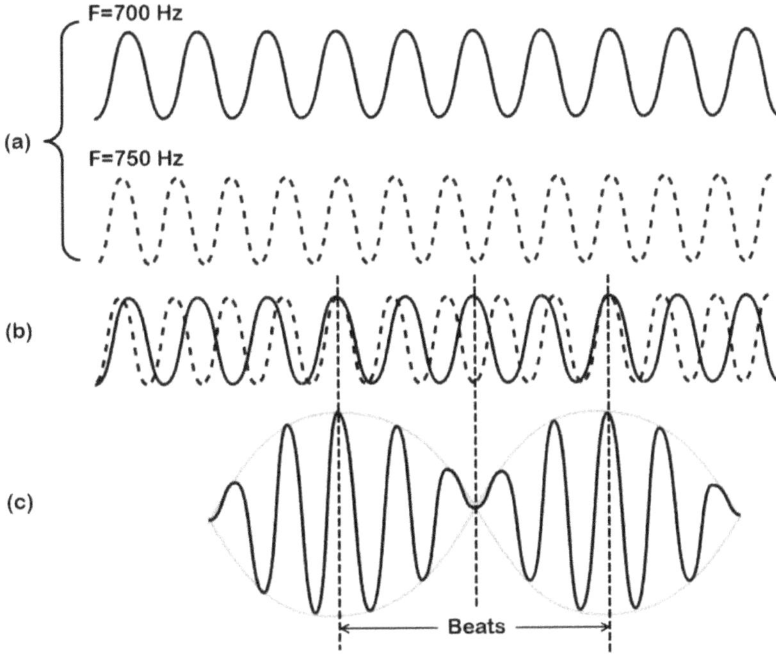

Figure 4.5: Formation of beats by combination of two waves of slightly different frequencies (a) individual waves (b) Combination of waves (c) resultant wave

Let us assume that a particle like an electron can be described by the expression

$$\Psi = A\sin(kx - \omega t) \tag{4.27}$$

It represents a pure sine wave that has no beginning and no end as shown in Figure 4.4. It is characterized by a precise wavelength λ and momentum $\hbar k$. It is of infinite extent and completely non-localized. Hence a mono-frequency wave cannot represent a particle which is an entity confined to a very small volume. It implies that de Broglie waves are not harmonic waves but could be a combination of several waves. It is known that a superposition of several waves having slightly different frequencies gives rise to a *wave packet*. Such a wave packet possesses both wave and particle properties. The regular separation λ_{ave} between successive maxima in a wave packet is characteristics of a wave and at the same time it has a particle-like localization in space.

Beats produced by sound waves are a familiar example of wave packets. When two sound waves of same amplitude but of slightly different frequencies combine, they produce a sound which has a frequency equal to the average of the two original frequencies and its amplitude rises and falls periodically. The formation of beats is schematic shown in Figure 4.5.

The actual formation of a wave packet requires the superposition of large number of waves. Thus,

$$\Psi(x,t) = \int A(k)\sin(kx - \omega t)\,dk \tag{4.28}$$

A wave packet produced by such superposition is shown in Figure 4.6. The packet is centred on ν_0. As $|\nu - \nu_0|$ increases the amplitude of the resultant wave diminishes. The spread of wave packet is given by Δx.

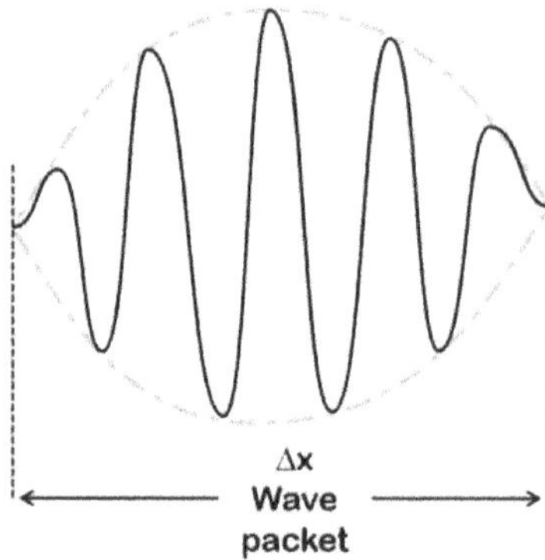

Figure 4.6: Wave packet

If the velocities of the constituent waves in wave packets are the same, the wave packet travels with the phase velocity v_p given by

$$v_p = \frac{\omega}{k} \tag{4.29}$$

If the wave velocities vary with wavelength, the different individual waves do not travel together. As a result the wave packet travels with a group velocity v_g which is given by

$$v_g = \frac{d\omega}{dk} \tag{4.30}$$

The particles can be therefore represented by wave packets.

4.4.2 Wave function Ψ

Now we turn to the second question raised in previous section. Waves represent the propagation of a disturbance in a medium. Light waves, sound waves, water waves are example of waves. They are all characterized by some quality that varies with position and time. In a light wave the electromagnetic field varies in space and time while in sound wave propagation, the pressure of sound wave varies in space and time. What is it whose variation leads to de Broglie waves? The variable quantity characterizing the de Broglie waves is called the *wave function* which is denoted by symbol Ψ. The wave function mathematically describes the motion of an electron. Since Ψ (x, y, z, t) is a function of space and time co-ordinate, we might expect to represent position of a particle at some time t. In general, it is not possible to locate a particle precisely at a position x, y, z, there is only a probability P of the particle being a specific point (x, y, z). Further, Ψ is usually a complex quantity. It has no direct physical significance as it is not an observable quantity. Max Born, a German physicist, showed in 1926 that the square of absolute value of the wave function $|\Psi|^2$ is proportional to the probability of a particle being in unit volume of space, centered at the point where Ψ is evaluated, at time t. A larger value of $|\Psi|^2$ means stronger possibility of the particle's presence while a small value of $|\Psi|^2$ means only slight possibility of its presence. As long as $|\Psi|^2$ is not actually 'zero' somewhere, there is definite chance of detecting the particle.

The wave function Ψ is complex quantity with both real and imaginary parts. The complex conjugate of Ψ is denoted by Ψ*

$$\Psi = x + iy$$
$$\Psi^* = x - iy$$

Therefore $\Psi \cdot \Psi^*$ is always positive and real as

$$\Psi\Psi^* = x^2 + y^2$$

4.4.3 Physical significance of Ψ

The square of absolute magnitude of Ψ i.e. $|\Psi|^2 = \Psi \cdot \Psi^*$ at a particular time at a point is proportional to probability P of finding the particle at that point at the particular instant. The possibility of finding the particle within a volume element $dV = dxdydz$ is given by

$$P = \int_{-\infty}^{+\infty} |\Psi|^2 \, dV \tag{4.31}$$

Since the total probability of finding the particle somewhere at all times is unity, we impose the condition on Ψ that

$$\int_{-\infty}^{+\infty} |\Psi|^2 \, dV = 1 \tag{4.32}$$

The wave function which obeys the above condition is said to be normalized. Similarly, the following other conditions are also imposed on Ψ:

→ As the probability P can have only one value at a particular place and time, Ψ must be single-valued.

→ The particle exists somewhere in the space, therefore, the integral of $\Psi \cdot \Psi^*$ overall space must be finite.

→ Wave function Ψ and its partial derivatives, i.e. $\frac{\partial \Psi}{\partial x}, \frac{\partial \Psi}{\partial y}, and \frac{\partial \Psi}{\partial z}$ must be also continuous everywhere.

4.5 Heisenberg uncertainty principle:

The fact that a moving particle must be regarded as a de Broglie wave group rather than as a localized entity suggests that there is a fundamental limit to the accuracy with which we can measure its particle properties. According to classical mechanics, a moving particle at any instant has a fixed position in space and a definite momentum which can be determined simultaneously with any desired accuracy. In recent years it has become apparent that the classical point of view represents an approximation which is adequate for the objects of appreciable size; but does not describe satisfactorily the behaviour of particles of atomic dimensions.

Since a moving atomic particle has to be regarded as a de Broglie wave group, there is a limit to the accuracy with which we can measure its particle properties. According to Born's probability interpretation, the particle may be found anywhere within the wave group, moving with the group velocity. If the group is considered to be narrow, it is easier to locate its position but the uncertainty in calculating its velocity or momentum increases. On the other hand, if the group is considered to be wide, its momentum can be estimated satisfactorily, but there is a great uncertainty about the exact location of the particle. Heisenberg, a German scientist, enunciated in 1927 the *indeterminacy* or *uncertainty principle*, which states that the simultaneous determination of the exact position and momentum of a moving particle is impossible. In general if Δx denotes the error in the measurement of the position of the particle along x-axis and Δp represents the error in the measurement of momentum, then

$$\Delta \mathbf{x} \cdot \Delta \mathbf{p} = \mathbf{h} \tag{4.33}$$

where, h is Planck's constant. The above relation represents the extent of the uncertainty involved in the measurement of both the position and momentum of the particle.

When one defines (Δx) and (Δp) as r.m.s. deviations and assumes the optimum measurement procedure, it turns out that the lower limit in Eq. (4.33) is

$$\frac{h}{4\pi} \text{ or } \frac{\hbar}{2}$$

where,

$$\hbar = \frac{h}{2\pi}$$

Thus

$$(\Delta x)(\Delta p) \geq \frac{\hbar}{2} \tag{4.34}$$

Eq. (4.33) is one form of the uncertainty principle first obtained by Werner Heisenberg in 1927. It states that the product of uncertainty Δx in the position of a body at some instant, and the uncertainty Δp in its momentum at the some instant, is at best equal to Planck's constant. We cannot measure simultaneously both position and momentum with perfect accuracy. In fact, Eq. (4.34) tells us that we could locate a particle exactly ($\Delta x \to 0$) only at the expense of imparting to it an infinite momentum ($\Delta p \to \infty$); *i.e.*, an exact position measurement requires the expenditure of an infinite amount energy.

The uncertainty relation discussed above applies specifically to position and momentum. There is not an uncertainty relation between any pair of variables, but only between certain pairs. There are uncertainty relations, for instance, between position and momentum, energy and time, and angular momentum and angle. All these relations have the form as Eq. (4.34). Thus, if the time during which a system occupies a certain state is not greater than Δt, then the energy of the state cannot be known to within ΔE, where:

$$(\Delta E)(\Delta t) \geq \frac{\hbar}{2} \tag{4.35}$$

Thus, for example, if an electron remains in an excited state for 10^{-8} s, the *uncertainty* in the energy of that state must be:

$$\begin{aligned}(\Delta E) \geq \frac{\hbar}{2}\frac{1}{\Delta t} &= \frac{h}{4\pi \times 10^{-8}} \\ &= \frac{(6.62 \times 10^{-34} \times 10^{8})}{4\pi} \\ &= 0.527 \times 10^{-26}\ \mathrm{J} \\ &= \frac{0.527 \times 10^{-26}}{1.6 \times 10^{-19}} \\ &= 3.29 \times 10^{-8}\ \mathrm{eV}\end{aligned}$$

The uncertainty is best understood and illustrated by the example of diffraction through a slit. If we propose to regard the passage of an electron through a slit and the observation of the diffraction pattern as a simultaneous measurement of position and momentum from the stand point of the corpuscle concept, then the breadth of the slit gives the 'uncertainty' Δx in the specified position perpendicular to the direction of the flight. For the fact is that a diffraction pattern merely allows us to conclude that the electrons have passed through the slit; at what place in the slit the passage took place remains quite indefinite.

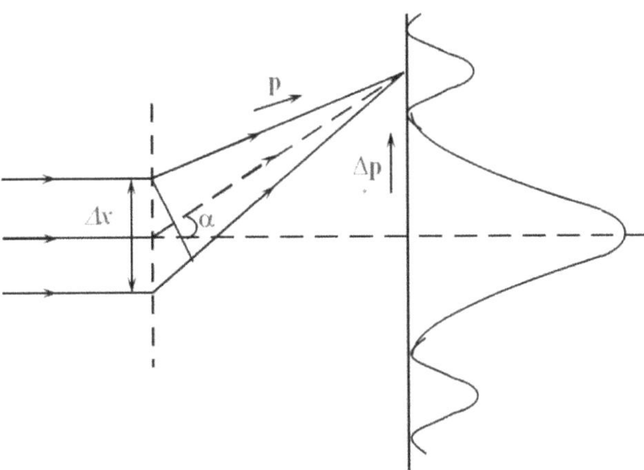

Figure 4.7: Diffraction of electrons at a slit

Again, from the standpoint of the corpuscular theory the occurrence of the diffraction pattern on the screen must be understood in the sense that the individual electron suffers deflection at the slit, upwards or downwards. It acquires component momentum perpendicular to its original direction of the flight, of amount Δp. The mean value of Δp in Figure 4.7 is given by $\Delta p = p \sin\alpha$, if α is the mean angle of deflection. We know that, the experimental results can be explained satisfactorily on the basis of the wave representation according to which α is connected with the slit width Δx and the wavelength $\lambda = \frac{h}{p}$, by the equations:

$$\Delta x \sin\alpha \cong \lambda = \frac{h}{p}$$

Thus,

$$\Delta p \cong p \sin\alpha = \frac{p\lambda}{\Delta x} = \frac{p\ h}{\Delta x\, p} = \frac{h}{\Delta x}$$

or

$$(\Delta x)(\Delta p) \cong h$$

which is Heisenberg's uncertainty principle.

One interesting question is whether electrons are present in atomic nuclei or not. As is known, typical nuclei are less than 10^{-14} m in radius. For an electron to be confined within such a nucleus, the uncertainty in its position may not exceed 10^{-14} m. The corresponding uncertainty in the electron's momentum is:

$$\Delta p \geq \frac{h}{4\pi\,(\Delta x)}$$

$$\Delta p \geq \frac{6.62 \times 10^{-34}}{4\pi \times 10^{-14}} = 0.526 \times 10^{-20}\ \mathrm{kg \cdot m/s}$$

If this is the uncertainty in the electron's momentum, the momentum itself must be atleast comparable in magnitude. An electron whose momentum is 0.5 x 10^{-20} kg·m/s has a kinetic energy E many times greater than its rest mass energy m_0c^2.

$$E = pc = \frac{0.526 \times 10^{-20} \times 3 \times 10^{8}}{1.6 \times 10^{-19}} \text{ eV}$$

$$E = 10 \text{ MeV}$$

The rest mass energy of the electron m_0c^2 is 0.5 MeV, which is negligible, compared to the kinetic energy. Experiments indicate that the electrons associated even with unstable atoms never have more than a fraction of this energy, and we thus conclude that electrons cannot be present within nuclei.

4.6 Schrödinger's wave equation

In 1926, developing further the de Broglie's ideas of the wave properties of matter, Erwin Schrödinger, an Austrian-Irish physicist, formulated the wave equation which is now known as the *Schrödinger equation*. This equation cannot be derived from any fundamental laws. It plays the same role in quantum mechanics as Newton's second law does in classical mechanics. We can determine the motion of an atomic particle using Schrödinger equation just as we determine the motion of a classical particle using Newton's laws.

Let us now explain how we can arrive at Schrödinger wave equation. Let us consider a micro-particle. We associate a wave function Ψ with the motion of this micro-particle. Ψ-function represents the wave field of the particle. According to de Broglie's hypothesis of matter wave, a particle of mass m moving with velocity v is associated with a wave system having wavelength

$$\lambda = \frac{h}{mv} = \frac{h}{p}$$

The wave disturbance is indicated by wave function Ψ, the periodic variation of which gives the complete description of the wave system associated with the moving particle.

The classical wave is described by the following wave equation Eq. (4.36)

$$\nabla^2\Psi(x, y, z, t) = \frac{1}{v^2}\frac{\partial^2\Psi}{\partial t^2} \qquad (4.36)$$

where ∇^2 is Laplacian operator represented by

$$\nabla^2 = \frac{\partial^2}{\partial x^2} + \frac{\partial^2}{\partial y^2} + \frac{\partial^2}{\partial z^2}$$

and v is velocity and $\Psi(x, y, z, t)$ is the wave function.

The solution of Eq. (4.36) gives Ψ as a periodic displacement in terms of time and is

$$\Psi(x, y, z, t) = \Psi_0(x, y, z)\, e^{-i2\pi\nu t} \qquad (4.37)$$

Here $\Psi_0(x, y, z)$ is the amplitude of the wave at the point (x, y, z) and ν is frequency. The position vector of point (x, y, z) is

$$\vec{r} = x\hat{i} + y\hat{j} + z\hat{k}$$

where $\hat{i}$, $\hat{j}$ and $\hat{k}$ are unit vectors along their respective axes.

Eq. (4.37) in terms of position vector is

$$\Psi(\vec{r}, t) = \Psi_0(\vec{r})\, e^{-i2\pi\nu t} \qquad (4.38)$$

Differentiating Eq. (4.38) with respect to time t twice, we get

$$\frac{\partial\Psi}{\partial t} = -i2\pi\nu\Psi$$

$$\frac{\partial^2\Psi}{\partial t^2} = -4\pi^2\nu^2\Psi \qquad (4.39)$$

Substituting Eq. (4.39) in Eq. (4.36), we get

$$\nabla^2\Psi = -\frac{4\pi^2\nu^2}{v^2}\Psi \qquad (4.40)$$

Since $v = \nu \times \lambda$, Eq. (4.40) reduces as

$$\nabla^2\Psi = -\frac{4\pi^2}{\lambda^2}\Psi \quad (4.41)$$

Now using de Broglie's wavelength $\lambda = \frac{h}{mv}$ in Eq. (4.41)

$$\nabla^2\Psi = -\frac{4\pi^2 m^2 v^2}{h^2}\Psi \quad (4.42)$$

The total energy E of the particle being the sum of its kinetic and potential energy.

$$E = KE + PE$$

$$= \frac{1}{2}mv^2 + V$$

$$\therefore 2(E - V) = mv^2$$

$$\therefore 2m(E - V) = m^2v^2 \quad (4.43)$$

Using Eq. (4.43) in Eq. (4.42), we get

$$\nabla^2\Psi + \frac{8\pi^2 m}{h^2}(E - V)\Psi = 0 \quad (4.44)$$

Putting $\hbar = \frac{h}{2\pi}$, Eq. (4.44) can be rewritten as

$$\nabla^2\Psi + \frac{2m}{\hbar^2}(E - V)\Psi = 0 \quad (4.45)$$

Eq. (4.44) or Eq. (4.45) is called Schrödinger's time-independent wave equation.
The Schrödinger's time-dependent wave equation may be obtained from Eq. (4.45) as follow:

$$\nabla^2\Psi = -\frac{2m}{\hbar^2}(E - V)\Psi$$

Or

$$-\frac{\hbar^2}{2m}\nabla^2\Psi = (E - V)\Psi$$

Or

$$\left(-\frac{\hbar^2}{2m}\nabla^2 + V\right)\Psi = E\Psi$$

i.e.

$$H\Psi = E\Psi \quad (4.46)$$

where $H = -\frac{\hbar^2}{2m}\nabla^2 + V$ is called Hamiltonian operator.
We know

$$\Psi = \Psi_0 e^{-i2\pi\nu t}$$

$$\frac{\partial\Psi}{\partial t} = -i2\pi\nu\Psi$$

$$= -i2\pi\frac{E}{h}\Psi \qquad (\because E = h\nu)$$

$$= -i\frac{E}{\hbar}\Psi$$

$$\therefore i\hbar\frac{\partial\Psi}{\partial t} = E\Psi = H\Psi \quad (4.47)$$

Eq. (4.47) is called Schrödinger's time-dependent wave equation.

4.7 Particle in a one-dimensional rigid box:

We can apply Schrödinger equation to study particle restricted to move within walls of a box (a deep potential well). For, simplicity we assume the potential well to be a one dimensional well, bounded on either side by infinitely high potential barriers, as shown in Figure 4.8. The particle is travelling along x-axis between $x = 0$ and $x = \mathrm{L}$ enclosed by infinitely hard walls. A particle does not loose energy when it collides with such walls so that its total energy remains constant. From the quantum mechanical point of view, the potential energy V of the particle is constant, taken zero for convenience inside the box (V = 0) while it is infinite on both sides of the box (V = ∞). Since the particle cannot have an infinite amount of energy it cannot exist outside the box and so its wave function Ψ is zero for $x \leq 0$ and $x \geq \mathrm{L}$. Our task is to find what Ψ is within the box, namely, $x = 0$ and $x = \mathrm{L}$.

Within the box, the Schrödinger equation becomes

$$\frac{d^2\Psi}{dx^2} + \frac{8\pi^2 mE}{h^2}\Psi = 0 \tag{4.48}$$

Let

$$\frac{8\pi^2 mE}{h^2} = \omega^2$$

Box or Potential well

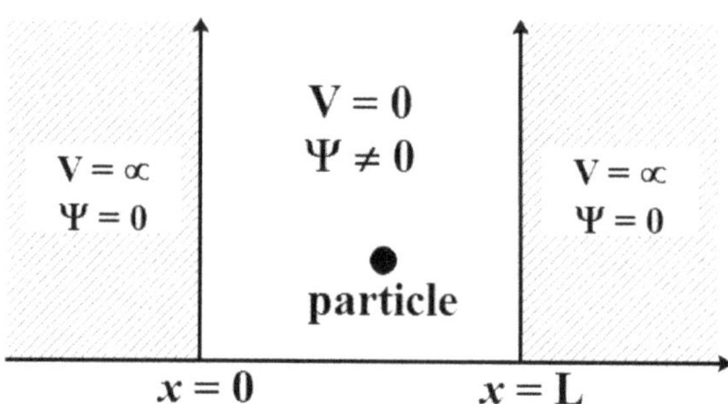

Figure 4.8: particle confined to a one-dimensional potential well

Eq. (4.48) becomes

$$\frac{d^2\Psi}{dx^2} + \omega^2\Psi = 0 \tag{4.49}$$

Let

$$\Psi = Ae^{\alpha x} \tag{4.50}$$

$$\frac{d\Psi}{dx} = A\alpha e^{\alpha x}$$

$$\frac{d^2\Psi}{dx^2} = A\alpha^2 e^{\alpha x} \tag{4.51}$$

Putting Eq. (4.50) and Eq. (4.51) in Eq. (4.49), we have

$$A\alpha^2 e^{\alpha x} + \omega^2 Ae^{\alpha x} = 0$$

$$\alpha^2 + \omega^2 = 0$$

$$\alpha = \pm i\omega$$

i.e. Eq. (4.50) becomes

$$\Psi = A_1 e^{i\omega x} + A_2 e^{-i\omega x} \tag{4.52}$$

Where A_1 and A_2 are arbitrary constants.

Eq. (5.52) can be expanded in following form as

$$\begin{aligned}\Psi &= A_1(\cos\omega x + i\sin\omega x) + A_2(\cos\omega x - i\sin\omega x)\\ &= (A_1 + A_2)\cos\omega x + i(A_1 - A_2)\sin\omega x\\ &= c_1\cos\omega x + c_2\sin\omega x\end{aligned} \tag{4.53}$$

Where c_1 and c_2 have the values of $(A_1 + A_2)$ and $i(A_1 - A_2)$, respectively.

To estimate the constants c_1 and c_2, let us now apply the boundary conditions. Since electrons are bound inside the crystal of length L, the electron wave function has to satisfy the following boundary conditions simultaneously.

i.e. at $x = 0$, $\Psi = 0$; this gives $c_1 = 0$

at $x = L$, $\Psi = 0$; this gives $c_2 \sin \omega L = 0$

Since $c_2 \neq 0$, $\sin \omega L = 0$

This is possible only when

$$\omega L = n\pi \tag{4.54}$$

$$\therefore L = \frac{n\pi}{\omega}$$

From Eq. (4.54)

$$\omega = \frac{n\pi}{L}$$

i.e.

$$\omega^2 = \frac{n^2\pi^2}{L^2}$$

$$\frac{8\pi^2 mE}{h^2} = \frac{n^2\pi^2}{L^2}$$

$$\therefore E = \frac{n^2h^2}{8mL^2} \tag{4.55}$$

Thus, the wave function

$$\Psi = c_2 \sin \omega x$$

$$= c_2 \sin\left(\frac{n\pi}{L}x\right) \tag{4.56}$$

Eq. (4.54) shows that

1. The bound electrons have only discrete energy values corresponding to n = 1, 2, 3, etc. and not any arbitrary values of energy.
2. The lowest energy of the particle is obtained by putting n = 1 in Eq. (4.55)

   i.e.

$$E_1 = \frac{h^2}{8mL^2}$$

In general,

$$E_n = \frac{n^2h^2}{8mL^2} = n^2E_1$$

3. The spacing between consecutive levels increases as

$$(n+1)^2E_1 - n^2E_1 = (2n+1)E_1$$

Figure 4.9 shows the energy level diagram for the particle.

The value of c_2 in Eq. (4.56) may be evaluated by normalizing the wave function according to which the total probability that the particle is somewhere inside the box must be unity, i.e.

$$\int_0^L |\Psi_n|^2\, dx = 1 \tag{4.57}$$

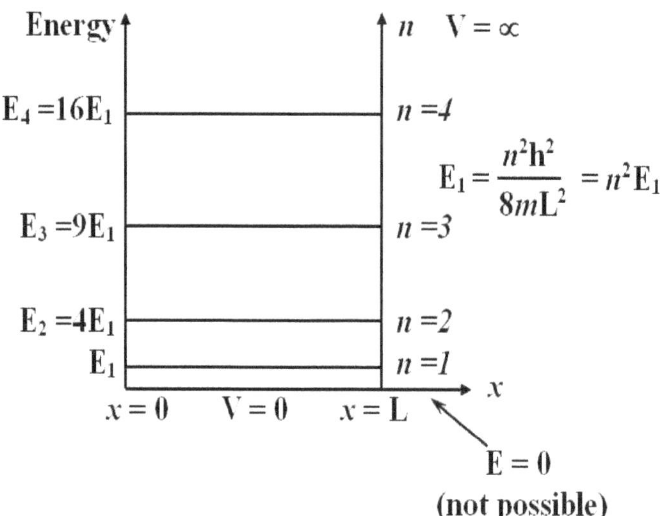

Figure 4.9: Schematic representation of energy level

$$\int_0^L c_2^2 \sin^2\frac{n\pi x}{L}dx = 1$$

$$c_2^2\int_0^L \frac{1}{2}\left(1-\cos\frac{2\pi nx}{L}\right)dx = 1$$

$$\frac{c_2^2}{2}\left[x-\frac{L}{2\pi n}\sin\frac{2\pi nx}{L}\right]_0^L = 1$$

Since the second term of the integrated expression becomes zero for both $x = 0$ and $x = L$, we get

$$\frac{c_2^2 L}{2} = 1$$

$$c_2 = \sqrt{\frac{2}{L}} \tag{4.58}$$

Using Eq. (4.58) in Eq. (4.56), the normalized wave function can be written as

$$\Psi_n = \sqrt{\frac{2}{L}}\sin\frac{n\pi x}{L} \tag{4.59}$$

And

$$|\Psi_n|^2 = \frac{2}{L}\sin^2\frac{n\pi x}{L} \tag{4.60}$$

4.8 Quantum mechanical tunneling:

4.8.1 Concepts of quantum mechanical tunneling

According to classical ideas, a particle striking a hard wall has no chance of leaking through it. But the behaviour of a quantum particle is different owing to the wave nature associated with it. We know that when an electromagnetic wave strikes at the interface of two media, it is partly reflected and partly transmitted through the interface and enters the second medium. In a similar way the de Broglie wave also has a possibility of getting partly reflected from the boundary of the potential well and partly penetrating through the barrier.

Figure 4.10 represents a *potential barrier* of height V and thickness L. A *potential barrier* is opposite of a potential well; it is a potential-energy function with a maximum. The potential energy is zero for $x < 0$ and $x > L$ has a value V for $0 < x < L$. An electron of total energy E approaches barrier from the left. From the view-point of classical physics, the electron would be reflected from the barrier because its energy E is less than V. For the particle to overcome the potential barrier, it must have energy equal to or greater than V. Quantum mechanics leads to an entirely new result. It shows that there is a finite chance for the electron to leak to the other side of the barrier. We say that the electron tunneled through the potential barrier and hence in quantum mechanics, the phenomenon is called *tunneling*.

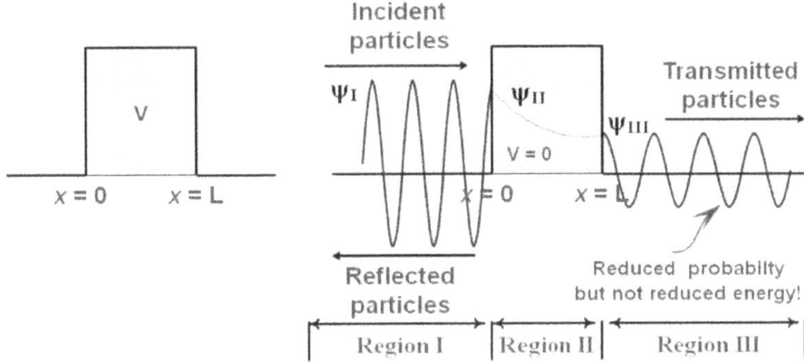

Figure 4.10: Quantum mechanical tunneling through potential barrier

The region around the barrier can be divided into three regions as shown in Figure 4.10. We can write the Schrödinger wave equation for the electron wave in the three regions and solve them. The Schrödinger wave equation for different regions has the forms given below.

For regions (I) and (III)

$$\frac{d^2\Psi}{dx^2} + \frac{8\pi^2 mE}{h^2}\Psi = 0 \tag{4.61}$$

And for region (II)

$$\frac{d^2\Psi}{dx^2} + \frac{8\pi^2 m}{h^2}(E - V)\Psi = 0 \tag{4.62}$$

The solution of equation (4.61) is found to be sinusoidal. The solution of equation (4.62) is found to be exponential. The form of the wave function in the region (I), (II) and (III) is also shown in the Figure 4.10. The wave function Ψ (I) corresponds to the free electron with momentum $p = \sqrt{2mE}$, The wave function Ψ (II) is not zero inside the barrier (the region forbidden by classical mechanics), but decreases exponentially. Since Ψ (II) is not equal to zero at x = L, there is a finite probability finding the electron in the region III. That means the electron that is initially to the left of the barrier has some probability of being found to the right of the barrier. The wave function Ψ (III) represents the wave transmitted through the barrier and the free electron on the right side of the barrier. The free electron has the same momentum as the incident electron but has smaller amplitude. The electron propagates to the right as a free particle. Thus, it is possible for a particle to penetrate through the potential barrier even if its kinetic energy is less than the height of the potential barrier. The probability that the particle gets through the barrier is called the *transmission coefficient*. The probability of particle penetration through a potential barrier depends on the height and width of the barrier.

Tunneling is significant in many areas of physics. The tunnel diode is a semiconductor diode in which electrons tunnel through a potential barrier. The current can be switched on and off very quickly by varying the height of the barrier, which is done with an applied voltage. The scanning tunneling electron microscope uses electron tunneling to produce images of surfaces down to the scale of individual atoms. The quantum possibility of penetrating potential barriers is the basis of the explanation of the α–decay of radioactive nuclei.

4.8.2 Scanning Tunneling Microscope (STM) as application of quantum mechanical tunneling:

Scanning tunneling microscopy (STM) is the ancestor of all scanning probe microscopies, which allow the real space imaging of surfaces with atomic resolution and employ no illumination and no lenses! The experimental arrangement is shown in Figure 4.11. A sharp conducting tip

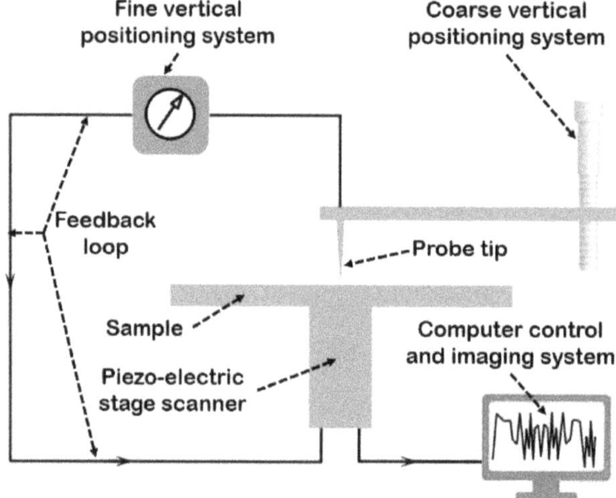

Figure 4.11: Experimental setup for scanning tunneling microscope

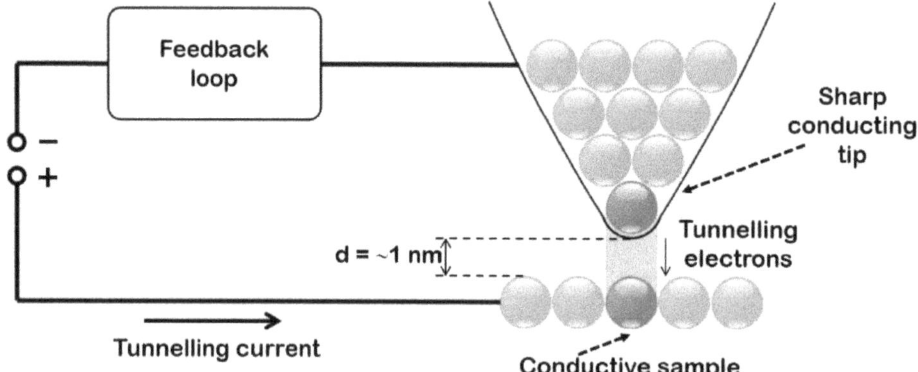

Figure 4.12: Schematic of tip and sample interaction for STM

(often tungsten), acting as the anode, is brought close to the surface of the specimen (the cathode). A bias voltage ranging from 1 mV to 1 V is applied between the tip and the sample. Above-the specimen surface there is an electron cloud due to surface atoms, and when the tip is brought within about 1 nm of the sample surface, electrons can quantum mechanically tunnel across the gap, causing a current to flow. The direction of electron tunneling across the gap depends on the sign of the bias voltage. It is this current that is used to generate an STM image. The tunneling current falls off exponentially with distance between tip and surface, and if the tip or sample is scanned laterally using piezoelectric drivers, the STM image reflects the variation in the sample surface topography. If the system is carefully damped from mechanical vibrations, the STM image will possess a sub-angstrom resolution vertically and atomic resolution laterally. The tunneling current also depends on the atomic species present on the surface and their local chemical environment. In principle, no vacuum is required except when studying adsorption of species on surfaces. However, many STMs are operated under ultra high vacuum (UHV) as any oxide or contaminant can interfere with the tunneling current. Furthermore, it is important to note that an STM cannot image insulating materials, except under conditions where they have appreciable conductivity, such as at high temperature.

An STM can be designed to scan a sample in one of two different modes: *constant height* or *constant current*. In constant-height mode, the tip travels in a horizontal plane above the sample and the tunneling current varies as a function of the surface topography and the local surface electronic states of the sample. The tunneling current, measured at each location on the sample surface, constitutes the data set, the topographic image. In constant-current mode, the STM uses a feedback system to keep the tunneling current constant by adjusting the height of the scanner at each measurement point. For example, when the system detects an increase in tunneling current, it adjusts the voltage applied to the piezoelectric scanner to increase the distance between the tip and the sample. In constant-current mode, the motion of the scanner therefore constitutes the data set. If the system keeps the tunneling current constant to within a few percent, the tip-to-sample distance will be constant to within < 0.01 nm. Comparing the two modes, constant-height mode is faster because the system doesn't have to move the scanner up and down, but it provides useful information only for relatively smooth surfaces. Constant-current mode can measure irregular surfaces with high precision, although the measurement takes considerably more time.

The ability of the STM to probe the local electronic structure of a surface, in principle with atomic resolution, leads to the various techniques of scanning tunneling spectroscopy (STS). STS techniques may involve recording 'topographic' (i.e., constant-current) images of the surface using different bias voltages and then directly comparing them, or taking current (i.e., constant-height) images at different heights z. STS methods are extremely powerful as they allow the surface electronic properties of a material to be investigated with near atomic resolution.

-: POINTS TO REMEMBER:-

- According to Plank's hypothesis, the atomic oscillator emitting radiation exists in discrete energy states.
- Wien's law and Rayleigh-Jeans law were deduced from Plank's equation of black body radiation under suitable conditions.
- De Broglie proposed the dual nature of matter. The waves associated with moving particles are called *matter waves* or *de Broglie waves*. The de Broglie wavelength of a particle in motion is given by, $\lambda = \frac{h}{p} = \frac{h}{mv}$.
- When a very large number of harmonic waves of slightly different frequencies combine, a *wave packet* is produced. A wave packet may be used to describe a microparticle.
- A wave function Ψ is used to represent the state of microparticle.
- The square of the wave function $|\Psi|^2$ gives the probability of finding a particle in space.
- It is impossible to determine simultaneously the position and the momentum of a microparticle with finite precision. This is known as Heisenberg's uncertainty principle. It is stated as

  $$\Delta x \cdot \Delta p \geq \hbar$$

  Where Δx is the uncertainty in position and Δp is uncertainty in momentum.
- The *Schrödinger equation* is the fundamental equation in quantum mechanics.
- The Schrödinger's time-independent equation is given by

  $$\nabla^2\Psi + \frac{2m}{\hbar^2}(E - V)\Psi = 0$$

- The Schrödinger's time-dependent equation is given by

  $$i\hbar\frac{\partial\Psi}{\partial t} = E\Psi = H\Psi$$

  where $H = -\frac{\hbar^2}{2m}\nabla^2 + V$ is called Hamiltonian operator.
- A free particle can have any energy and its energy spectrum is continuous.
- A particle confined to move in a one-dimensional infinite potential well cannot have any arbitrary energy. If L is the width of the well, the allowed energies are given by

  $$E_n = \frac{n^2h^2}{8mL^2}$$

- For a particle in three-dimensional box, the energy is

$$E_n = \frac{h^2}{8mL^2}(n_x^2 + n_y^2 + n_z^2)$$

- *Tunneling* is a quantum mechanical phenomenon when a particle is able to penetrate through a potential energy barrier that is higher in energy than the particle's kinetic energy.

-: SOLVED NUMERICALS:-

1) An electron is accelerated by 50 kV. Calculate the wavelength associated with electron.

Given: Voltage, V= 50,000 V Wavelength of electron, λ = ?

Solution:

The wavelength of electron is given by an expression

$$\lambda = \frac{1.227}{\sqrt{V}} \text{ nm}$$

$$= \frac{1.227}{\sqrt{50000}} = 5.48 \times 10^{-3} \text{ nm}$$

The wavelength of electron is 5.48×10^{-3} nm.

2) Assume 40 W sodium lamp (λ = 5893 Å) emitting light in all directions. Calculate the rate at which the photons cross an area placed normally to the beam at a distance of 10 m from the source.

Given: wavelength, λ = 5893 Å Power, P = 40 W Radius of surface area = 10 m

Solution:

Surface area for radius of 10 m, $A = 4\pi r^2$

$$= 4 \times 3.14 \times (10)^2$$

$$= 1256.6 \text{ m}^2$$

Total energy of the photons emitted out per second, $E = P \times t$

$$E = 40 \frac{J}{\text{sec.}} \times 1 \text{ sec.} = 40 \text{ J}$$

Total number of photons, $n = \frac{E}{h\nu} = \frac{E\lambda}{hc}$

$$\therefore n = \frac{40 \times 5893 \times 10^{-10}}{6.62 \times 10^{-34} \times 3 \times 10^{8}}$$

$$= 1.186 \times 10^{20}$$

Rate of flow of photons per unit area at a distance of 10 m from source,

$$R = \frac{\text{Total number of photons per second}}{\text{Total surface area}} = \frac{n}{A}$$

$$R = \frac{1.186 \times 10^{20}}{1256.6} = 9.44 \times 10^{6} \text{ /m}^2$$

Rate of flow of photons per unit area at a distance of 10 m from source is $9.44 \times 10^{6}\ /m^2$.

3) Determine the energy values of an electron confined in a box of width 2 Å.

Given:

Width of a box, $L = 2$ Å $= 2 \times 10^{-10}$ m Energy E of an electron = ?

Solution:

The energy of an electron in potential well is given by equation

$$E = \frac{n^2h^2}{8mL^2}$$

$$= \frac{n^2 \times (6.62 \times 10^{-34})^2}{8 \times 9.1 \times 10^{-31} \times (2 \times 10^{-10})^2}$$

$$= 1.5 \times 10^{-18} n^2 \text{ J}$$

$$= \frac{1.5 \times 10^{-18} n^2}{1.6 \times 10^{-19}} \text{ eV}$$

$$= 9.375 \text{ eV}$$

Energy of an electron is $9.375\ eV$ or $1.5 \times 10^{-18} n^2\ J$.

4) Find the lowest energy level and the momentum of an electron in one-dimensional potential well of width 2 Å.

Given:

Width of potential well, L = 2 Å = 2×10^{-10} m

Lowest energy of an electron, E_1 = ?

Momentum of an electron, p = ?

Solution:

a) The energy of an electron in potential well is given by equation

$$E_n = \frac{n^2 h^2}{8mL^2}$$

For the lowest energy level, $n = 1$, therefore

$$E_1 = \frac{h^2}{8mL^2}$$

$$= \frac{(6.62 \times 10^{-34})^2}{8 \times 9.1 \times 10^{-31} \times (2 \times 10^{-10})^2}$$

$$= 1.5 \times 10^{-18} \text{ J}$$

b) Energy of an electron is also given by

$$E = \frac{1}{2} mv^2 = \frac{p^2}{2m}$$

Therefore

$$E = \frac{p^2}{2m} = \frac{h^2}{8mL^2}$$

$$\therefore \text{momentum}, p = \frac{h}{2L}$$

$$= \frac{6.62 \times 10^{-34}}{2 \times 2 \times 10^{-10}}$$

$$= 1.655 \times 10^{-24} \text{ kg} \cdot \text{m/s}$$

5) A particle is confined to one-dimensional infinite potential well of width 0.2×10^{-9} m. It is found that when energy of the particle is 230 eV its eigenfunctions have 5 antinodes. Find the mass of the particle.

Given:

Width of potential well, L = 0.2×10^{-9} m

Energy of an electron for n = 5, E_5 = 230 eV = $230 \times 1.6 \times 10^{-19}$ J

Mass of the particle, m = ?

Solution:

The energy of the particle in one-dimensional potential well is given by

$$E_n = \frac{n^2 h^2}{8mL^2}$$

For n = 5, energy becomes

$$E_5 = \frac{5^2 h^2}{8mL^2} = 5^2 E_1$$

$$\therefore\ E_1 = \frac{E_5}{5^2} = \frac{230 \times 1.6 \times 10^{-19}}{25}$$
$$= 14.7 \times 10^{-19}\ J$$

Now,

$$E = \frac{h^2}{8mL^2}$$
$$\therefore\ m = \frac{h^2}{8EL^2}$$
$$= \frac{(6.62 \times 10^{-34})^2}{8 \times 14.7 \times 10^{-19} \times (0.2 \times 10^{-9})^2}$$
$$= 9.3 \times 10^{-31}\ kg$$

Mass of the particle is 9.3×10^{-31} kg.

6) A particle is moving in one-dimensional potential box of width 50 Å. Calculate the probability of finding particle within an interval of 5 Å at the centre of the box when it is in its state of least energy.

Given:

state of least energy, n = 1

Width of potential box, L = 50 Å = 50×10^{-10} m

Position interval, Δx = 5 Å = 5×10^{-10} m

Solution:

Probability of finding particle P within interval Δx is given by

$$P = |\Psi(x)|^2 \cdot \Delta x$$

For that wave function Ψ is given by

$$\Psi(x) = \sqrt{\frac{2}{L}} \cdot \sin\frac{n\pi x}{L}$$
$$= \sqrt{\frac{2}{L}} \cdot \sin\frac{\pi x}{L} \quad (\therefore n = 1)$$

At the centre of box, x = L/2

$$|\Psi(x)|^2 = \frac{2}{L} \cdot \left[\sin\frac{\pi(\frac{L}{2})}{L}\right]^2$$
$$= \frac{2}{L} \cdot \text{Sin}^2\frac{\pi}{2} = \frac{2}{L}$$

$$\therefore\ P = |\Psi(x)|^2 \cdot \Delta x$$
$$= \frac{2}{L} \cdot \Delta x$$
$$= \frac{2}{50 \times 10^{-10}} \times 5 \times 10^{-10}$$
$$= 0.2$$

The probability of finding the particle is 0.2

7) If a dust particle of mass 1 μg requires time of 100 s to cross a distance of 1 mm which is the separation between two rigid walls of the potential, determine quantum number describe by it.

Given:

Mass of particle, m = 1 μg = 10^{-9} kg

Time to cross distance of 1 mm, t = 100 s

Width of potential well, L = 1 mm = 1×10^{-3} m

quantum number, n = ?

Solution:

The distance covered by particle in 100 s is 1×10^{-3} m. Hence, the distance covered by particle in one second is

10^{-5} m, which is the velocity of a particle.

$$\therefore \text{energy, } E = \frac{1}{2}mv^2$$
$$= \frac{1}{2} \times 10^{-9} \times (10^{-5})^2$$
$$= 5 \times 10^{-20}\ J$$

We know energy of a particle in potential well is given by

$$E = \frac{n^2h^2}{8mL^2}$$

$$\therefore n^2 = \frac{8mL^2}{h^2}E$$
$$= \frac{8 \times 10^{-9} \times (10^{-3})^2}{(6.62 \times 10^{-34})^2} \times 5 \times 10^{-20}$$
$$= 9.11 \times 10^{32}$$
$$n = 3 \times 10^{16}$$

The number of the quantum state is 3×10^{16}.

8) Find the lowest energy of an electron confined to move in a cubical box of length 0.5 Å.

Given:

For the lowest energy $n_x = n_y = n_z = 1$

Length of cube, L = 0.5 Å = 0.5×10^{-10} m

Solution:

Energy in the lowest level in three-dimensional potential well is given by

$$E = \frac{h^2}{8mL^2} \cdot (n_x^2 + n_y^2 + n_z^2)$$
$$= \frac{h^2}{8mL^2}(1 + 1 + 1) = \frac{3h^2}{8mL^2}$$
$$= \frac{3 \times (6.62 \times 10^{-34})^2}{8 \times 9.1 \times 10^{-31} \times (0.5 \times 10^{-10})^2}$$
$$= 7.22 \times 10^{-17}\ J$$
$$= \frac{7.22 \times 10^{-17}}{1.6 \times 10^{-19}}\ eV$$
$$= 451\ eV$$

The lowest energy level will have energy 451 eVor 7.22×10^{-17}.

9) An electron and a 150 g base ball are travelling at 220 m/s measured to an accuracy of 0.065%. Calculate and compare uncertainty in position of each of the bodies.

Given:

Velocity of electron v_e = 220 m/s, and accuracy = 0.065%

Mass of base ball, M = 150 g = 0.15 kg

Velocity of base ball v_M = 220 m/s, and accuracy = 0.065%

Solution:

According to Heisenberg's uncertainty principle, we can write

$$\Delta x \times \Delta p \approx \hbar = \frac{\hbar}{m \cdot \Delta v}$$

1) For an electron

$$\Delta v_e = v_e \times 0.065 = 220 \times \frac{0.065}{100}$$
$$= 0.143\ m/s$$
$$\Delta x_e = \frac{\hbar}{m_e \cdot \Delta v_e}$$

$$= \frac{1.05 \times 10^{-34}}{9.1 \times 10^{-31} \times 0.143}$$
$$= 0.80 \times 10^{-3} \text{ m}$$

2) For a base ball

$$\Delta v_M = 0.143 \frac{m}{s}$$
$$\Delta x_M = \frac{\hbar}{M \cdot \Delta v_M}$$
$$= \frac{1.05 \times 10^{-34}}{0.15 \times 0.143}$$
$$= 4.9 \times 10^{-33} \text{ m}$$

The uncertainty in position of an electron is very large compared to its dimensions whereas the uncertainty in position of the base ball is as small as zero.

10) An electron is confined to a box of length 10^{-9} m, Calculate the minimum uncertainty in its velocity.

Given: $\Delta x = 10^{-9}$ m,

$\Delta v = ?$

Solution:

From the Heisenberg uncertainty principle, we can write

$$\Delta p \times \Delta x = \hbar$$
$$m \cdot \Delta v \times \Delta x = \hbar$$
$$\Delta v = \frac{\hbar}{m \cdot \Delta x}$$

$$= \frac{1.05 \times 10^{-34}}{9.1 \times 10^{-31} \times 10^{-9}}$$
$$= 0.1154 \times 10^{6} \text{ m/s}$$
$$= 1.15 \times 10^{5} \text{ m/s}$$

The uncertainty in velocity of electron is 1.15×10^{5} m/s.

-:UNSOLVED NUMERICALS:-

1. How many photons of red light $\lambda = 6 \times 10^{-7}$ m have the same energy as one photon of γ–rays $\lambda = 1.6 \times 10^{-13}$ m?

   [Ans: 3.75×10^{-6}]

2. Calculate the number of photons of yellow light of wavelength $\lambda = 6 \times 10^{-7}$ m required to produce one joule of energy.

   [Ans: 3×10^{18} photons]

3. An electron is bound by a potential box of infinite height having width 2.5 Å. Calculate the lowest three permissible energies that the electron can have.

   [Ans: 6 eV, 24 eV, 54 eV]

4. Find the lowest energy of a neutron confined to a box 10-14 m across.

   [Ans: 2.1 MeV]

5. Determine the wavelength and momentum associated with an electron having kinetic energy equal to 1 MeV.

   [$\lambda = 0.87 \times 10^{-3}$ m]

-: SHORT QUESTIONS:-

1. Define black body.
2. Sate the Wien's displacement law.

3. State Rayleigh-Jeans law of radiation.
4. Write down Plank's assumption for a black body radiation.
5. Mention the properties of photons.
6. Write down Plank's expression for the energy density of black body in terms of wavelength and frequency.
7. Mention the characteristics of the matter waves.
8. What are the de Broglie's matter waves?
9. Write an equation for wavelength of matter wave in term of applied voltage and energy.
10. State equation for Heisenberg's uncertainty principle.
11. Give the physical significance wave function Ψ.
12. Write down the Schrödinger's time-dependent and Schrödinger's time-independent equations.
13. What is potential well?
14. Write down an expression for energy and wave function of a particle in a one-dimensional potential well.
15. Write down an expression for energy and wave function of a particle in a three-dimensional potential well.
16. What is quantum mechanical tunneling?
17. Mention the applications of de Broglie's matter waves.
18. Mention full name of STM.
19. Name the different working modes of STM.
20. What are the limitations of STM?

-: DESCRIPTIVE QUESTIONS:-

1. Describe the Plank's law of radiation and obtain an expression for energy density.
2. Write down the Plank's expression for energy density in terms of wavelength and deduce Wien's law and Rayleigh-Jeans law from it.
3. Discuss the de Broglie's hypothesis of duality for material particles.
4. Derive the formula for a wavelength of matter waves in terms of applied potential difference V and energy E.
5. Give the statement of Heisenberg's uncertainty principle. Discuss its significance and importance.
6. Explain physical significance of Ψ–function. Why normalization of Ψ is required?
7. Derive the Schrödinger's time-dependent and Schrödinger's time-independent equations.
8. Derive equation for energy and wave function for a particle in a one-dimensional infinite potential well.
9. Discuss the phenomenon of quantum mechanical tunneling of a microparticle by considering a potential barrier.
10. Discuss the construction and working of scanning tunneling microscope using schematic diagram. Also, discuss about its different kinds of working modes.

* * * * *

CHAPTER-V LASER

Learning goals:

At the end of this chapter reader will be able to

✓ Derive the relationship between Einstein's coefficients.

✓ Explain the principle construction and working mechanism of Ruby and He-Ne laser.

✓ Explain various applications of laser.

PREREQUISITES

What is Light?

Light is a kind of energy released by an atom. Light is made up of very small particles called photons. Atoms are the basic units of matter. Each atom consists of a nucleus and a set of electrons orbiting the nucleus. Nucleus is formed as a result of strong nuclear force between the protons and neutrons. Protons have positive charge so they are referred as positively charged particles. Neutrons do not have charge so they are referred as neutral particles. Neutrons do not have charge so the overall charge of the nucleus is positive.

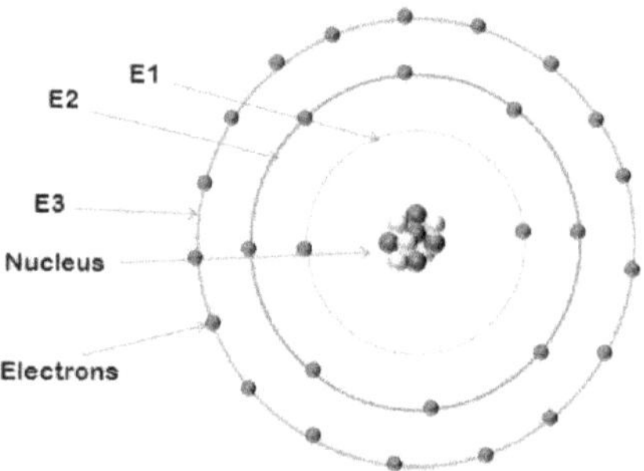

Electrons have negative charge so they are referred as negatively charged particles. Electrons always orbit around the nucleus because of the electrostatic force of attraction present between them. Electrons revolve around the nucleus in different orbits or shells. Each orbit has a unique energy level. Electrons orbiting at a larger distance from the nucleus have higher energy level whereas the electrons orbiting at a smaller distance from the nucleus have lower energy level. Electrons in the lower energy level need some extra energy to jump from lower energy level to the higher energy level. This extra energy can be supplied from various types of energy sources such as heat, electric field or light.

Light shows properties of both waves and particles so it can behave simultaneously as a particle or a wave. Einstein believed that light is a particle or photon and the flow of photons is a wave. Light is obtained from various sources like candles, lamps and sun-rays. Candles and lamps are called as the man made light sources and sun-rays is called natural light source. Incandescent light bulb was invented in 1879 by Thomas Edison. In incandescent light bulb, electric current flows through a filament inside the bulb. When sufficient electric current is passed through the filament, it gets heated up and emits visible light. Thus, visible light is emitted from the incandescent light bulb.

5.1 INTRODUCTION:

The word Laser is an acronym for **Light Amplification by Stimulated Emission of Radiation.** Laser is a device that generates a light through a process called stimulated emission of radiation, amplifies this light and then emit it.

In general, when electron jumps from a higher energy level to a lower energy level, it emits light or photon. The energy of the emitted photon is equal to the energy difference between the energy levels. The loss of electron energy is attributed to the entire atom. Therefore, it can be thought that the atom is moving from a higher energy state to a lower energy state.

Laser light is different from the conventional light. Laser light has extra-ordinary properties which are not present in the ordinary light sources like sun and incandescent lamp.

The conventional light sources such as electric bulb or tube light does not emit highly directional and coherent light whereas lasers produce highly directional, monochromatic, coherent and polarized light beam.

In conventional light sources, excited electrons emit light at different times and in different directions so there is no phase relation between the emitted photons.

On the other hand, the photons emitted by the electrons of laser are in same phase and move in the same direction.

Einstein gave the theoretical basis for the development of laser in 1917, when he predicted the possibility of stimulated emission. In 1954, C. H. Townes and his co-workers put Einstein's prediction for practical realization. They developed a microwave amplifier based on stimulated emission of radiation. It was called as MASER (Microwave Amplification by Stimulated Emission of Radiation. Maser operates on principles similar to laser but generates microwaves rather than light radiation.

In 1958, C. H. Townes and A. Schawlow extended the principle of masers to light. In 1960, T.H. Maiman built the first laser device.

Lasers of different wavelength and different type of lasing mechanism are available today. Each type of laser has suitability to various applications like optical communication, printing, material processing/ manufacturing, automobiles, computer technology, military, medical fiend and several others.

In this chapter, properties, basic principles and few different types of laser has been discussed in detail.

5.2 PROPERTIES/CHARACTERISTIC OF LASER

Some extraordinary properties of laser which makes it different from ordinary light sources are as discussed below.

Intensity:

A laser emits light radiation into narrow beam, and its energy is concentrated at small region. Intensity of laser beam is 10^{12} to 10^{28} $W \cdot m^{-2}$ while for ordinary light it is ≈ 100 $W \cdot m^{-2}$.

We know that the intensity of a wave is the energy per unit time flowing through a unit normal area. In an ordinary light source, the light spreads out uniformly in all directions. In laser, the light spreads in small region of space and in a small wavelength range. Hence, laser light has much greater intensity when compared to the ordinary light.

Directionality:

In conventional light sources (lamp, sodium lamp and torchlight), photons will travel in random direction. Therefore, these light sources emit light in all directions.

On the other hand, in laser, all photons will travel in same direction. Therefore, laser emits light only in one direction. This is called directionality of laser light. The width of a laser beam is extremely narrow. Hence, a laser beam can travel to long distances without spreading.

Monochromacity:

Monochromatic light means a light containing a single colour or wavelength. The photons emitted from ordinary light sources have different energies, frequencies, wavelengths, or colours. Hence, the light waves of ordinary light sources have many wavelengths or colours. Therefore, ordinary light is a mixture of waves having different frequencies or wavelengths.

On the other hand, in laser, all the emitted photons have exactly the same energy, frequency, or wavelength. Hence, the light waves of laser have single wavelength or colour. Therefore, laser light covers a very narrow range of frequencies or wavelengths.

In general, a laser beam is highly monochromatic beam than any other conventional monochromatic sources.

4. Coherence:

Coherence is a property of a wave being in phase with itself and also with another wave over a period of time and distance. In other words, coherence is the predictability of amplitude and phase at any point on the wave by knowing the amplitude and phase at any other point on it. Laser have following two type of coherences.

Temporal coherence: The condition in which each cycle of the wave takes exactly the same time to pass a given point in space.

Spatial coherence: The condition in which the light waves passing through space is not only of same frequency but also in constant phase with each other.

Divergence:

Light emitted from conventional sources spreads out spherically as it propagates and hence it is highly divergent. But the light emitted by a laser is confined to a rather narrow cone. As it propagates, it diverges very less compared to normal light.

For an electromagnetic beam, beam divergence is the angular measure of increase in diameter with distance from the source.

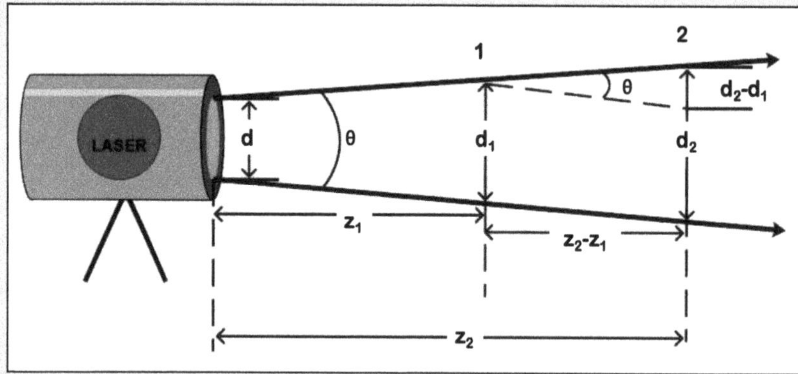

The divergence of a laser beam can be calculated if the beam diameter d_1 and d_2 at two separate distances are known. Let z_1 and z_2 are the distances along the laser axis, from the end of the laser to points "1" and "2".

Usually, divergence angle is taken as the full angle of opening of the beam. Then,

$$\theta = \frac{d_1 - d_2}{z_1 - z_2}$$

Speckles:

When laser light illuminates a diffuse surface, the high coherences of the light produce a random granular effect known as speckle.

Laser speckle is an interference pattern produced by light reflected or scattered from different parts of the illuminated surfaces. It is random phenomenon and describes statically.

GROUND STATE: The ground state of a quantum-mechanical system is its lowest-energy state; the energy of the ground state is known as the zero-point energy of the system.

EXCITED STATE: An excited state is any state with energy greater than the ground state.

In general if an electron is in any particular energy level than it is said to be in ground state if all the energy levels below it are filled and it is said to be in excited state if any energy level below it is empty.

LIFETIME: It is a time period for which an electron stay in a particular energy state. For excited state the lifetime is of the order of 10^{-6} seconds, while for metastable state it is of the order of 10^{-3} seconds.

5.3 PRINCIPLE OF LASER

There are basically three processes for interaction between a photon and an electron in a solid: absorption, spontaneous emission, and stimulated emission. For the simplicity consider two energy levels $\mathbf{E_1}$ and $\mathbf{E_2}$ of an atom, where $\mathbf{E_1}$ corresponds to ground state and $\mathbf{E_2}$ corresponds to excited state. Any transition between these states involves the emission or absorption of a photon with frequency ν_{12} given by $h\nu_{12} = E_2 - E_1$.

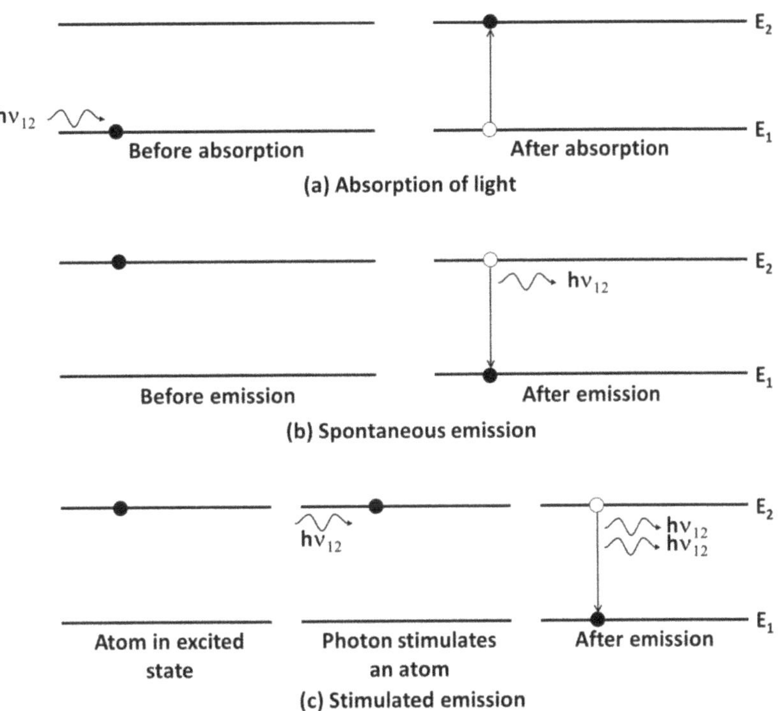

Figure 5.1: Three basic optical transition processes: (a) absorption of light, (b) spontaneous emission, (c) stimulated emission.

ABSORPTION: At room temperature, most of the atoms in a solid are at the ground state. This situation is disturbed when a photon of energy exactly equal to $\mathbf{h\nu_{12}}$ is incident on the system. An atom in state $\mathbf{E_1}$ absorbs the photon and gets excited to state $\mathbf{E_2}$. This process is called absorption of photon (Figure 5.1(a)).

SPONTANEOUS EMISSION: Excited state of atom is unstable (typical lifetime is of the order of 10^{-6} second). Therefore after a short time, without any external stimulus, it makes a transition to the ground state, by emitting a photon of energy $\mathbf{h\nu_{12}}$. This process is called spontaneous emission (Figure 5.1(b)).

STIMULATED EMISSION: In certain cases when an atom is in excited state but the transition from excited state to ground state is not allowed by the selection rules, atom will remain in excited state for more time (typical lifetime is of the order of 10^{-3} second). When a photon of energy $\mathbf{h\nu_{12}}$ impinges on such atom, it can be stimulated to make a transition to the ground state and emit a photon of energy $\mathbf{h\nu_{12}}$, which is in phase with the incident photon. This process is called stimulated emission. The radiation from stimulated emission is monochromatic because each photon has precisely an energy $\mathbf{h\nu_{12}}$ and is coherent because all emitted photons are in phase (Figure 5.1(c)).

5.4 EINSTEIN'S THEORY FOR STIMULATED EMISSION

In 1917, Einstein proposed a mathematical expression for the existence of stimulated emission of light. This expression known as ''Einstein's expression''.

Let us assume that the instantaneous populations of $\mathbf{E_1}$ and $\mathbf{E_2}$ are $\mathbf{n_1}$ and $\mathbf{n_2}$, respectively. Under a thermal equilibrium condition, population can be given by Boltzmann distribution as:

$$\mathbf{n_1 = e^{\frac{-E_1}{kT}}} \text{ and } \mathbf{n_2 = e^{\frac{-E_2}{kT}}}$$

$$\therefore \frac{n_1}{n_2} = e^{\frac{(E_2-E_1)}{kT}} = e^{\frac{h\nu_{12}}{kT}} \qquad \mathbf{(5.1)}$$

Now the rate of absorption $\mathbf{R_{12}}$ is directly proportional to the population of $\mathbf{E_1}$ and density of incident photons ρ_ν.

$$\mathbf{R_{12} \propto n_1} \quad \text{and} \quad \mathbf{R_{12} \propto \rho_\nu}$$

$$\therefore \mathbf{R_{12} = B_{12}\rho_\nu n_1} \tag{5.2}$$

Here $\mathbf{B_{12}}$ is the coefficient of photon absorption.

Similarly the rate of spontaneous emission $\mathbf{R_{21}(sp)}$ is directly proportional to the population of $\mathbf{E_2}$.

$$\mathbf{R_{21}(sp) \propto n_2}$$

$$\therefore \mathbf{R_{21}(sp) = A_{21}n_2} \tag{5.3}$$

Here A_{21} is the coefficient of spontaneous emission.

Similarly the rate of stimulated emission $\mathbf{R_{21}(st)}$ is directly proportional to the population of $\mathbf{E_2}$ and density of incident photons $\boldsymbol{\rho_\nu}$.

$$\mathbf{R_{21}(st) \propto n_2} \quad \text{and} \quad \mathbf{R_{21}(st) \propto \rho_\nu}$$

$$\therefore \mathbf{R_{21}(st) = B_{21}\rho_\nu n_2} \tag{5.4}$$

Here B_{21} is the coefficient of stimulated emission.

Now in equilibrium condition absorption and emission are equally possible. Therefore

Rate of absorption = Rate of emission = Rate of spontaneous emission + Rate of stimulated emission

$$\therefore \mathbf{R_{12} = R_{21}(sp) + R_{21}(st)}$$

$$\therefore \mathbf{B_{12}\rho_\nu n_1 = A_{21}n_2 + B_{21}\rho_\nu n_2}$$

$$\therefore \mathbf{B_{12}\rho_\nu n_1 - B_{21}\rho_\nu n_2 = A_{21}n_2}$$

$$\therefore \mathbf{\rho_\nu(B_{12}n_1 - B_{21}n_2) = A_{21}n_2}$$

$$\therefore \mathbf{\rho_\nu n_2\left(B_{12}\frac{n_1}{n_2} - B_{21}\right) = A_{21}n_2}$$

$$\therefore \mathbf{\rho_\nu = \frac{A_{21}}{B_{12}\frac{n_1}{n_2} - B_{21}}} \tag{5.5}$$

Putting the value of $\mathbf{\frac{n_1}{n_2}}$ from eqn. (5.1) in to eqn. (5.5), we get

$$\mathbf{\rho_\nu = \frac{A_{21}}{B_{12}e^{\frac{h\nu_{12}}{kT}} - B_{21}}} \tag{5.6}$$

Here eqn. (5.6) seem to be similar to the equation for the Plank's radiation law which is

$$\mathbf{\rho_\nu = \frac{8\pi h\nu^3}{c^3}\frac{1}{e^{\frac{h\nu}{kT}} - 1}} \tag{5.7}$$

Comparing eqn. (5.6) and eqn. (5.7) we get the relationship between the coefficients $\mathbf{A_{21}}$, $\mathbf{B_{12}}$ and $\mathbf{B_{21}}$ which are known as Einstein's coefficients as below.

$$\mathbf{B_{12} = B_{21}} \quad \textbf{and} \quad \mathbf{\frac{A_{21}}{B_{12}} = \frac{8\pi h\nu^3}{c^3}} \tag{5.8}$$

From equations (5.3) and (5.4), the ratio of stimulated emission to spontaneous emission is given by,

$$\mathbf{\frac{R_{21}(ST)}{R_{21}(SP)} = \frac{B_{21}N_2\rho_\nu}{A_{21}N_2} = \frac{1}{e^{\frac{h\nu}{kT}} - 1}} \tag{5.9}$$

Equation (5.9) proved the existence of stimulated emission of radiation.

The spontaneous emission produces incoherence light, while the stimulated emission produces coherence light. In an ordinary conventional light source, the spontaneous emission is dominant. For laser action stimulated should be predominant over spontaneous emission and absorption. To achieve this, an artificial condition is known as ''population inversion''.

ACTIVE MEDIUM: It is a material being used in laser which contains metastable states.

The active medium is excited by the external energy source (pump source) to produce the population inversion. In active medium, spontaneous and stimulated emission of photons takes place, leading to the phenomenon of optical gain, or amplification.

Examples of different gain media include:

→ Liquids, such as dye lasers. These are usually organic chemical solvents, such as methanol, ethanol or ethylene glycol, to which are added chemical dyes such as coumarin, rhodamine, and fluorescein. The exact chemical configuration of the dye molecules determines the operation wavelength of the dye laser.

→ Gases, such as carbon dioxide, argon, krypton and mixtures such as helium–neon. These lasers are often pumped by electrical discharge.

→ Solids, such as crystals and glasses. The solid *host* materials are usually doped with an impurity such as chromium, neodymium, erbium or titanium ions. Typical hosts include YAG (yttrium aluminium garnet), YLF (yttrium lithium fluoride), sapphire (aluminium oxide) and various glasses. Examples of solid-state laser media include Nd:YAG, Ti:sapphire, Cr:sapphire (usually known as ruby), Cr:LiSAF (chromium-doped lithium strontium aluminium fluoride), Er:YLF, Nd:glass, and Er:glass. Solid-state lasers are usually pumped by flash lamps or light from another laser.

→ Semiconductors, a type of solid, crystal with uniform dopant distribution or material with differing dopant levels in which the movement of electrons can cause laser action. Semiconductor lasers are typically very small, and can be pumped with a simple electric current, enabling them to be used in consumer devices such as compact disc players.

PUMPING: Pumping is the process of exciting electrons to higher energy states by providing external energy.

The pump source is the part that provides energy to the laser system. Examples of pump sources include electrical discharges, flash lamps, arc lamps, light from another laser, chemical reactions and even explosive devices. The type of pump source used principally depends on the active medium, and this also determines how the energy is transmitted to the medium. A helium–neon (HeNe) laser uses an electrical discharge in the helium-neon gas mixture, a Nd:YAG laser uses either light focused from a xenon flash lamp or diode lasers, and excimer lasers use a chemical reaction.

5.5 SPONTANEOUS EMISSION VS STIMULATED EMISSION

Sr	Spontaneous Emission	Stimulated Emission
1	Emission of a light photon takes place without any influence of external photon	Emission of a light photon takes place with influence of external photon
2	Polychromatic radiation	Monochromatic radiation
3	Less Intense	More Intense
4	Random Process	Not a random Process
5	Uncontrollable Process	Controllable Process
6	The photons do not multiply through chain reaction	The photons multiplied through chain reaction
7	Less Directionality, so more angular spread during propagation	High Directionality, so less angular spread during propagation
8	e.g. Light	e.g. Laser

5.6 POPULATION INVERSION

Population inversion stage is responsible for stimulated emission of multiple photons. This remarkable stage is the basic condition for light amplification in a laser. In order to set the condition of population inversion i.e. making $N_2 > N_1$, various methods are used known as pumping.

If energy state E containing N atoms per unit volume. This number N is called population and given by Boltzmann's equation

$$\mathbf{N = N_0 e^{\frac{-E}{KT}}} \qquad \textbf{(5.10)}$$

Where N_0 is the population of the ground state with E=0, K is the Boltzmann constant.

From above expression it is clear that the population is maximum in the ground state and decrease exponentially as we go to a higher energy state.

$$\mathbf{N_1 = N_0 e^{\frac{-E_1}{KT}}} \quad \text{and} \quad \mathbf{N_2 = N_0 e^{\frac{-E_2}{KT}}}$$

Therefore

$$\mathbf{\frac{N_2}{N_1} = e^{\frac{-(E_2-E_1)}{KT}}}$$

Thus under the normal situation when $\mathbf{E_2 > E_1 \Rightarrow N_2 < N_1}$

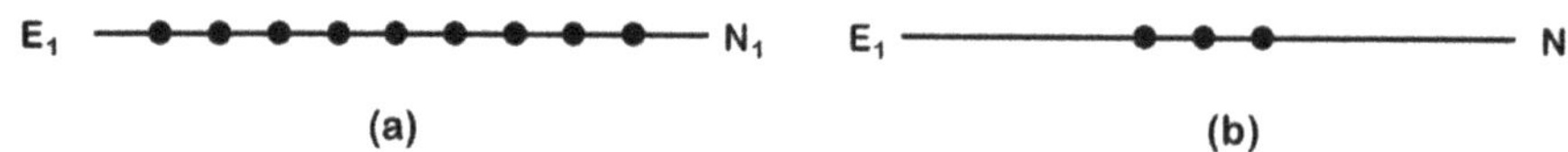

Figure 5.2: (a) Normal population and (b) Population inversion.

If the process of stimulated emission predominates over the process of spontaneous emission, it may then be possible that $N_2 > N_1$. If this happens then state is known as population inversion. If such inversion can be achieved by optical energy than it called optical pumping.

OPTICAL RESONATOR: The optical resonator, or optical cavity, in its simplest form is two parallel mirrors placed around the gain medium which provide feedback of the light. The mirrors are given optical coatings which determine their reflective properties. Typically one will be a high reflector, and the other will be a partial reflector. The latter is called the output coupler, because it allows some of the light to leave the cavity to produce the laser's output beam.

Light from the medium, produced by spontaneous emission, is reflected by the mirrors back into the medium, where it may be amplified by stimulated emission. The light may reflect from the mirrors and thus pass through the gain medium many hundreds of times before exiting the cavity. In more complex lasers, configurations with four or more mirrors forming the cavity are used. The design and alignment of the mirrors with respect to the medium is crucial for determining the exact operating wavelength and other attributes of the laser system.

Other optical devices, such as spinning mirrors, modulators, filters, and absorbers, may be placed within the optical resonator to produce a variety of effects on the laser output, such as altering the wavelength of operation or the production of pulses of laser light.

Some lasers do not use an optical cavity, but instead rely on very high optical gain to produce significant amplified spontaneous emission (ASE) without needing feedback of the light back into the gain medium. Such lasers are said to be super-luminescent, and emit light with low coherence but high bandwidth. Since they do not use optical feedback, these devices are often not categorized as lasers.

During population inversion excitation of atom or particles take places. A very short time in which particles or atoms remain in the excited state is known as "life time". It is normally 10^{-8} second. Population inversion is completed in the certain medium so that laser beam can be produced. Such a medium is known as active medium, medium can be liquid (dye laser), gas(He-Ne laser,CO_2 laser), solid (Ruby laser, Nd-YAG laser) and plasma.

Normal population: Generally in the atomic structure of materials, at the thermal equilibrium the total numbers of atoms in the ground energy state are much greater than higher energy state. This is known as ''normal population''.

Population inversion: It is a situation in which number of atoms in a higher energy state becomes more compared to that of lower energy state.

Light amplification can be achieved if the stimulated emission occur almost exclusively. In practice light absorption, spontaneous emission and stimulated emission takes place simultaneously. Lasing action can be achieved when stimulated emission exceeds the spontaneous emission.

5.7 AMPLIFICATION OF LIGHT BY POPULATION INVERSION

Conditions under which this can be achieved are discussed below.

1. Condition for stimulated emission to dominate spontaneous emission:

Ratio of stimulated to spontaneous emission can be written from eqn. (5.9) as:

$$\frac{R_{21}(ST)}{R_{21}(SP)} = \frac{B_{21}N_2\rho_v}{A_{21}N_2} = \frac{B_{21}}{A_{21}}\rho_v \quad (5.11)$$

This indicates that the stimulated emission will dominate the spontaneous emission if the radiation density 'ρ_v' is very large. Thus the presence of a large number of photons are required. However this will lead to more absorption. Hence large number of photons only will not serve the lasing action.

2. Requirement of states of larger life time:

Equation (5.11) also indicates that the stimulated emission will dominate the spontaneous when the ratio B_{21}/A_{21} is large. This can be achieved by increasing the life time of electrons in higher energy states considerably.

3. Condition for stimulated emission to dominate absorption:

Ratio of Eqn. (5.4) to Eqn. (5.2) can be given as

$$\frac{R_{21}(st)}{R_{12}} = \frac{B_{21}\rho_v n_2}{B_{12}\rho_v n_1} = \frac{B_{21}\rho_v n_2}{B_{12}\rho_v n_1} \quad (5.12)$$

This condition clearly indicates that the stimulated emission will dominate the absorption only when N_2 is greater than N_1. This means more number of electrons shall be present in higher energy state compared to that in lower energy state.

A medium will amplify the light only if all the above three conditions are fulfilled. Therefore to achieve the higher percentage of stimulated emission, an artificial situation known as population inversion shall be created in the medium.

5.8 TYPES OF LASER

There are many **types of lasers** available for different purposes. Depending upon the sources they can be described as below.

Solid State laser: In this kind of lasers solid state, materials are used as active medium. The solid state materials can be ruby, neodymium-YAG (yttrium aluminum garnet) etc.

Gas laser: These lasers contain a mixture of helium and Neon. This mixture is packed up into a glass tube. It acts as active medium. We can use Argon or Krypton or Xenon as the medium. CO_2 and Nitrogen laser can also be made.

Dye or Liquid laser: In this kind of lasers organic dyes like Rhodamine 6G in liquid solution or suspension used as active medium inside the glass tube.

Excimer laser: Excimer lasers (the name came from excited and dimers) use reactive gases like Chlorine and fluorine mixed with inert gases like Argon or Krypton or Xenon. These lasers produce light in the ultraviolet range.

Chemical laser: A chemical laser is a **laser** that obtains its energy from a chemical reaction. Examples of chemical lasers are the chemical oxygen iodine laser (COIL), all gas-phase iodine laser (AGIL), and the hydrogen fluoride laser, deuterium fluoride laser etc.
Semiconductor laser: In these **lasers**, junction diodes are used. The Semiconductor is doped by both the acceptors and donors. These are known as injection laser diodes. Whenever the current is passed, light can be seen at the output.

5.9 RUBY LASER

It is a solid-state laser, in which a rod of a synthetic ruby crystal is used as an active medium.

Construction:

The ruby crystal is obtained by doping a small amount (about 0.05% by weight) of chromium oxide (Cr_2O_3) in Aluminum oxide (Al_2O_3), so that some of the aluminum ions (Al^{3+}) are replaced by chromium ions (Cr^{3+}). These chromium ions give the crystal a pink or red colour depending upon the doping concentration. Al_2O_3 only acts as the host while the chromium ions act as active centres in ruby crystal and responsible for the laser action. The length of the ruby rod is usually 2 cm to 30 cm and the diameter is 0.5 cm to 2 cm.

To construct the optical resonator cavity, ends of the rod are polished such that they become flat and parallel to each other. Now one of the ends is coated with silver completely while the other one is partially silvered. Thus, the two silver-coated ends of the rod act as an optical resonator system.

The ruby rod is placed inside a helically shaped xenon flash lamp to excite the Cr^{3+} ions. Thus, in ruby laser population inversion is achieved by using optical pumping.

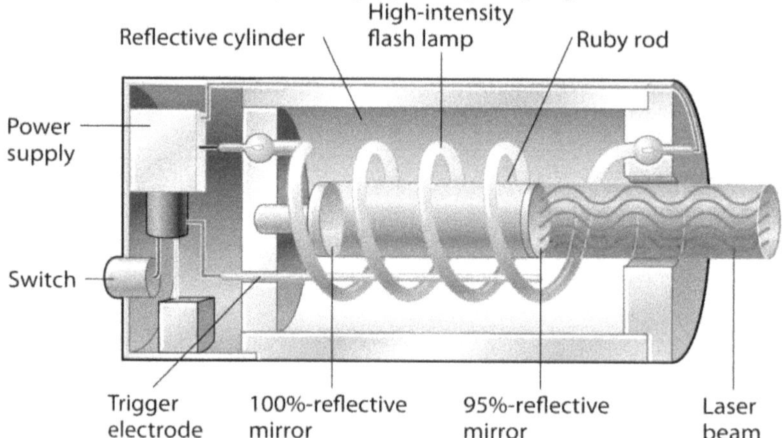

Figure 5.3: Construction of Ruby laser.

Working:

Ruby is a three energy level laser system. After absorbing light photons of wavelength 5500 Å from xenon flash lamp, some of the Cr^{3+} ions at ground energy level E_1 get excited to higher energy level E_3. At this energy level, they are unstable and by losing a part of their energy to the crystal lattice, they fall to the meta-stable energy level E_2, whose lifetime is much longer (about 10^{-3}s). Therefore, the number of Cr^{3+} ions goes on increasing in E_2 state while the number of these ions in ground state E_1 goes on decreasing due to pumping by the flash lamp and soon the population inversion is achieved between states E_2 and E_1.

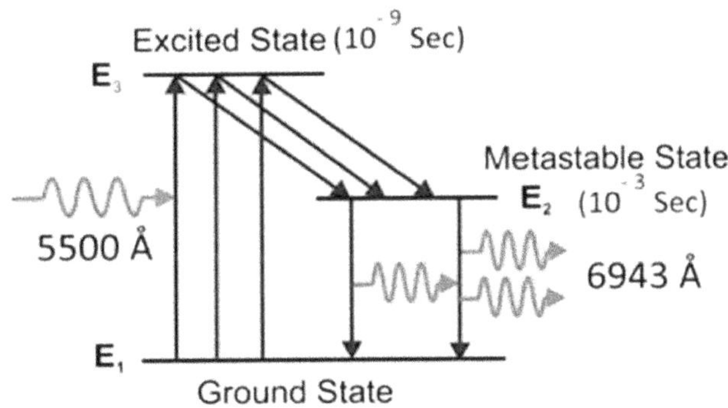

Figure 5.4: Energy level diagram of Ruby laser.

Now some of the Cr^{3+} ions will decay spontaneously to the ground state E_1 by emitting photons of wavelength 6943 Å. The photons that are moving parallel to the axis of the rod will reflect back and forth by the silvered ends of the rod and stimulate other excited Cr^{3+} ions to radiate another photon with the same phase. Thus, due to successive reflections of these photons at the ends of the rod, the number of photons multiplies. After a few microseconds, a monochromatic, intense and collimated beam of red light of wavelength 6943 Å emerges through the partially silvered end of the rod. The Ruby laser is a pulsed laser that emits light in the form of very short pulses.

Advantages:

1. It is economically affordable.
2. 3D hologram can be obtained.
3. High quality holes of drilling.

5.10 HELIUM-NEON LASER

Helium-Neon laser is a type of gas laser in which a mixture of helium and neon gas is used as a gain medium. Helium-Neon laser is also known as He-Ne laser.

A gas laser is a type of laser in which a mixture of gas is used as the active medium or laser medium. Gas lasers are the most widely used lasers. Gas lasers range from the low power helium-neon lasers to the very high power carbon dioxide lasers. The helium-neon lasers are most commonly used in laboratories whereas the carbon dioxide lasers are used in industrial applications. The main advantage of gas lasers (eg: He-Ne lasers) over solid state lasers is that they are less prone to damage by overheating so they can be run continuously.

The helium-neon laser was the first continuous wave laser ever constructed. It was built in 1961 by Ali Javan, Bennett, and Herriott at Bell Telephone Laboratories. Helium-neon lasers are the most widely used gas lasers. These lasers have many industrial and scientific uses and are often used in laboratory demonstrations of optics. In He-Ne lasers, an electrical pumping method is used. The excitation of electrons in the He-Ne gas active medium is achieved by passing an electric current through the gas.

The helium-neon laser operates at a wavelength of 632.8 nm, in the red portion of the visible spectrum.

Construction:

The helium-neon laser consists of three essential components:

1. Pump source (high voltage power supply)
2. Gain medium (laser glass tube or discharge glass tube)
3. Resonating cavity

High voltage power supply or pump source: In He-Ne laser, a high voltage DC power supply is used as the pump source which passes electric current through the gas mixture of helium and neon.

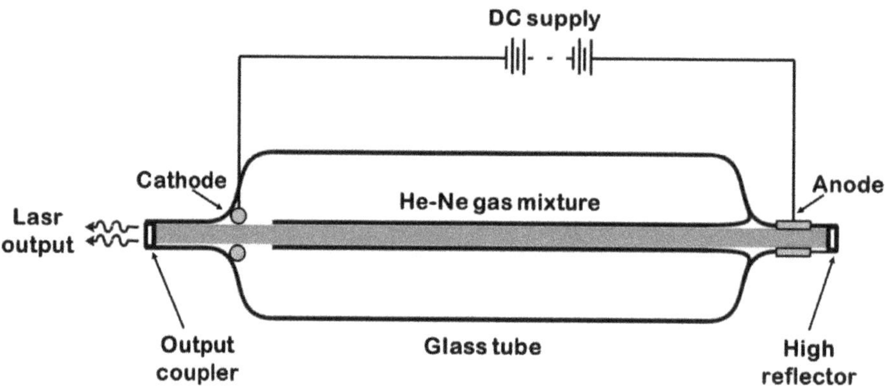

Figure 5.5: Construction of He-Ne Laser.

Gain medium (discharge glass tube or glass envelope): The gain medium of a helium-neon laser is made up of the mixture of helium and neon gas contained in a glass tube at low pressure. The partial pressure of helium is 1 mbar whereas that of neon is 0.1 mbar. The gas mixture is mostly comprised of helium gas. Therefore, in order to achieve population inversion, we need to excite primarily the lower energy state electrons of the helium atoms. Neon atoms are the active centres and have energy levels suitable for laser transitions while helium atoms help in exciting neon atoms.

Electrodes (anode and cathode) are provided in the glass tube to send the electric current through the gas mixture. These electrodes are connected to a DC power supply.

Resonating cavity: The glass tube (containing a mixture of helium and neon gas) is placed between two parallel mirrors. These two mirrors are silvered or optically coated. Each mirror is silvered differently. The left side mirror is partially silvered and is known as output coupler whereas the right side mirror is fully silvered and is known as the high reflector or fully reflecting mirror. The fully silvered mirror will completely reflect the light whereas the partially silvered mirror will reflect most part of the light but allows some part of the light to produce the laser beam.

Working:

In order to achieve population inversion, we need to supply energy to the gain medium. In helium-neon lasers, we use high voltage DC of 10 kV as the pump source. The gas mixture in helium-neon laser is mostly comprised of helium atoms. Therefore, helium atoms observe most of the energy supplied by the high voltage DC.

When the power is switched on, gas mixture gets excited and discharge electrons are produced which are accelerated between the electrodes (cathode and anode) through the gas mixture.

In the process of flowing through gas, energetic electrons transfer some of their energy to helium atoms in the gas. As a result, the lower energy state electrons of the helium atoms gain enough energy and jumps into the excited states or metastable states. Let us assume that these metastable states are F_3 and F_5.

The meta-stable state electrons of the helium atoms cannot return to ground state by spontaneous emission. However, they can return to ground state by transferring their energy to the lower energy state electrons of the neon atoms by collision.

The energy levels of some of the excited states of neon atoms are identical to the energy levels of meta-stable states of helium atoms. Let us assume that these identical energy states are $F_3 = E_3$ and $F_5 = E_5$. E_3 and E_5 are excited states or meta-stable states of neon atoms.

Unlike the solid, a gas can move or flow between the electrodes. Hence, when the excited electrons of the helium atoms collide with the lower energy state electrons of the neon atoms, they transfer their energy to the neon atoms. As a result, the lower energy state electrons of the neon atoms gain enough energy from the helium atoms and jumps into the higher energy states or meta-stable states (E_3 and E_5)

whereas the excited electrons of the helium atoms will fall into the ground state. Thus, helium atoms help neon atoms in achieving population inversion.

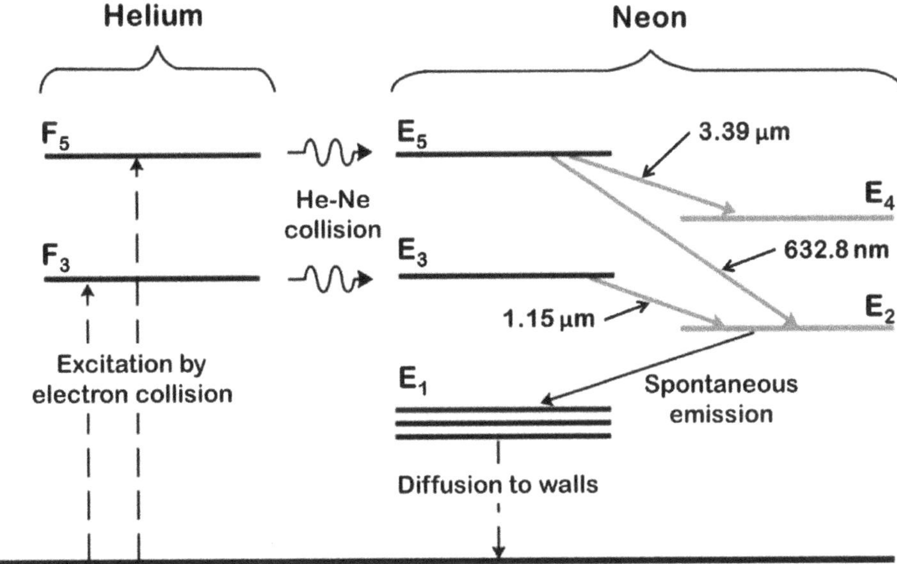

Figure 5.6: Energy level diagram of He-Ne laser.

Likewise, millions of ground state electrons of neon atoms are excited to the meta-stable states. The meta-stable states have longer lifetime. Therefore, a large number of electrons will remain in the meta-stable states and hence population inversion is achieved.

After some period, electrons of neon atoms will spontaneously fall from meta-stable states (E_3 and E_5) to lower energy states (E_2 and E_4) by releasing photons or red light. This is called spontaneous emission.

The neon excited electrons continue on to the ground state through radiative and non-radiative transitions. It is important for the continuous wave (CW) operation.

The light or photons emitted from the neon atoms will moves back and forth between two mirrors until it stimulates other excited electrons of the neon atoms and causes them to emit light. Thus, optical gain is achieved. This process of photon emission is called stimulated emission of radiation.

The light or photons emitted due to stimulated emission will escape through the partially reflecting mirror or output coupler to produce laser light.

Advantages of helium-neon laser

1. Helium-neon laser emits laser light in the visible portion of the spectrum.
2. High stability & Low cost
3. Operates without damage at higher temperatures

Disadvantages of helium-neon laser

1. Low efficiency & Low gain
2. Helium-neon lasers are limited to low power tasks

Applications of helium-neon lasers

1. Helium-neon lasers are used in industries, fabrication of scientific instrument.

5.11 APPLICATIONS OF LASER

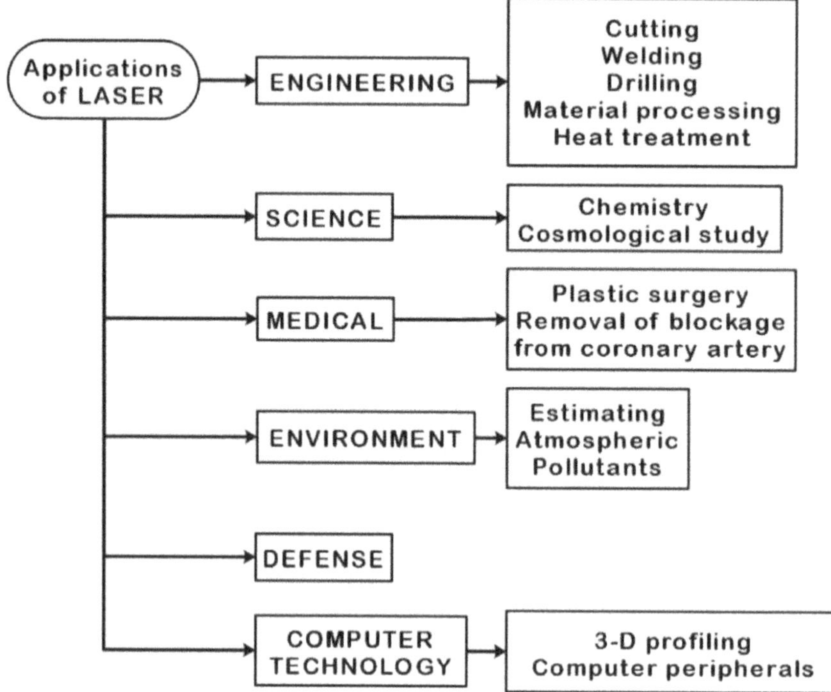

Figure 5.7: Applications of Laser.

5.11.1 Engineering Applications

Cutting:

To cut very small precious metal with high accuracy co_2 gas laser is used. In this purpose, high power laser beam along with inert gas are injected to reduce oxidation it also remove the molten material from cutting process. High power laser beam focusing through lens via nozzle on a metal. Using laser cutting 60 to 70 % power save compared to conventional cutting in aerospace and textile industry.

Welding:

Laser welding is thermal technique in which two or more similar or dissimilar metals are join together, in this process high intense ND-YAG or CO2 gas laser beam focus on two edge of metals through optical arrangement. Incident laser beam convert into heat energy in such way that vaporisation temperature of work piece are kept below. It is non-contact process method having ability to weld smaller and thinner components, it also provided excellent metallurgical quality.

Drilling:

High energetic beam is used to drill small hall in material at very high speed with good quality. When energetic beam incident on surface, its rise surface temperature at its evaporation level hence create a cavity on it.

Material processing:

There are mainly two methods; diffraction and opto-acoustic image processing are employed in which high intensity laser beam is used to study the surface defects in material, such as ICs, aircrafts, automobile tyres etc.

Heat treatment:

It is widely used for surface Hardening: nowadays it is popular to change metallurgical and mechanical properties of materials, as a results, increasing in hardness, strength, and fatigue life can be achieved by them. For examples;

Temperature dependent structural changes are observed in iron or steel at different temperature like below 1085k iron is BCC, 1085K to 1667K iron is FCC and beyond 1667k it is again BCC.

Computer technology:

1. 3-D profiling:

Monochromatic, high directionality, high coherence laser beam are used to storing and retrieving the 3D image of an object by laser scanner. It is same as holography. Information are store in computer in the form of matrix and using signal processing software it generate 3D image.

2. Computer peripherals:

Now a days optical discs have high storage capacity than conventional magnetic discs, similarly data transferring from one computer to other computer through optical wave guides play an immerse role, both of above are possible due to laser beam.

5.11.2 Medical Applications

Plastic surgery

In reconstructive surgery, replacing skin of some part of body insert or patch to other part of body in this process laser beam play vital role to remove skin accurately.

Removal of blockage from coronary artery:

Now days blockages inside coronary artery is common in any human body which result into the high blood pressure and heart attack, such a blockage are remove by injecting laser beam on it via optical fibre in a artery and blockage can be removed by vaporization process in accurate manner.

Estimating Atmospheric Pollutants

Dust, smokes, gases and chemicals like carbon monoxide, carbon dioxide, all are pollutants which are non-uniformly distributed in atmosphere. In conventional method, samples of such pollutants are collecting from different location and analyzed in lab. Hence results give only concentration of pollutants at time of collection which is not real time analysis. So real time data are analyzed using laser beam via absorption and Raman back scattering techniques.

Defense:

1. A powerful laser beam can be used to destroy big size objects like aeroplane, missile etc by pointing the laser beam on them, and hence laser beam also called death ray.
2. Laser beam can be used to determine accurately distance, velocity, direction, size and the nature of reflected light in radar.

5.11.3 Science Applications

Chemistry:

3. It is used to accelerate some chemical reactions to create new chemicals complexes and destroying atomic bonds between molecules.
4. To study the brownian motion of particles.

Cosmological study:

1. For astrophysical observations, understanding the dynamics of cosmological phenomenon.

5.11.4 Miscellaneous Applications

1. Using laser beam blood less cancer surgery can be carried out, here focus beam incident on small area of any part therefore only the harmful tissues can be destroyed without damaging the surrounding region tissues.
2. Laser beam can be used for eye surgery. laser probes can be used as dental clinic with and advantage of no heating, no pain.

3. It is used in optical fiber in communication purpose,
4. Retina surgery in eyeball.
5. In construction purpose to construct tunnel, dam, bridges etc.

-: POINTS TO REMEMBER:-

→ **LASER:** light amplification by stimulated emission of radiation.

→ **Three basic phenomena involved in LASER action.**

Absorption: it is process in which a photon energy hν, get absorbed by an atom and it goes from a lower energy state E_1 to a higher energy state E_2.

Spontaneous emission: an electron which is reached to an excited state E_2, spontaneously decay back to a lower energy level E_1 and radiate an energy level to E_2-E_1. Such as emission called as spontaneous emission.

Stimulated emission: A photon of energy $h\nu = E_2 - E_1$ triggers an excited atom to drop to the lower energy level giving up a photon. This phenomenon of forced emission of photons is called stimulated emission.

→ **Meta-stable state:** The upper energy level in which excited state of the atom or molecule, have a long lifetime compared to normal excited state.

→ Relationship between Einstein's coefficients can be given as, $\mathbf{B_{12} = B_{21}}$ and $\mathbf{\frac{A_{21}}{B_{12}} = \frac{8\pi h\nu^3}{c^3}}$.

→ **Population inversion:** The process of getting large percentage of atoms into an excited state is called as population inversion.

→ **Pumping:** A method of rising atoms from lower energy to higher energy level is called pumping.

→ Ruby laser is three level of laser system.

→ Ruby laser employs optical pumping mechanism.

→ Wavelength of ruby laser is 6943 Å or 694.3 nm.

→ He-Ne laser employs DC discharge or electrical pumping mechanism.

→ Wavelength of He-Ne laser is 632.8 nm.

-: SOLVED NUMERICALS:-

1) In a ruby laser, total no of cr^{+3} ions is 2.5×10^{23}. If the laser emits radiation of 8000Å, then calculate energy of an emitted photon and total energy available per laser pulse.

Given: Total no. of photons = Total no. of ions = 2.5×10^{23}

$\lambda = 8000$ Å $= 8000\times10^{-10}$

Solution:

Energy of single photon is

$$E = \frac{hc}{\lambda}$$

$$\therefore E = \frac{6.625\times10^{-34}\times3\times10^{8}}{8000\times10^{-10}}$$

$$\therefore E = 2.48\times10^{-19}\text{ joule}$$

Now

Energy per unit pulse = energy of single photon × total no of photons

$= 2.48\times10^{-19}\times 2.5\times10^{23}$

Energy per unit pulse $= 6.2\times10^{4}$ joule

2) Calculate the wavelength of radiation emitted by an LED made up of semi-conductivity materials with band gap energy of 2.8 eV.

Given: $E_g = 2.8\text{ eV} = 2.8\times1.6\times10^{-19}$ J

Solution:

We know that

$$E_g = \frac{hc}{\lambda}$$

$\therefore \lambda = \frac{hc}{E_g}$

$\therefore \lambda = \frac{6.625\times10^{-34}\times3\times10^{8}}{2.8\times1.6\times10^{-19}}$

$\therefore \lambda = 4419.6 \times 10^{-10}$ m

$\boxed{\therefore \lambda = 4419.6\ \text{Å}}$

3) Calculate the long wavelength limit of an extrinsic semiconductor if the ionization energy is 0.02 eV.

Given: $E = 0.02$ eV $= 0.02\times1.6\times10^{-19}$ J

Solution:

We know that

$E = \frac{hc}{\lambda}$

$\therefore \lambda = \frac{hc}{E}$

$\therefore \lambda = \frac{6.625\times10^{-34}\times3\times10^{8}}{0.02\times1.6\times10^{-19}}$

$\therefore \lambda = 6.2109 \times 10^{-5}$m

4) For InP laser diode, the wavelength of light emission is 1.55 μm. What is its band gap in eV.

Given: $\lambda = 1.55$ μm $= 1.55\times10^{-6}$ m, $E_g = ?$

Solution:

We know that

$E_g = \frac{hc}{\lambda}$

$\therefore E_g = \frac{6.625\times10^{-34}\times3\times10^{8}}{1.55\times10^{-6}\times1.6\times10^{-19}}$

$\boxed{\therefore E_g = 0.8014\ \text{eV}}$

5) In ruby laser two states at 300K and 500K. If it emits light 7000Å, then calculate relative population. (given $k_B = 8.6\times 10^{-5}$eV /k).

Given: $T_1 = 300$ K $T_2 = 500$ K $\lambda = 8000$ Å $k_B = 8.6\times 10^{-5}$eV /k $N_2/N_1 = ?$

Solution:

We know that the population ratio can be given as,

$\frac{N_2}{N_1} = e^{-\frac{h\nu}{kT}} = e^{-\frac{hc}{\lambda kT}}$

Here

$\frac{hc}{\lambda} = \frac{6.625\times10^{-34}\times3\times10^{8}}{7000\times10^{-10}}$

$\therefore \frac{hc}{\lambda} = 1.775$ eV

Now the population ratio at 300 K will be

$\frac{N_2}{N_1} = e^{-\frac{hc}{\lambda kT}} = e^{-\frac{1.775}{kT}} = e^{-\frac{1.775}{300\times80617\times10^{-5}}}$

$\therefore \frac{N_2}{N_1} = e^{-\frac{1.775}{0.0258}}$

$\boxed{\therefore \frac{N_2}{N_{1[at\ 300\ K]}} = 1.51 \times 10^{-30}}$

Now the population ratio at 500 K will be

$$\frac{N_2}{N_1} = e^{-\frac{hc}{\lambda kT}} = e^{-\frac{1.775}{kT}} = e^{-\frac{1.775}{500\times80617\times10^{-5}}}$$

$$\therefore \frac{N_2}{N_1} = e^{-\frac{1.775}{0.0431}}$$

$$\therefore \frac{N_2}{N_{1[at\ 500\ K]}} = 1.28 \times 10^{-18}$$

-: UNSOLVED NUMERICALS: -

1. A typical laser emits a 6940 Å wavelength. Find the energy difference (in eV) between the energy levels of this laser.
   (Ans: ΔE = 1.78 eV)
2. In a laser, energy difference between two levels is 1.21 eV. Calculate the wavelength of radiation.
   (Ans: λ = 1022.7 nm)
3. What is the wavelength of light of Ruby Laser if the separation between metastable state and lower energy state is 1.79 eV. Given that Planck's constant = 6.64×10^{-34} Js.
   (Ans: λ = 695.5 nm)

-: SHORT QUESTIONS: -

1. What is laser?
2. List out four unique properties of laser.
3. What is ground state?
4. What is excited state?
5. What is life time?
6. What is meta-stable state?
7. What is population inversion?
8. What is pumping?
9. What is active medium?
10. What is optical resonator?
11. What is essential condition for population inversion?
12. Define: Absorption of light.
13. Define: spontaneous emission.
14. Define: stimulated emission
15. Write the equations showing the relationship between Einstein's coefficients.
16. Describe classification of lasers.
17. In population inversion, number of excited atoms is more than __________.
18. In ruby laser population inversion is achieved by ____________________.
19. In He-Ne laser population inversion is achieved by ____________________.
20. Wavelength of ruby laser is ____________________.

-: DESCRIPTIVE QUESTIONS: -

1. Describe and differentiate ordinary light and Laser light.
2. Briefly explain properties of Laser light.
3. Describe population inversion with suitable diagram.
4. Describe role of stimulated emission in lasing action.
5. Prove that the ratio of spontaneous emission and stimulated emission is proportional to the cube of frequency.

   OR

   Derive the relation between Einstein's coefficients A and B.
6. Explain the construction and working of He-Ne laser.
7. Explain the construction and working of ruby laser.
8. Write down the various applications of LASER.

* * * * *

CHAPTER-VI NEW ENGINEERING MATERIALS

Learning goals:

At the end of this chapter reader will be able to

- ✓ Understand the Group IV elements and their properties.
- ✓ Analyze the characteristics and theories in semiconductor materials in terms of charge carriers and energy bands.
- ✓ Explain the properties of n-type and p-type semiconductors.
- ✓ Describe the I-V characteristics of P-N junction diode and Zener diode
- ✓ Explain superconductivity and general properties of superconductors.
- ✓ Differentiate between type-1 and type-2 superconductors.
- ✓ Explain the origin of superconductivity using BCS theory.
- ✓ Derive London's equations.
- ✓ Explain various applications of superconductors
- ✓ Get the knowledge about nanomaterials and their classifications.
- ✓ Understand the methods of preparing the nanomaterials.
- ✓ Explain various applications of nanomaterials.

PREREQUISITES:

- Understanding of atoms, protons, neutrons, electrons, and how they interact in chemical bonds.
- Knowledge of how electrons are arranged in atomic orbitals and their significance in bonding and energy states.
- Familiarity with the periodic table, especially the significance of Group IV elements (e.g., Carbon, Silicon, Germanium)
- A basic understanding of how electric charge moves through materials and the concept of electric current
- Understanding of the relationship between voltage, current, and resistance in electrical circuits
- Familiarity with the idea of discrete energy levels in atoms

Maxwell's equations:

Name	Differential Equations
Gauss's law	$\nabla \cdot E = \frac{\rho}{\varepsilon_0}$
Gauss's law for magnetism	$\nabla \cdot B = 0$
Maxwell–Faraday equation (Faraday's law of induction)	$\nabla \times E = -\frac{\partial B}{\partial t}$
Ampère's circuital law (with Maxwell's addition)	$\nabla \times B = \mu_0 \left(J + \epsilon_0 \frac{\partial E}{\partial t}\right)$

6.1 INTRODUCTION:

In this chapter, we explore three pivotal categories of materials—semiconductors, superconductors, and nanomaterials—that have significantly influenced modern technology. Semiconductor materials, primarily composed of Group IV elements, are foundational to electronic devices due to their ability to control electrical conductivity through doping, forming the basis of components like diodes and transistors. Superconducting materials, known for their zero electrical resistance at low temperatures, have enabled advancements in applications such as magnetic levitation and MRI technologies.

Nanomaterials, with their extraordinary properties at the nanoscale, represent a new frontier in materials science, finding applications in electronics, medicine, and energy. By understanding the properties, synthesis methods, and applications of these materials, this chapter provides a comprehensive overview of their roles in shaping the future of technology.

6.2 SEMICONDUCTOR MATERIALS

A semiconductor, as the name suggests, is a material whose electrical conductivity falls between that of an insulator (or bad conductor) and a good conductor (such as metals). Insulators typically exhibit conductivities in the range of 10^{-12} to 10^{-18} S/cm, while good conductors have conductivities between 10^4 to 10^7 S/cm. In contrast, semiconductors have conductivities ranging from approximately 10^{-6} to 10^3 S/cm. So, Semiconductor is a material whose conductivity lies between that of conductors and insulators. The reason for their vast range of applications lies in their ability to have their conductivity altered by several orders of magnitude. This unique property arises from three key factors:

Doping: The conductivity of a semiconductor can be significantly modified by introducing impurities into the material, a process known as doping. Depending on the type of doping—either P-type or N-type—the material's conductivity can be controlled and varied drastically.

Temperature Variation: Changing the temperature of a semiconductor influences its conductivity. Typically, as temperature increases, the conductivity of semiconductors increases, unlike metals where conductivity decreases with rising temperature.

Illumination: Semiconductors also exhibit a change in conductivity when exposed to light of the appropriate wavelength. This property is the basis for devices like photodetectors and solar cells.

Thus, semiconductors are materials whose conductivity can be adjusted by doping, temperature changes, or illumination, making them essential for a wide range of modern electronic devices.

6.3 PROPERTIES OF SEMICONDUCTORS

- The resistivity of semiconductors lies between that of a good conductor and a bad conductor, typically in the range of 10^{-4} to 10^8 $\Omega\cdot$cm.
- The electrical conductivity of a semiconductor is significantly affected by doping with suitable impurities, such as trivalent and pentavalent elements.
- The band gap of semiconductors typically ranges from 0.1 to 3 eV.
- The resistivity of semiconductors decreases with increasing temperature up to a certain limit. The variation of resistivity with temperature for semiconductors is shown in Figure 6.1. It is evident that semiconductors have a negative temperature coefficient of resistivity.
- The conductivity of semiconductors can be altered by exposing them to radiation of a suitable frequency.
- Most semiconductors crystallize in the Zinc Blende or Wurtzite structure, where atoms form covalent bonds with each other.
- Both electrons and holes contribute to electrical conduction in semiconductors.
- All semiconductors behave as insulators at absolute zero temperature.
- Semiconductors are nonlinear conductors of electricity and therefore do not obey Ohm's law.
- Binary semiconductors, also known as compound semiconductors, are formed by combining one element from Group III and one element from Group V, creating III-V semiconductors. Similarly, Group II and Group VI elements form II-VI semiconductors.

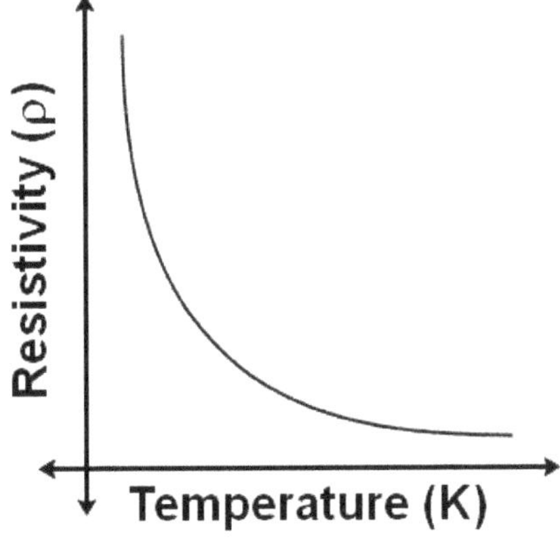

Figure 6.1 Plot of resistivity versus temperature for semiconducting material

6.4 INTRODUCTION TO GROUP IV ELEMENTS

The most common elemental semiconductors comprise of group IV elements, like Silicon, Germanium and Tin. These atoms are bound with neighboring atoms by covalent bonds. The valence electrons are responsible for the chemical bond. As for e.g. the electronic configuration of silicon is $1s^2$ $2s^2$ $2p^6$ $3s^2$ $3p^2$. The inner most shells are completely filled shells and outer most shell has four valence electrons. Therefore, they form covalent bonds sharing four electrons with four nearest silicon atoms to make an Octet, i.e., eight electron shell, which completes the Octet. The above situation is shown is shown in Figure 6.2.

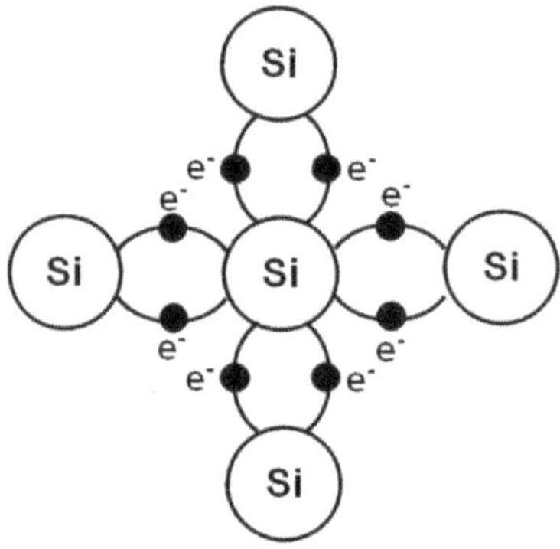

Figure 6.2: Sharing of electrons in silicon atoms

At absolute zero temperature each of the valence electrons of Si is bounded by the covalent bond. As a consequence Si behaves as insulators at absolute zero temperature. The atoms of the crystal perform thermal oscillations at the room temperature. This results in the breaking of several covalent bonds and results in the electrons freeing from the covalent bond. These free electrons are responsible for electrical conduction. Deficiency of electron is created at place where the electron is free. This deficiency has the ability of attracting the electrons. An electron which has become free from any other covalent bond can get trapped in this place. This deficiency of electron is known as hole. It behaves as if it has positive electric charge. It has to be remembered that hole is not a real particle and it neither has any positive electric charge.

We also have binary semiconductors, or compound semiconductors; these are stable compounds formed by one element from group III and one element from group V. These are also sometimes called as III-V semiconductors. We could also have one element from group II and one element from group VI forming a compound. These are called II-VI compounds.

6.5 CONCEPT OF CARRIERS

We have just seen an electron leaves behind a hole on becoming free. In this situation on applying a potential difference between the two ends of a crystal, electric current is constituted (refer to Figure 6.3). Apart from the above phenomenon, thermal oscillations and external electric field causes the bound electron to break free from the covalent bond and gets trapped in the hole. The trapped electron in the hole would fill the hole, but a new hole is created at the place where the electron is breaking free from the covalent bond.

The motion of the electron involved in the creation of the hole is from negative end towards the positive end. In which case, the motion of the hole is from the positive end towards the negative end. Hence we get two types of electric current in a semiconductor. (1) one due to the motion of the free electrons and (2) due to motion of the electron (bound) responsible for the hole and filling another hole. Such an electron becomes free from a bound state and is again gets bound in the nearest hole. To differentiate the motion of the bound and free electron, one can consider the motion of the hole in a direction opposite to the direction of the motion of the bound electron. The hole behaves as a particle having positive charge. Since it's motion is in the opposite direction to that of the electron that is from the positive end towards the negative end. We will have to remember that the conduction of holes means that the conduction is due to bound electrons. In the case of a pure semiconductors like Si an Ge the electrical conduction is due to both electrons as well as holes.

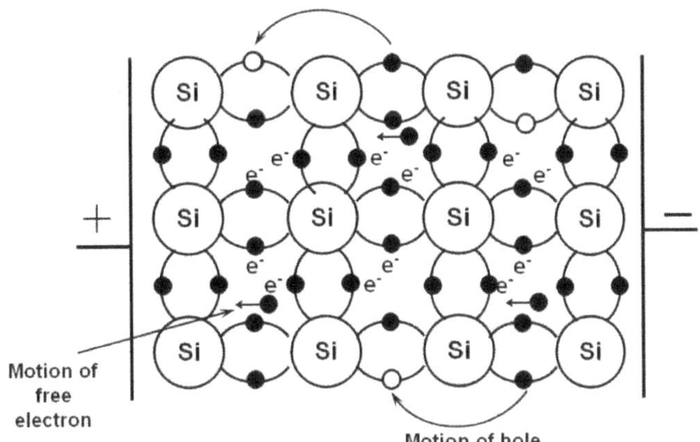

Figure 6.3: Motion of electrons and holes in pure silicon crystal under external potential difference

6.6 CONCEPT OF BANDS AND BAND GAP

6.6.1 Formation of energy bands in solid

The energy spectrum of an electron moving within a crystalline solid can be understood through band theory. This theory begins by examining the energy levels of a free atom and gradually extends to describe how these levels change as atoms come together to form a solid structure.

Let's take lithium as an example. In an isolated lithium atom, electrons occupy discrete energy levels, such as 1s, 2s, and 2p, with the three electrons of lithium occupying the 1s and 2s levels (refer to Figure 6.4a). When two lithium atoms combine to form a Li_2 molecule, the potential energy experienced by the electrons doubles, and each atomic energy level—1s, 2s, 2p, etc.—splits into two closely spaced sublevels (refer to Figure 6.4b) due to the interaction between the atoms. This splitting occurs because of Pauli's exclusion principle, which states that no two electrons can occupy the same quantum state simultaneously. As the lithium atoms move closer together, the influence of one atom's electrons on the other becomes significant, lifting the degeneracy of energy levels and resulting in the formation of molecular sublevels.

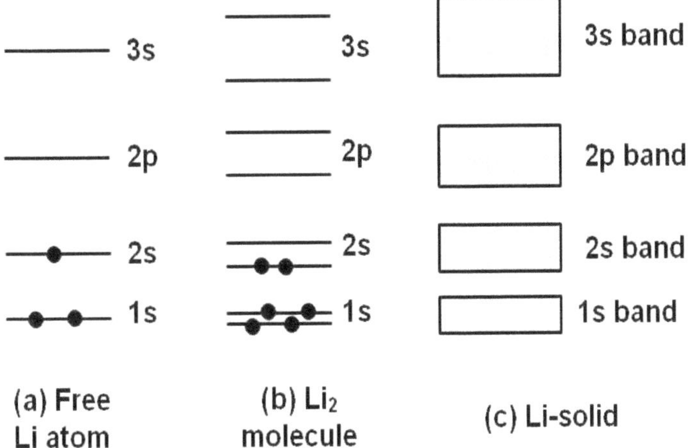

Figure 6.4: Formation of energy bands in solids (a) Free Li atom (b) Li2 molecules (c) Li-solid

Each molecular level can accommodate at most two electrons with opposite spins, according to the exclusion principle. In the Li_2 molecule, the six electrons occupy the available sublevels: four in the 1s molecular doublet and two in the lower sublevel of the 2s doublet.

This concept can be generalized to polyatomic lithium molecules with an arbitrary number of atoms. For example, in a 3-atom molecule, each atomic level splits into a triplet; in a 4-atom molecule, it splits into a quadruplet, and so on. In solid lithium, where there are approximately 10^{23} atoms, each atomic level is split into an extremely large number of closely spaced sublevels. As the number of atoms increases, these sublevels become so close to one another that they merge into continuous energy bands (refer to Figure 6.4c).

To illustrate how tightly packed these sublevels are, consider the following example: if the width of a band is 5 eV, the energy interval between two adjacent levels is approximately $5/10^{23} \approx 5 \times 10^{-23}$ eV. Since this value is extremely small, individual sublevels become indistinguishable, and we treat their distribution as a continuous energy band.

In general, the energy spectrum of a solid consists of multiple energy bands, with regions between them called energy gaps, or forbidden zones, where no electron can exist. The energy band occupied by valence electrons is called the valence band, which may be either completely or partially filled. Bands below the valence band are fully occupied. The energy band immediately above the valence band, known as the conduction band, is where conduction electrons reside. In insulators, the conduction band is empty, while in conductors it is partially filled.

The amount of energy level splitting depends strongly on the distance between nuclei in the molecule. The closer the nuclei, the stronger the interaction and the larger the splitting of the energy levels. Additionally, the degree of splitting varies with the atomic orbitals. For example, the 2p level splits more than the 2s level, which, in turn, splits more than the 1s level. This is because the 1s orbital is smaller and more tightly bound to its nucleus, making it less affected by interactions, whereas the larger 2s and 2p orbitals are more loosely bound and thus more influenced by the interaction. In general, higher energy orbitals experience greater splitting.

6.6.2 Classification of Solids Based on Band Diagram

The concept of energy bands is crucial for classifying solids into three categories: conductors, semiconductors, and insulators. The nature of these energy bands determines whether a solid conducts electricity or acts as an insulator. According to band theory, a solid is characterized by the energy gap (E_g) that separates the valence band from the conduction band. The electrical conductivity of the material depends on the magnitude of this energy gap.

Conductors: In good conductors, such as metals, the valence band and conduction band overlap, as shown in Figure 6.5a. This overlap allows valence electrons to move freely from the valence band into the conduction band, where they act as conduction electrons. When an external electric field is applied, these conduction electrons can easily flow, resulting in electrical conduction.

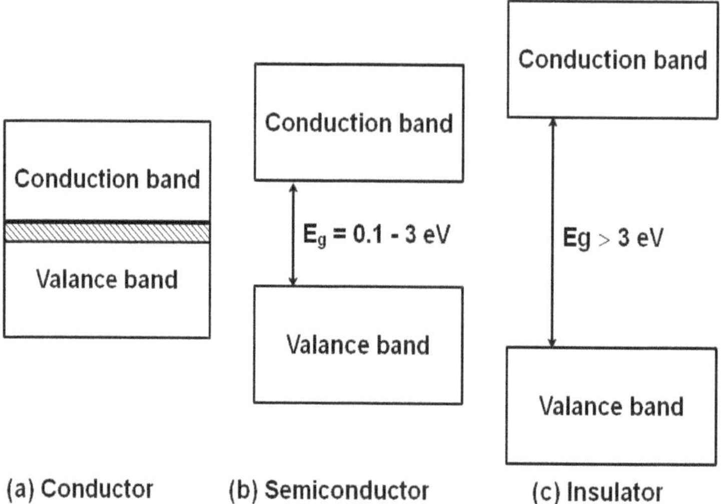

Figure 6.5: Classification of solids based on band diagram

Semiconductors: In some solids, the band gap is narrow, typically less than 3 eV, as shown in Figure 6.5b. This means only a small amount of energy is required to excite electrons from the valence band to the conduction band. At room temperature, thermal energy from atomic vibrations is enough to raise some valence electrons into the conduction band, partially filling it. When a potential difference is applied, these electrons move to higher energy levels within the conduction band, allowing current to flow. Such materials are classified as semiconductors. However, at absolute zero temperature, semiconductors behave like insulators. The energy gap for germanium is 0.7 eV, while for silicon, it is 1.1 eV.

Insulators: In insulators, the energy gap between the valence and conduction bands exceeds 3 eV at room temperature. As a result, there is not enough thermal energy to break covalent bonds and excite electrons into the conduction band. Even when a large electric field is applied, it is insufficient to liberate electrons, making the conductivity of insulators nearly zero. For instance, the energy gap for diamond is 6 eV, and for glass, it is around 10 eV.

6.7 EXTRINSIC SEMICONDUCTORS:

The application of intrinsic (pure) Semiconductors is restricted due to their low conductivity. In electronic devices, high conducting Semiconductors are more essential. The concentration of either electrons or holes in a Semiconductor is increased depending upon the requirements in the electronic devices.

This can be carried out simply by impurities (one atom in 10^7 host atoms) to the intrinsic Semiconductors. The process of adding an impurity to the intrinsic Semiconductors is known as *doping*. The doped Semiconductors are called *extrinsic Semiconductors*. The concentration of electrons and holes are not equal in an extrinsic Semiconductor.

Extrinsic Semiconductors are classified into two categories based on the basis of charge carriers: (1) n-type Semiconductors (2) p-type Semiconductors

6.7.1 n-type Semiconductors:

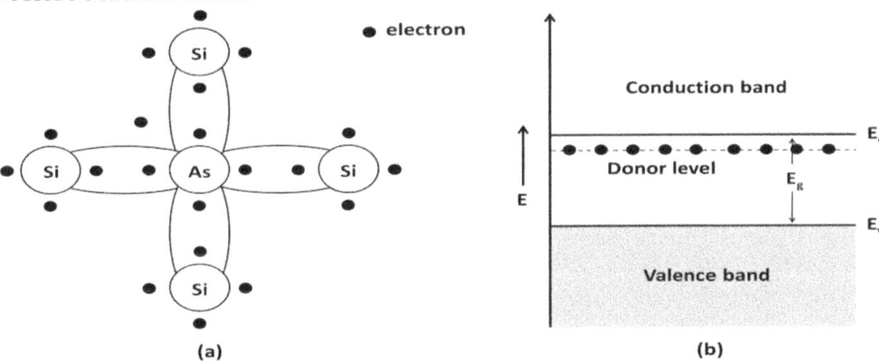

Figure 6.6: n- type doping in silicon; (a) Two-dimensional arrangement of atoms, (b) Energy band diagram.

When a pentavalent atom such as arsenic (antimony, bismuth, phosphorus) is added as a dopant to the tetravalent silicon atom, the arsenic atom will occupy one site of the silicon atom. Thus, out of five free electrons in arsenic, four electrons make covalent bonds with the four neighbouring silicon atoms and the fifth one loosely bound to the silicon atom, as shown in Figure 6.6a.

The energy required to ionize the fifth electron is very less and hence, the thermal energy of the material shifts the free electron to the conduction band, each arsenic atom contributes one free electron to the crystal and hence, it is called a donor impurity. In this type of Semiconductors, the concentration of electrons is more than that of holes. Therefore, these Semiconductors are called n-type Semiconductors. Here majority charge carriers are electron and minority charge carrier are holes.

6.7.2 p-type Semiconductors:

Instead of a penta-valent atom, the addition of a trivalent atom indium (In) to the tetravalent silicon atom, occupies the crystal site of the silicon atom as shown in Figure 6.7a.

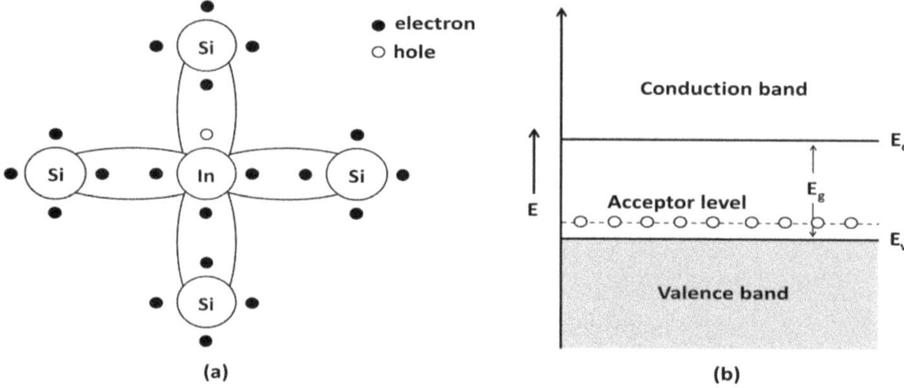

Figure 6.7: p- type doping in silicon; (a) Two-dimensional arrangement of atoms, (b) Energy band diagram.

The three valence electrons in indium make covalent bonds with the three neighbouring silicon atom. Whereas the fourth bond has an empty space known as hole due to the deficiency of one electron. Therefore, when a trivalent atom is added to silicon, it creates a hole in the valence band, the dopant (indium) accept an electron from the neighbouring silicon atom to from a covalent bond and hence, it is called an acceptor. The hole in the valence band moves freely and hence, the current flows through material. This type of electrical conduction will take place only when the dopant valency is less than that of the parent atom. Such Semiconductors are called p-type Semiconductors. In p-type Semiconductors, holes are the majority current carriers and electrons are the minority current carriers.

6.8 P-N JUNCTION:

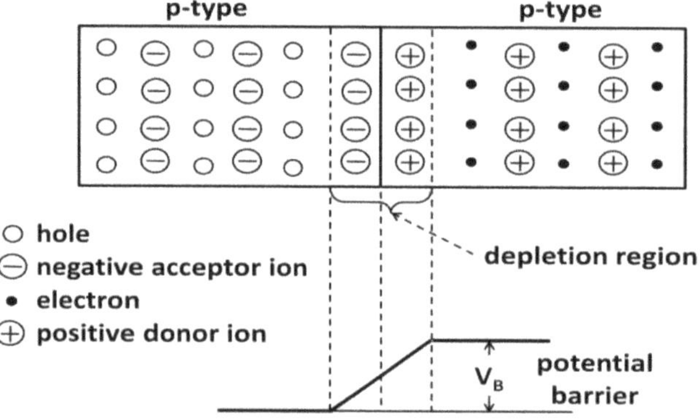

Figure 6.8: Formation of depletion region and junction potential in a pn-junction diode.

P-N junction is metallurgical boundary in a semiconductor crystal in which holes are the majority charge carrier on P side and, electron are the majority charge carrier in other side N side. If Ge is doped with P type material from one side and other half side is doped with N type material then zone forms P-N junction. Electron have high concentration in N side and holes has high concentration on P side ,so electron in N region tend to diffuse to the P region and holes from P region tend to diffuse in N side this process called Diffusion . The diffusion charge carrier combine at the junction to neutralized to each other. Hence development of immobile positive ions in N region and negative ions in P region near the junction take place and a charge free space called depletion layer. It is order of some micron near the junction. The diffusion process continues till Fermi levels are equalize on the both side. The immobile ions form parallel rows of opposite charges facing each other across the depletion layer. Because of this charge separation electric potential V_B is developed across the junction under equilibrium condition shown in Figure 6.8. This potential is called junction potential or barrier potential it prevent the further diffusion of majority carrier across the junction. Also outside the barrier each side of the junction the material is still neutral.

6.8.1 I-V Characteristic of P-N junction:

Figure 6.10 show the current Vs voltage feature in forward and reverse bias. Very low forward bias needed to overcome the potential barrier at the junction and permit current to flow in the forward direction

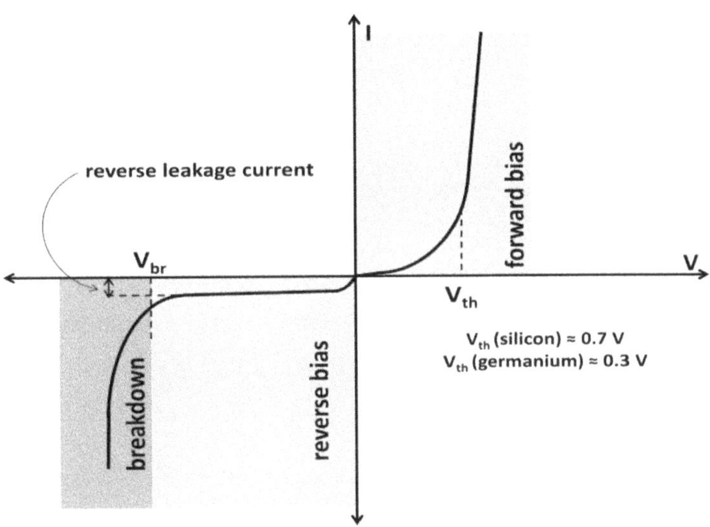

Figure 6.10: IV-characteristics of a pn-junction diode.

6.9 ZENER DIODE

When the reverse bias applied to a crystal diode is increased, a critical point, known as the breakdown voltage, is reached. At this point, the reverse current rapidly increases to a high value. The region where this sharp rise in current occurs is referred to as the breakdown region, or the knee of the reverse characteristics, as shown in Figure 6.11. The specific breakdown voltage at which this happens is called the Zener voltage, and the resulting rapid increase in current is termed the Zener current.

The breakdown voltage of the diode is influenced by the level of doping. In heavily doped diodes, the depletion region is thin, resulting in breakdown occurring at a lower reverse voltage. Conversely, in lightly doped diodes, the breakdown voltage is higher. A diode that is specifically doped to achieve a precise breakdown voltage is known as a Zener diode.

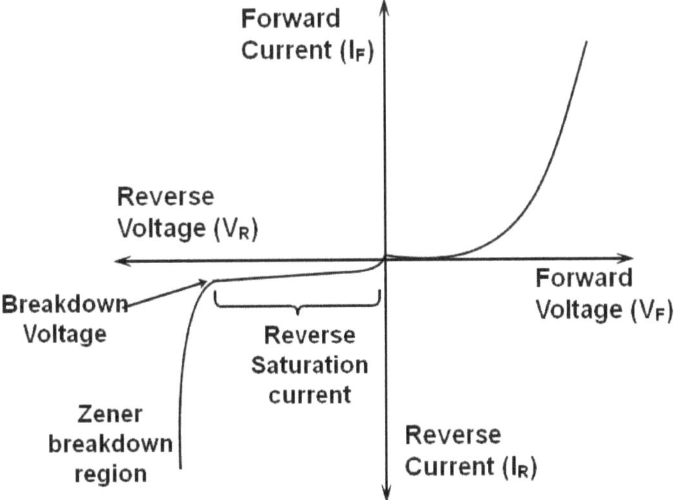

Figure 6.11: Forward and reverse IV characteristics of Zener diode

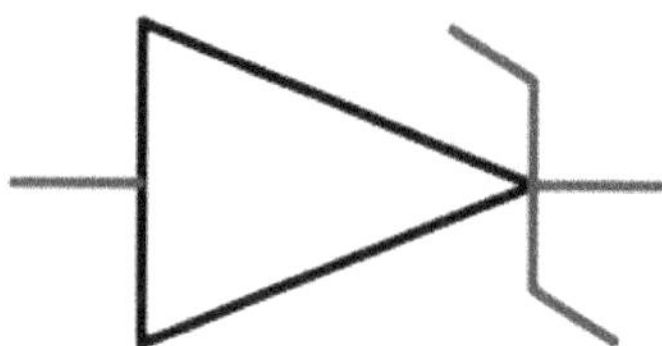

Figure 6.12: Circuit symbol of Zener diode

Figure 6.12 depicts the symbol of a Zener diode, which closely resembles that of an ordinary diode, except that the bar is replaced by a Z-shaped symbol. Key characteristics of a Zener diode include the following:

- A Zener diode is similar to an ordinary diode but is doped in such a way that it exhibits a sharp and well-defined breakdown voltage.
- It is always connected in reverse bias, meaning it operates in reverse mode.
- The Zener diode has a specific breakdown voltage, known as the Zener voltage (V_Z).
- When forward biased, its behavior is identical to that of a standard diode.

6.10 ZENER DIODE AS A VOLTAGE REGULATOR

A Zener diode can function as a voltage regulator to provide a stable output voltage from a source whose input voltage may fluctuate over a wide range. The circuit configuration for this is shown in Figure 6.13.

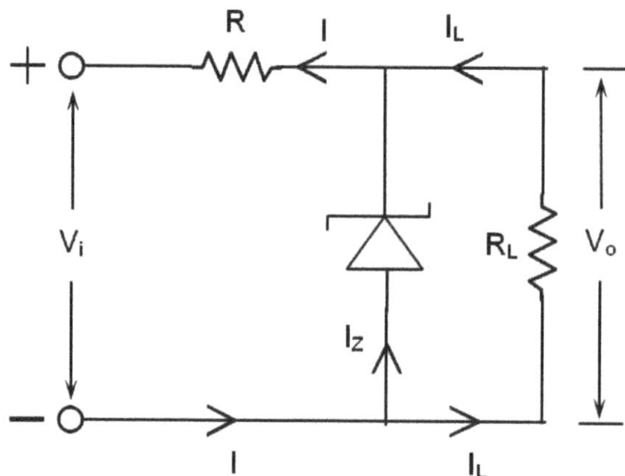

Figure 6.13: Zener diode as voltage regulator

In this setup, the Zener diode, with Zener voltage V_Z, is reverse-biased and connected across the load R_L, where a constant output voltage is desired. A series resistor R is used to absorb any fluctuations in the input voltage, ensuring the voltage across the load remains stable. The Zener diode will maintain a constant voltage of V_Z across the load as long as the input voltage does not drop below V_Z.

Variations in the input voltage V_i or the load resistance R_L do not affect the output voltage V_o. If the input voltage V_i increases, the Zener diode, operating in its breakdown region, acts like a constant voltage source equivalent to a battery with voltage V_Z. Therefore, the output voltage remains fixed at V_Z , and any excess voltage is dropped across the series resistor R. This leads to an increase in the total current I, with the Zener diode conducting the excess current while the load current remains unchanged. As a result, the output voltage V_o remains constant, regardless of variations in the input voltage V_i.

6.11 INTRODUCTION TO SUPERCONDUCTING MATERIALS:

The Helium gas was liquefied at 4.2K by Kamerlingh Onnes in 1908. Liquid He has a temperature of 4.2K. Further, he studied the properties of Hg at very low temperatures. He found that the resistivity of Hg suddenly dropped nearly to zero at 4.2K (liquid He temperature). At 4.2K, the resistivity of Hg is in the order of 10^{-5} Ω·cm, i.e., at 4.2K, Hg is converted into a superconducting material.

For a normal conductor, the relation between temperature and resistivity is shown in Figure 4.1. At very low temperature, a normal conductor has some resistivity. But for a superconductor, the resistivity is suddenly drops to zero at very low temperatures. This is shown in Figure 6.14. Let T_c be the transition temperature. It is defined as the temperature at which a normal conductor is converted into a superconductor. It is also known as critical temperature. For superconductor, T_c varies from 0.3K (GeTe) to 1.25K (NbO); for metals, T_c varies from 0.35K (Hafnium) to 9.22 K (Niobium); and for alloys, from 18.1K (Nb3Sn) to 22.65K (Nb3Ge). Nowadays, can be achieved at higher transition temperatures.

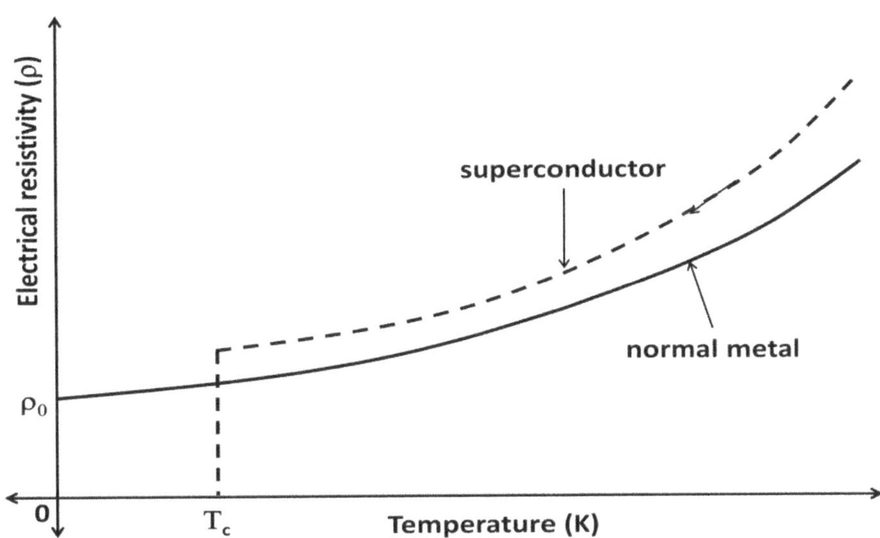

Figure 6.14: Electrical resistivity Vs Temperature curve for superconductor and normal material.

Good electric conductors like copper and gold are not good superconductors. Addition of impurity destroys the superconducting property. A normal conductor is brought into a superconducting state by increasing its pressure.

6.12 GENERAL PROPERTIES OF SUPERCONDUCTING MATERIALS

At the transition temperature, the following changes are observed.

→ The electrical resistivity drops to zero.

→ The magnetic flux lines are expelled from the material.

→ There is a discontinuous change in specific heat.

→ Further, there is also small change in the thermal conductivity and the volume of the material.

6.12.1 Electrical Resistance

The Electrical resistivity of a super conducting material is of the order of 10^{-5} Ω·cm. The ratio of the resistivity of a material in the superconducting state (ρ_s) to the resistivity of material in normal state (ρ_n) is less than 10^{-5} (i.e., $\rho_s/\rho_n < 10^{-5}$)

6.12.2 Magnetic properties

When superconducting materials are subjected to a large value of magnetic field, it will result in the destruction of superconducting property. The minimum field required to destroy the superconducting property is given by

$$H_c = H_0\left[1 - \left(\frac{T}{T_c}\right)^2\right] \quad (6.1)$$

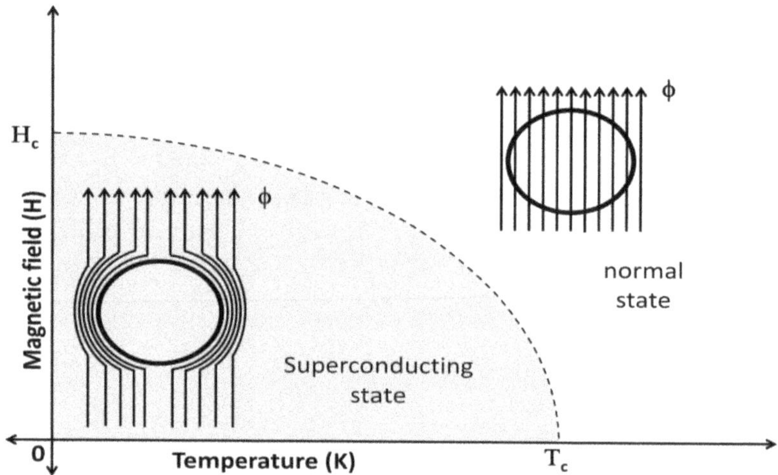

Figure 6.15: Magnetic field versus temperature

Where $\mathbf{H_0}$ is the field required to destroy the superconducting property at 0K, $\mathbf{H_c}$ is the minimum field required to destroy the superconducting property at given temperature **T** and $\mathbf{T_c}$ is the transition temperature of material. Magnetic properties of the material can be represented graphically as shown in Figure 6.15.

6.12.3 Diamagnetic property/ Meissner effect

When a normal conducting material is placed in a magnetic field of flux density "**B**", the lines of forces penetrate through the material, at $T > T_c$. On the other hand, if the material is cooled (at $T < T_c$) for superconductivity, magnetic lines of forces are ejected out from the material, as shown in Figure 4.3. A diamagnetic material also repels the magnetic field. Therefore, a superconducting material behaves as a perfect diamagnetic material. This behavior was observed by Meissner & hence, this property is known as Meissner effect.

$$\mathbf{B = \mu_0(M + H)} \quad \textbf{(6.2)}$$

$\mathbf{B = 0}$ inside the superconductor therefore magnetic susceptibility $\chi = \mathbf{M}/\mathbf{H}$ = -ve value so it is diamagnetic.

Distinction between a perfect conductor and a superconductor

Superconductors, in addition to having no electrical resistance, exhibit quantum effects such as the Meissner effect and quantization of magnetic flux. In perfect conductors, the interior magnetic field must remain fixed but can have a zero or nonzero value. In real superconductors, all magnetic flux is expelled during the phase transition to superconductivity (the Meissner effect), and the magnetic field is always zero within the bulk of the superconductor.

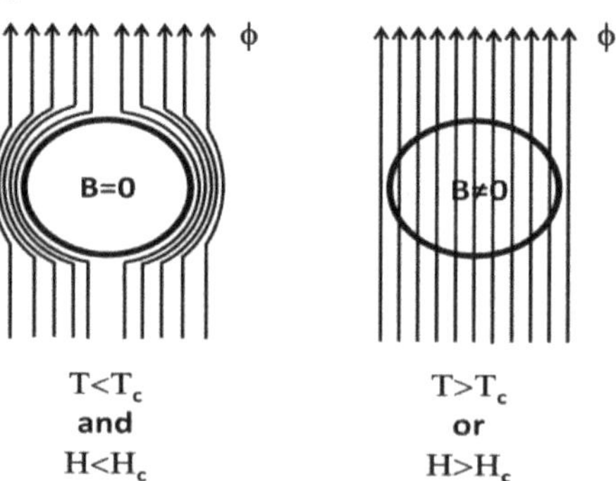

Figure 6.16: Meissner effect

6.12.4 Effect of Pressure

Certain materials are brought into the superconducting state by increasing the pressure. For example, cesium is a normal conductor at atmospheric pressure. While increasing the pressure of Cs, it is converted into a superconductor at 110 Kbar ($T_c = 1.5$ K).

6.12.5 Effect of Electric Current

The application of a large value of electric current to a superconducting material destroys the superconducting property. Consider a coil of wire wound on a superconductor as shown in figure. Let **I** be the current flowing through the wire. The application of the current induces a magnetic field. Thus, the induced magnetic field in the conductor destroys the superconducting property. The induced critical current $\mathbf{I_c}$ required to destroy the superconducting property is given by $\mathbf{2\pi r H_c}$ Where $\mathbf{H_c}$ is the critical magnetic field required and r the radius of the superconductor. Therefore $I_c = 2\pi r H_c$.

6.12.6 Isotopic Effect

The presence of isotopes slightly changes the transition temperature of the superconductor. The atomic mass of Hg varies from 199.5 gm to 203.4 gm. Due to the variation in atomic mass, the transition temperature of isotopes of Hg varies from 4.185 K to 4.146 K. Maxwell showed that the transition temperature is inversely proportional to the square root of the atomic mass of the isotope of a single superconductor.

$$\mathbf{T_c \propto \frac{1}{M^{\alpha}}} \tag{6.3}$$

Where α is a constant equal to 1/2 and **M** the atomic weight.

6.13 TYPE OF SUPERCONDUCTORS

Superconductors are classified into two types. They are type I superconductors and type II superconductors. Type I superconductors are known as soft superconductors and type II superconductors are known as hard superconductor.

6.13.1 Type I Superconductors

Type I superconductors behave as perfect diamagnetic materials and obey the Meissner effect. Figure 4.4 shows the relation between the magnetization produced and the applied magnetic field for type I superconductors. A negative sign is introduced in the magnetization value to represent the diamagnetic property of the superconductor. The material produces a repulsive force up to the critical field H_c Therefore, due to the repulsive force; it does not allow the magnetic field to penetrate through it. Hence, the Material behaves as a superconductor. At H_c the repulsive force is zero and hence, the material behaves as normal conductor. Sn, Hg, Nb, and V are some examples of type I superconductors.

6.13.2 Type II superconductors

Do not perfectly obey the Meissner effect. These materials behave as a perfect superconductor up to $\mathbf{H_{c1}}$ above $\mathbf{H_{c1}}$ the repulsive force decreases, resulting in decrease in the magnetization M and hence, the magnetic flux starts to penetrate through the material. The magnetic field penetrates up to the value $\mathbf{H_{c2}}$. In the region up to $\mathbf{H_{c2}}$, the material behaves as superconductor, as shown in Figure 4.4 Let $\mathbf{H_{c1}}$ and $\mathbf{H_{c2}}$ be the lower and upper critical fields. This region is known as vortex state or mixed state. Above $\mathbf{H_{c2}}$, the materials behave as normal conductors. Examples for type II superconductors are Nb_3Sn, Nb_3Ge, $YBa_2Cu_3O_7$.

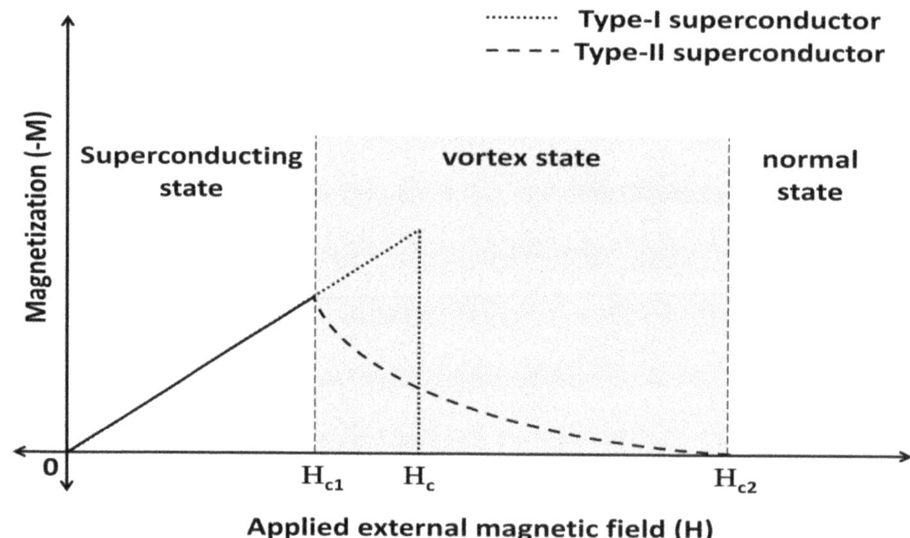

Figure 6.17: Type I superconductors and Type II superconductor

6.14 APPLICATIONS OF SUPERCONDUCTOR

6.14.1 Superconducting Quantum Interface Device (SQUID)

The superconducting quantum interference device (SQUID) consists of two superconductors separated by thin insulating layers to form two parallel Josephson junctions as shown in Figure 4.7. SQUID is a magnetometer, which is involves the super current properties of the Josephson junction.

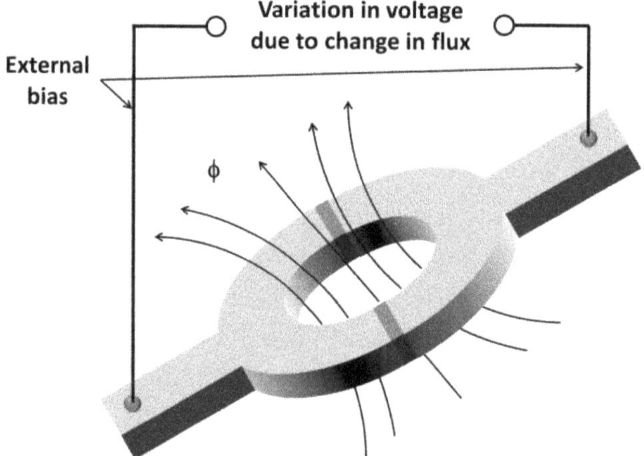

Figure 6.18: Superconducting QUantum Interference Device (SQUID).

The low temperature superconductors are being used for fabricating this SQUID. The main applications of SQUID are to detect a small fractional change in flux, geological layers in different minerals, to detect NMR signals at low temperature, etc.

6.14.2 Maglev

Magnetically levitated (Maglev) trains are known as Maglev vehicles. Maglev trains are faster, quieter and smoother than the current wheeled manual trains. Maglev trains are very popular as they can travel fast for long distance within a short time, the transportation speed for maglev trains are comparable to that of commercial airplane, due to the absence of direct contact between the trains and rail. The comfort for a passenger is a Maglev train is almost same as that available in airplane travel. Maglev trains are already commercialized for passenger use in Japan.

6.14.3 Principal of Maglev Vehicles

In Maglev vehicles, the levitation is brought about due to the presence of enormous repulsion between two highly powerful magnetic fields. When a small magnet is brought close to the superconducting magnet, the magnet gets repelled. The strength of repulsion is very strong which is due to the existence of a persistent current in the superconductor. The persistent current exists in superconductors due to its zero resistance properties. The magnetic fields produced by this induced current repel very strongly the field produced by the magnet. Therefore, the magnet is levitated above the superconductor. Maglev vehicles are configured employing the following two types:

(a) **Electrodynamic suspension (EDS):** In this technique, electromagnets are used to levitate the vehicle above the track employing magnets on both vehicle and track.

(b) **Electromagnetic suspension (EMS):** The alternative controlled electromagnetic suspension is used to attract the vehicle to a magnetic iron rail which is fixed on the track.

In a Maglev vehicle, the contact between the moving and stationary system is absent. The absence of contact eliminates friction during the levitation of the vehicle and also helps to achieve great speed with very low energy consumption.

6.14.4 High-speed train (Bullet train)

The high speed long distance train is commercially used in Japan. The Maglev train is operated employing the EDS concept. The train contains superconducting magnetic coils while the guideways contains passive levitation coils. Maglev is a system used to run the vehicle levitated from the guideway i.e., the rail tracks of conventional railways. The principle behind maglev is the electromagnetic forces between the superconductivity magnets.

The guideways for the maglev trains are similar to the rail tracks of the conventional railways. An electric current is induced within the levitation coils. Thus, the levitation coil acts as an electromagnet and hence, produces electromagnetic forces which push the onboard superconducting magnet upward. Therefore, the maglev system is levitated and hence, the onboard vehicle is levitated from the ground. The levitation coils which are facing each other are connected through a loop under the guideway. When the onboard vehicle is levitated laterally, an electric current is induced in the loop and hence, creates repulsive and attractive forces. The repulsive force is acting on the levitation coil which is near the onboard vehicles, while attractive force is acting on the levitation coil side further apart from the onboard vehicle. Therefore, the running on board vehicle is always located at the centre of the guideway.

The onboard superconductivity magnet is accelerated employing the repulsive force and attracted force induced between the magnets. The propulsion coils which are fitted on the sidewall on both sides of guide tube is used to accelerate onboard vehicle. The acceleration is achieved by giving a sufficient energy (three phase a.c) to the propulsion coils from the substation. Therefore, the onboard vehicle is accelerated.

6.14.5 Other applications of Superconductor

1. Superconducting electric generators are small in the size compared to conventional electric generators. Superconductivity generators produce more power compared to ordinary generators.
2. Superconducting materials are used as no loss transmission lines.
3. In Japan, Superconducting materials are used as levitate a train above its rail.
4. Superconducting materials are used as a storage device in computers.
5. Superconducting materials are used as relay in switching circuits.

6.15 INTRODUCTION TO NANO MATERIALS

Nano Science:

Nanoscience is the study of phenomena and manipulation of materials at atomic, molecular and macromolecular scales: where properties differ significantly from those at larger scale.

Or Nanoscience is the study of atoms, molecules and objects whose size is of the order of nano meter scale (1-100nm).

Nanotechnology:

Nanotechnology is the applications of the properties of nanoscience into useful nanodevices and components, by manipulating the concepts of nanoscience, nanotechnology aims at improving the life style of the human race.

Or Nanotechnology is the technique of design, production of devices and systems by controlling the shape and size at the nanometer scale.

Nanoparticle:

A particle with size in the range of the 1-100nm is called nanoparticle.

Nanomaterials:

Materials classified as nanoscale are those whose minimum dimension is smaller than about 100 nanometers. One millionth of a millimeter, or 100,000 times smaller than the diameter of a human hair (refer to Figure 1), is called a nanometer. Because distinct optical, magnetic, electrical, and other properties occur at this scale, nanomaterials are of interest.

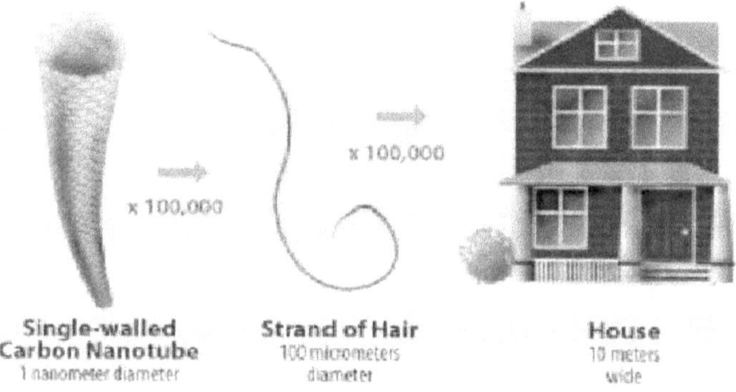

Figure 6.19: Comparison of nano-tube with respect to human hair.

Nanomaterials are materials containing nanocrystals i.e. their grain size is in the 1 to 100 nm range. The nanomaterials may be metals, alloys, intermetallics and ceramics.

Some nanomaterials occur naturally, but of particular interest are, engineered nanomaterials which are developed for the use in many commercial products. For examples electronic devices, sporting goods, cosmetics, textiles, sunscreens, tyres, paints, vanishes etc. In medical field, they are used for the purpose of imaging targeted drug delivery, diagnosis etc.

There are novel UV-blocking coatings on glass bottles which protect beverages from damage by sunlight, and longer-lasting tennis balls using butyl rubber/nano-clay composites. Nanoscale titanium dioxide, for instance, is finding applications in cosmetics, sun-block creams and self-cleaning windows, and nanoscale silica is being used as filler in a range of products, including cosmetics and dental fillings.

6.16 CLASSIFICATION OF NANOMATERIALS

Nanomaterials are incredibly small, with a minimum dimension of 100 nm or less. One dimension (such as surface coatings), two dimensions (such as strands or fibers), or three dimensions (such as particles) can all be considered nanoscale for nanomaterials. They can have spherical, tubular, or irregular shapes and can exist in solitary, fused, aggregated, or agglomerated forms. Quantum dots, fullerenes, dendrimers, and nanotubes are examples of common nanomaterials. Nanomaterials exhibit distinct physical and chemical properties from conventional chemicals, making them useful in the field of nanotechnology (i.e., silver nano, carbon nanotube, fullerene, photocatalyst, carbon nano, silica).

On the basis of the dimensions they are classifies as, Zero dimension(0D), One dimension(1D), Two dimension(2D) and Three dimension(3D). They are nanocrystalline or amorphous in nature.

Zero dimensional (0D) nanostructure: In 0D nanostructure (refer to Figure 2a) all three dimensions are in nanometer size range and the third dimension remains large. Electrons are confined in three dimensions, e.g. nanopowders, quantum dots.

One dimensional (1D) nanostructure: In 1D nanostructure (refer to Figure 2b), two dimensions are in the nanometer size range and the third dimension remains large. Electrons confined in two dimensions. These structures have shape like rod. Examples are nanotubes, nanorods, nanoneedles and quantum wires.

Two dimensional (2D) nanostructure: In 2D nanostructure (refer to Figure 2c), one dimension is reduced to nanometer size and the other two remains large. Electrons confined in one dimension. This 2D display plane like structures.

Three dimensional (3D) nanostructure: In 3D nanostructures (refer to Figure 2d), have all the three dimensions out of nanometer size. A 3D nanostructure can include different distribution of nanocrystallirtes, nanocomposites, group of nanowires and nano tubes and different nanolayers.

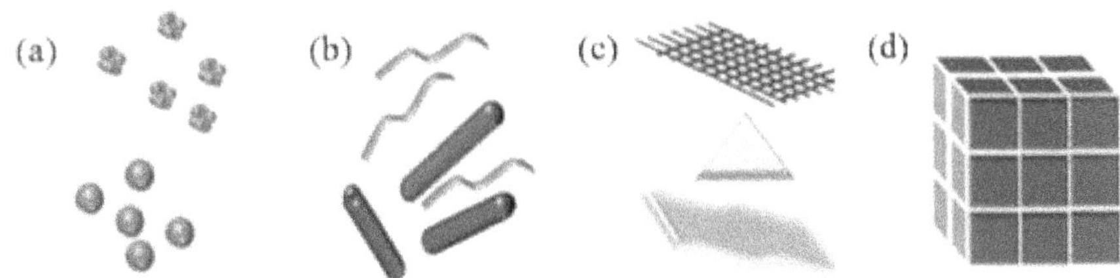

Figure 6.20: Classification of Nanomaterials (a) 0D spheres and clusters, (b) 1D nanofibers, wires, and rods, (c) 2D films, plates, and networks, (d) 3D nanomaterials

Materials with ultra-fine grain sizes (less than 50 nm) or dimensionalities under 50 nm are referred to as nanomaterials. According to Richard W. Siegel, nanomaterials can be produced with one modulation dimensionality (multilayers), two modulation dimensionalities (ultrafine-grained over layers or buried layers), three modulation dimensionalities (nanophase materials made of equiaxed nanometer-sized grains), and zero (atomic clusters, filaments, and cluster assemblies), as illustrated in Figure 2 above.

6.17 PROPERTIES OF NANOMATERIALS

The structural characteristics of bulk materials and atoms are intermediated in nanomaterials. The properties of materials with nanoscale dimensions differ greatly from those of bulk materials, even though most microstructured materials share similarities with their equivalent bulk materials.

This is mainly due to the nanometer size of the materials which render them:

(i) Large fraction of surface atoms; (ii) high surface energy; (iii) spatial confinement and (iv) reduced imperfections, which do not exist in the corresponding bulk materials.

Nanomaterials have a very large surface area to volume ratio because of their small size, which leads to more "surface" dependent material characteristics. The surface characteristics of nanomaterials will have an impact on the entire material, particularly when the diameters of nanoparticles are similar to their lengths. The bulk materials' characteristics could then be improved or changed as a result. Additionally, materials at the nanoscale have a quantum confinement effect. The electrical and optical properties of nanomaterials are altered by their quantum effects.

Most important, properties are listed below.

- ✓ The strength, toughness, hardness, and formability of the nanomaterials are high.

- ✓ More fragile materials are these.
- ✓ Even at low temperatures, these materials show hyper plasticity, or the ability to undergo significant deformation without necking or breaking.
- ✓ Reducing the particle size of nanomaterials can increase their magnetic moment.
- ✓ These materials' optical densities can be adjusted based on their diameter.
- ✓ Grain size regulates optical, chemical, mechanical, electrical, semiconducting, and magnetic characteristics.
- ✓ Reducing the particle size lowers the melting point of nanomaterials.
- ✓ There is more coercivity and magnetism.

6.18 NANOMATERIAL - SYNTHESIS AND PROCESSING

Nanomaterials deal with very fine structures: a nanometer is a billionth of a meter. This indeed allows us to think in both the 'bottom up' or the 'top down' approaches to synthesize nanomaterials, i.e. either to assemble atoms together or to dis-assemble (break, or dissociate) bulk solids into finer pieces until they are constituted of only a few atoms (refer to Figure 6.21). This domain is a pure example of interdisciplinary work encompassing physics, chemistry, and engineering up to medicine.

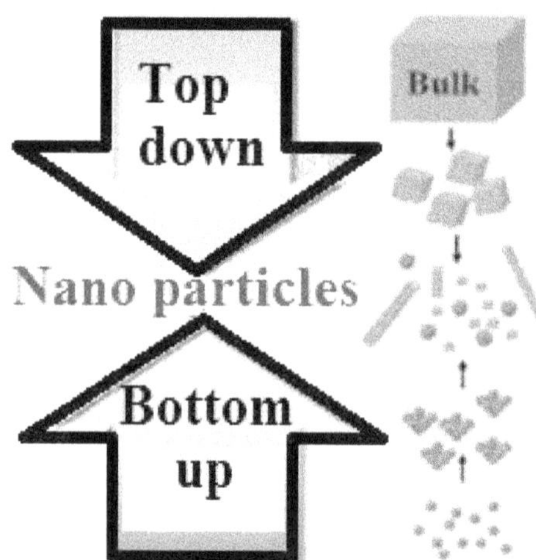

Figure 6.21: Schematic illustration of the preparative methods of nanoparticles

Nanostructures can be made in numerous ways. A broad classification divides methods into either those which build from the bottom up, atom by atom or those which construct from the top down using processes that involve the removal or reformation of atoms to create the desired structure.

Top down approach: the top down approaches are simpler and rely either on the removal or division of bulk material or on the miniaturization of bulk fabrication process to produce the desired structure with the appropriate properties. E.g. Milling lithographic process and machining.

Bottom up approach: In the bottom up approach atoms, molecules and even nanoparticles themselves can be used as the building blocks for the creation of complex nanostructures, the useful size of building blocks depends on the properties to be engineered.

Various techniques are adopted for the synthesis of nanomaterials based on the two processes, top down and bottom-up.

Top down processes are,

1. Milling
2. Lithography
3. Machining

Bottom up processes are,

1. Plasma assisted deposition process

2. Vapour deposition methods
3. Liquid phase processes
4. Molecular Beam Epitaxy
5. Laser, Synthesis, etc.

6.19 BALL MILLING (MECHANICAL CRUSHING)

By smashing balls against finely ground powdered particles, the ball milling technology creates nanoparticles. To obtain nanoparticles, this procedure is repeated several times. Through mechanical deformation, the grain size of powder samples is lowered to the nanoscale range. The most widely used industrial method for creating nanomaterials is high-energy ball milling. Also known as mechanical alloying.

It is a solid state method that produces a variety of energy nanopowders. At room temperature, this high energy ball milling technique causes chemical reactions and structural alterations. As seen in Figure 6.22, the powder material is mechanically crushed by putting it inside a revolving stainless steel drum filled with hard steel or tungsten carbide balls. As a result, the hard balls mechanically crush the powder materials when the steel drum rotates. As seen in Figure 4, this repeated deformation can result in a significant reduction in the grain size of the powder particles. Nanostructured alloys can be created by mechanically alloying several components together using cold welding.

Mechanical crushing is performed under controlled atmospheric conditions to prevent unwanted reactions such as oxidation.

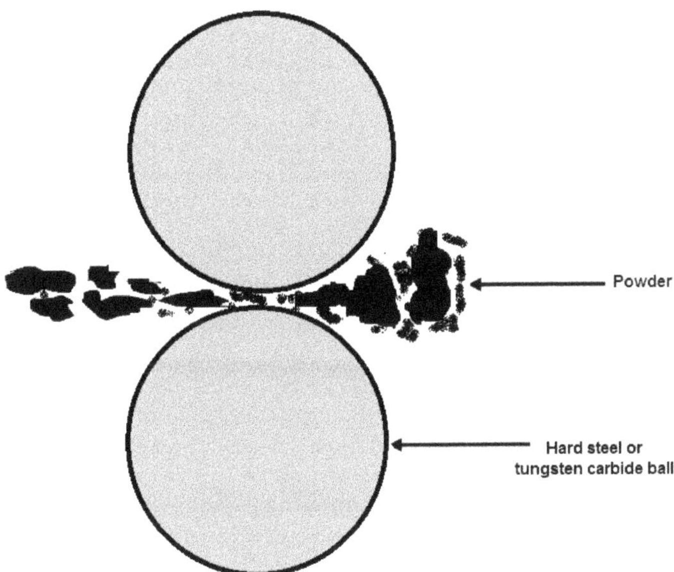

Figure 6.22: High energy ball Milling

Merits

1. This method can be used on a bigger scale.
2. It is possible to synthesis several kilograms or a few milligrams of nanomaterials in a short amount of time.
3. This technology will be used to fabricate alloys that can't be made with traditional methods.

Demerits

1. The nanomaterials produced by this method is contaminated with impurities.
2. This technique also produces a variety of non-equilibrium structures that include amorphous, quasi-crystalline and nanocrystalline materials.

Uses

1. High energy mechanical milling is a very effective process for synthesising metal-ceramic composite powders.
2. It is also used for the production of nanocomposites, nanotubes, nano rods, nanowires, etc.

6.20 VAPOUR PHASE DEPOSITION METHODS

It is possible to create thin films, multilayers, nanotubes, Nano filaments, and particles the size of nanometers using vapour phase deposition. The general techniques can be classified broadly as either physical vapour deposition (PVD) or chemical vapour deposition (CVD).

6.20.1 PHYSICAL VAPOUR DEPOSITION (PVD)

The objective of Physical Vapour Deposition (PVD) process is to controllably transfer atoms from a source to substrate where film formation and growth proceed atomistically. Plasma or ions are usually the elements of the vapour phase of the source material. Sometimes the reactive gas is passed through the substrate during the deposition process, which is termed as a reactive deposition.

The physical deposition is followed by evaporation or sputtering of target materials. To deposit onto surface of substrate, atoms or molecules of source materials are transported in the form of vapour through the vacuum or partial vacuum or plasma environment. Usually, thin films of nanometer to micron range have to be deposited using PVD. They can also apply for mono and multi-layer coatings, thick film depositions, functionally graded deposition and used in conjunction with other deposition method.

In evaporation, atoms are removed from the source by thermal means as shown in figure 6.23, whereas in sputtering they are dislodged from gaseous ions.

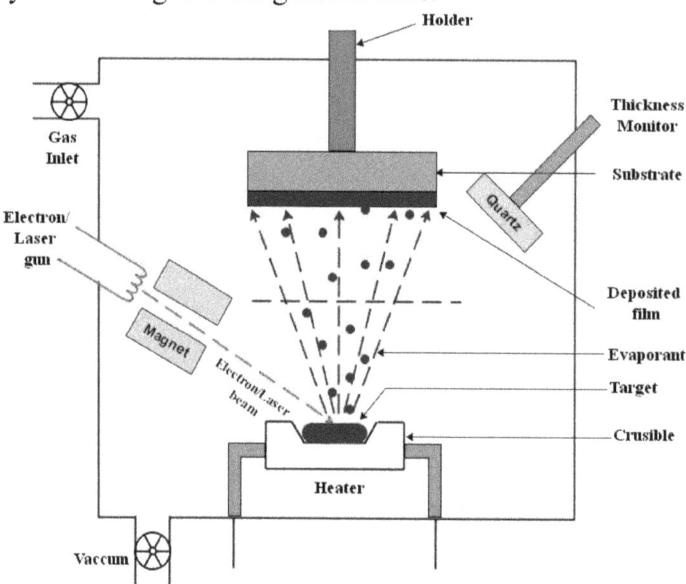

Figure 6.23: Physical vapour deposition method using thermal means

Each PVD process follows basic three steps.

Conversion of the target material into vapour phase species: in this step, target materials are converted into vapour phase by evaporation or sputtering.

Displacement of atoms from source to the substrate: in this step, the ejected atoms or molecules from the target materials will be reached at the substrate through molecular flow or thermal collision process. Some species of metal vapour are to be ionized due to large number of collision that occurs before reaching the substrate.

Growth of the film on the substrate: The transported vaporized atoms or molecules will start nucleation over the substrate's surface and subsequently resulting in film formation via different growth process. The interface between nucleated atoms and substrate determines the growth mechanism. The stoichiometry and micro surface of thin film can be modified by imparting ions from vapour phase onto the growing film. This process will result in sputtering, re-condensation and nucleation of the film atoms and increased surface activity of the atoms around the film's surface.

6.21 APPLICATIONS OF NANOMATERIALS

The emergence of nanomaterials has greatly accelerated scientific advancements across a wide range of disciplines. Due to their numerous uses in physics, chemistry, biology, medicine, material science, and transdisciplinary domains, nanomaterials with appealing electronic, optical, magnetic, thermal, and catalytic properties have garnered significant interest.

These days, nanomaterials are employed in the following fields:

Production technologies:

It is increasingly necessary and desirable to use nanoparticles in composites as components of diverse functionalities. Adding Nano powders to steels and alloys reduces porosity and improves the range of mechanical properties. The presence of super plasticity in nanostructured aluminum and titanium alloys makes them promising for the production of intricate shape details and as a connecting layer in welding distinct solid state materials. Nano powders with extremely large specific surface areas are ideal for use as catalysts in a variety of chemical processes.

Military engineering:

Ultra-fine powders are used in a number of radar absorbing coatings for aircraft, created with the use of technology "Stealth", and promising types of explosives and incendiary. Carbon nanofibers are used in special ammunition intended for the scrapping of the enemy power systems (so-called "graphite bomb").

Nuclear power engineering:

Ultra-fine powders provided the foundation for nuclear power engineering. These powders are widely employed in industrial operations that separate uranium isotopes. The prospects for developing nuclear energy by getting particles to the nanostate are mostly related with a reduction in the average consumption of natural uranium. This comes at the cost of increasing the depth of nuclear fuel combustion. To do this, scientists are investigating the prospect of creating coarse-grained nuclear structures that are porous. These nanoparticles will increase the retention of fission products.

Material surface protection:

In some circumstances, it is vital to ensure that the material surface has excellent water and oil repellent qualities. Such products include car windows, glass planes and ships, protective apparel, liquid storage tanks on walls, building construction, and so on. Currently, a titanium oxide nanoparticle coating (20-50 nm) with a polymer binder has been created. This coating significantly decreases the surface's wettability to water, oil, and alcohol solutions.

Medicine and biotechnology:

There are several fields where nanotechnology is effectively applied, including the following:

Delivery of drugs (molecules) to the target. In cancer treatment, targeted medication delivery will address a number of problems, including preventing drug deterioration and reversing interactions with biological molecules. Additionally, pharmacokinetics can be controlled, medication bioavailability in tumor cells can be increased, and drug absorption by tumor cells can be made more selective. In addition to medications, genes can be delivered into cells by nanoparticles.

Treatment and prosthetics using nanomaterials: The special qualities of nanomaterials enable the creation of a variety of implants and dentures. We can create implants that are reliable, biocompatible, and safe by using nanotechnology.

Diagnostics:

As a result of technological advancements, nanotechnology in biomedicine has grown, enabling high-resolution imaging, characterization, and analysis of biological material. One important source for biosensor manufacture is magnetic nanoparticles. The most widely utilized nanoparticles are made of iron oxide that has been covered with a variety of polymers. Moreover, different biospecific ligands can alter the surface. Consequently, the iron oxide nanoparticles' shell shields them from chemical reactions with tissues' and cells' constituent molecules. Certain nanomaterials, such as nanotubes and nanoparticles, are also employed in diagnostics as electrochemical sensors.

Electronic equipment:

The use of carbon nanotubes in electronics has greatly advanced nanotechnology. In addition to being able to take the role of transistors, they also give the innovative electronic circuits additional mechanical and optical characteristics, enabling the creation of transparent and flexible electronics. Because of their greater mobility and ability to retain light in thick layers, the nanotubes allow the experimental matrix integrated circuit to bend without losing its electrical characteristics. A further use of nanotechnology in electronics is the development of novel hard disks. Peter Grunberg and Albert Fert received the 2007 Nobel Prize in Physics for their discovery of the massive magneto resistance effect, or GMR-effect as some writers refer to it. This result opens the door to the development of magnetic field sensors that precisely read data stored on hard drives with nearly atomic densities.

Making solar cells is another potential use for nanomaterials. The energy received by a battery can be increased fifteen times using solar cells based on nanowires rather than conventional metal wires. Conductor nanoscale light absorption has special characteristics. Utilizing nanostructured materials during the solar cell production process can save costs and increase efficiency.

-: POINTS TO REMEMBER:-

- → Semiconductors are materials whose conductivity can be changed by orders of magnitude using means of doping, temperature changes, or illumination.
- → Semiconductors have conductivities ranging from approximately 10^{-6} to 10^{3} S/cm and band gap between the range of 0.1 – 3 eV.
- → All semiconductors behave as insulators at absolute zero temperature.
- → The resistivity of semiconductors decreases with increasing temperature up to a certain limit.
- → In semiconductors, both electrons and holes contribute to electrical conductivity.
- → The motion of electrons in a free atom is described by energy levels, while in a solid, it is described by energy bands.
- → Solids can be classified based on the energy gap. Typically, the band gap of a conductor is on the order of 0.01 eV, in semiconductors, it ranges between 0.1 and 3 eV, and in insulators, it is more than 3 eV.
- → In N-type semiconductors, pentavalent impurities like phosphorus, antimony, or arsenic are used, while in P-type semiconductors, impurities like aluminum, gallium, or indium are used.
- → In N-type semiconductors, electrons are the majority charge carriers, and holes are the minority charge carriers, while in P-type semiconductors, holes are the majority charge carriers, and electrons are the minority charge carriers.
- → The layer of neutralized charge, having a width on the order of microns across the junction in a P-N junction diode, is called the depletion region.
- → When a P-N junction is connected in an external circuit such that the P-type region is connected to the positive terminal and the N-type region to the negative terminal, the junction is called forward biased.
- → When the positive terminal of the battery is connected to the N-region and the negative terminal to the P-region, the junction is said to be reverse biased.
- → A Zener diode is a specially designed, heavily doped diode, where the depletion region decreases, and breakdown occurs at a lower reverse voltage (due to the Zener mechanism).
- → A Zener diode can be used as a voltage regulator.

→ Meissner effect is the exclusion of magnetic lines of force through the superconductor.
→ Behavior of the critical field versus temperature is Parabolic.
→ Above the critical temperature Super electrons do not contribute to conduction.
→ The variation of the critical field with temperature is expressed by $H(T) = H_c(0)[1-(\frac{T}{Tc})^2]$.
→ Cooper pair is a pair of Electrons bound together through lattice vibration.
→ Crystal lattice remains unchanged during the transition from the Normal to the superconducting state.
→ Superconductors are of great use as they consume very less energy and respond in a very short time.
→ Superconductivity emerges when on decreasing the temperature across a material, its resistivity drop to zero.
→ Superconductors have less number of applications because of the requirement of Low temperature.
→ Normal metals and superconductors differ from each other on the basic of Zero resistivity at low temperature.
→ The classification of different superconductors is done on the basis of Meissner effect.
→ Type-II superconductors are observed not to follow the Meissner effect strictly.
→ A superconductor contains normal and super electrons.
→ As the temperature is decreased, the conduction mechanism is controlled by super electrons.
→ If superconducting material is placed in the magnetic field and temperature across it is decreased, it converts from normal state to superconducting state.
→ A perfect conduction and a superconductor differ from each other on the basis of no magnetic field when the electric field is zero.
→ Type-II superconductors are known as hard superconductor because they require large critical field for the transfer from superconductor state to normal state.
→ Perfect diamagnetic behavior is only shown by superconductor.
→ A perfect conductor has zero electric field but constant magnetic field.
→ When a superconductor is heated above the critical temperature, its transforms into the normal state.
→ Superconducting state is more ordered then normal state.
→ The elements of higher isotopes mass show lower critical temperature.
→ High temperature superconductors are important as they contain higher critical temperature due to ceramic form.
→ If at low temperature, the magnetic field across a superconductor is increased, it regain its normal state beyond a value known as critical field.
→ BCS ground state is more stable than the ground state of a Fermi gas because Cooper pairs utilize maximum kinetic energy for many through the lattice.
→ A Josephson function is a combination of two superconducting materials connected through each other by an insulating layer.
→ The lattice vibration involved in the motion of cooper pair is known phonon.
→ The size of Cooper pair gives an indication of the extent to which the electrons overlap on each other through phonon.
→ The popular superconducting ceramic oxide $YBa_2Cu_3O_7$ is observed to show critical temperature up to 90 K.
→ SQUID works on the principal of macroscopic quantum interference.
→ The parts of super current shows interference and diffraction effect in terms of phase.
→ The flow of current between two superconductors separated from each other by an insulating layer is known as Josephson effect.
→ London penetration depth is defined as that distance in a superconductor up to which the Magnetic field reduces to 37% of its surface value.
→ A nanometer is one millionth of a millimeter - approximately 100,000 times smaller than the diameter of a human hair.
→ Classification of Nanomaterials (a) 0D spheres and clusters, (b) 1D nanofibers, wires, and rods, (c) 2D films, plates, and networks, (d) 3D nanomaterials.
→ Nanomaterials are materials which are characterized by an ultra-fine grain size (< 50 nm) or by a dimensionality limited to 50 nm.

- → Nanomaterials deal with very fine structures: a nanometer is a billionth of a meter. This indeed allows us to think in both the 'bottom up' and the 'top down' approaches to synthesize nanomaterials various techniques are adopted for the synthesis of nanomaterials based on the two processes, top down and bottom-up.
- → Top down processes includes Milling, Lithography, Machining etc.
- → Bottom up processes include Plasma assisted deposition process, Vapour deposition methods, Liquid phase processes, Molecular Beam Epitaxy, Laser Synthesis, etc.
- → PVD Means Physical Vapour Deposition.

-: SOLVED NUMERICALS:-

1) A superconducting tin has a critical temperature of 3.7 K in zero magnetic field and a critical field of 0.0306 T at 0 K. Find the critical field at 2 K.

Given: $H_c(0) = 0.0306$ T $\quad T_c = 3.7$ K $\quad T = 2$ K $\quad H_c = ?$

Solution:

Critical field at any temperature T kelvin is given as

$$H_c = H_c(0)\left[1-\left(\frac{T}{T_c}\right)^2\right]$$

$$\therefore H_c = 0.0306\left[1-\left(\frac{2}{3.7}\right)^2\right]$$

$$\therefore H_c = 0.0306 \times 0.708$$

$$\therefore H_c = 0.0216\text{ T}$$

2) The transition temperature for lead (Pb) is 7.2 K. However, at 5 K, it loses the superconducting property when subjected to a magnetic field of 3.3×10^4 A/m. Find the value of the magnetic field that will allow the metal to retain its superconductivity at 0 K.

Given: $H_c = 3.3 \times 10^4$ A/m $\quad T_c = 7.2$ K $\quad T = 5$ K $\quad H_c(0) = ?$

Solution:

Critical field at any temperature T kelvin is given as

$$H_c = H_c(0)\left[1-\left(\frac{T}{T_c}\right)^2\right]$$

$$\therefore 3.3 \times 10^4 = H_c(0)\left[1-\left(\frac{5}{7.2}\right)^2\right]$$

$$\therefore H_c(0) = \frac{3.3\times10^4}{0.5177}$$

$$\therefore \mathbf{H_c(0) = 6.37 \times 10^4 A/m}$$

3) At what temperature do we get $H_c = 0.1\, H_c(0)$ for lead(Pb) having $T_c = 7.2$ K?

Given: $H_c = 0.1\, H_c(0)$ A/m $\quad T_c = 7.2$ K $\quad T = ?$

Solution:

Critical field at any temperature T kelvin is given as

$$H_c = H_c(0)\left[1-\left(\frac{T}{T_c}\right)^2\right]$$

$$\therefore 0.1\, H_c(0) = H_c(0)\left[1-\left(\frac{T}{7.2}\right)^2\right]$$

$$\therefore 0.1 = \left[1-\left(\frac{T}{7.2}\right)^2\right]$$

$$\therefore \left(\frac{T}{7.2}\right)^2 = 0.9$$

$$\therefore T^2 = 46.656$$

$$\therefore T = 6.83\text{ K}$$

4) Calculate the critical field in lead (Pb) at T= 4.2 K when $H_c(0) = 0.0803$ Wb/m² and $T_c = 7.2$ K for lead.

Given: $H_c(0) = 0.0803\ Wb/m^2$ $T = 4.2\ K$ $Tc = 7.2\ K$ $H_c = ?$

Solution:
Critical field at any temperature T kelvin is given as

$$H_c = H_c(0)\left[1-\left(\frac{T}{T_c}\right)^2\right]$$

$$\therefore H_c = 0.0803\left[1-\left(\frac{4.2}{7.2}\right)^2\right]$$

$$\therefore H_c = 0.0803[0.6597]$$

$$\therefore H_c = 0.0529\ Wb/m^2$$

5) **Calculate the transition temperature of niobium for which the critical field is 1×10^5 A/m at 8 K and 2 X10^5 A/m at 0 K.**

Given: $H_c = 1\ X10^5\ A/m$ $H_c(0) = 2\ X10^5\ A/m$ $T = 8\ K$ $T_c = ?$

Solution:
Critical field at any temperature T kelvin is given as

$$H_c = H_c(0)\left[1-\left(\frac{T}{T_c}\right)^2\right]$$

$$\therefore 1\times 10^5 = 2\times 10^5\left[1-\left(\frac{8}{T_c}\right)^2\right]$$

$$\therefore \left[1-\left(\frac{8}{T_c}\right)^2\right] = 0.5$$

$$\therefore \left(\frac{8}{T_c}\right)^2 = 0.5$$

$$\therefore (T_c)^2 = 128$$

$$\therefore T_c = 11.31\ K$$

6) **What observation can you make with following data for lead(Pb)? Given** that $H_c(T) = 4\times 10^4$ A/m, $T_c = 7.26$ K, and $H_c(0)=8\times 10^5$ A/m.

Solution:
Critical field at any temperature T kelvin is given as

$$H_c = H_c(0)\left[1-\left(\frac{T}{T_c}\right)^2\right]$$

$$\therefore 4\times 10^4 = 8\times 10^5\left[1-\left(\frac{T}{7.26}\right)^2\right]$$

$$\therefore \left[1-\left(\frac{T}{7.26}\right)^2\right] = 0.5$$

$$\therefore \left(\frac{T}{7.26}\right)^2 = 0.5$$

$$\therefore (T)^2 = 26.35$$

$$\therefore T = 5.13\ K$$

This shows that the temperature of the Pb should be held at 5.13 K.

6) **For a specimen of V_3Ga, the critical fields are, respectively, 0.176 T and 0.528 T for 14 K and 13 K. Calculate transition temperature and critical field at 0 K and 4.2 K.**

Given: $H_{c1} = 0.176$ T $H_{c2} = 0.528$ T $T_1 = 14$ K $T_1 = 13$ K $T_c = ?$ $H_c(0)=?$
$H_C(4.2K) = ?$

Solution:
Critical field at any temperature T kelvin is given as

$$H_c = H_c(0)\left[1-\left(\frac{T}{T_c}\right)^2\right]$$

For the given set of values, the above equation becomes

$0.176 = H_c(0)\left[1 - \left(\frac{14}{T_c}\right)^2\right]$ and $0.528 = H_c(0)\left[1 - \left(\frac{13}{T_c}\right)^2\right]$

dividing above equation we get

$$\frac{\left[1-\left(\frac{14}{T_c}\right)^2\right]}{\left[1-\left(\frac{13}{T_c}\right)^2\right]} = 0.3333$$

$$\therefore \frac{1-\frac{196}{T_c^2}}{1-\frac{169}{T_c^2}} = 0.3333$$

$$\therefore 1 - \frac{196}{T_c^2} = 0.3333 - \frac{56.6277}{T_c^2}$$

$$\therefore \frac{196}{T_c^2} - \frac{56.6277}{T_c^2} = 0.6666$$

$$\therefore \frac{139.3723}{T_c^2} = 0.6666$$

$$\therefore T_c^2 = 209.08$$

$$\therefore T_c = 14.46\ K$$

Substituting the value of T in equation of critical field we get

$$0.176 = H_c(0)\left[1 - \left(\frac{14}{14.46}\right)^2\right]$$

$$\therefore 0.176 = H_c(0) \times 0.0626$$

$$\therefore H_c(0) = 2.811\ T$$

Now critical field at 4.2 K is given as

$$H_c = 2.811\left[1 - \left(\frac{4.2}{14.46}\right)^2\right]$$

$$\therefore H_c = 2.5738\ T$$

-: SHORT QUESTIONS:-

1. Define a semiconductor.
2. Mention the properties of semiconductors.
3. State the conductivity and resistivity range for semiconductors.
4. State the range of the energy gap for semiconductors.
5. Show the graph of resistivity vs. temperature for a semiconductor.
6. What are holes in a semiconductor?
7. State Pauli's exclusion principle.
8. Draw the band diagram for a semiconductor.
9. Name the elements used for doping to obtain an N-type semiconductor.
10. Name the elements used for doping to obtain a P-type semiconductor.
11. Define the potential barrier.
12. Define the depletion region.
13. What is a forward-biased P-N junction diode?
14. What is a reverse-biased P-N junction diode?
15. What is reverse saturation current?
16. What is the breakdown region?
17. Draw the I-V characteristics of a P-N junction diode.
18. What is a Zener diode?
19. Define superconductivity.
20. Explain Meissner effect.
21. Describe the relation between the temperature and the critical magnetic field in a superconductor.
22. Define (i) critical transition temperature and (ii) critical magnetic field.
23. What are the differences between perfect conductor and super conductor?

24. What is the isotropic effect?
25. What is the Josephson junction? Explain ac and dc Josephson effect.
26. Show that super conductor behave perfect diamagnetic under Meissner effect.
27. What are nanomaterials?
28. Mention some important properties of nanomaterials?
29. Mention some of the applications of nanomaterials.
30. List various techniques of synthesis of nano materials.
31. What are the merits and demerits of ball milling technique?

-: DESCRIPTIVE QUESTIONS:-

1. Discuss different properties of semiconductors.
2. Explain concepts of carriers in semiconductor.
3. Discuss about formation of energy band in solids and also classify solids based on band diagram.
4. Discuss about N-type and P-type semiconductor in detail.
5. Discuss about forward and reverse biased IV characteristics of P-N junction diode.
6. What is Zener diode? Discuss about Zener diode as voltage regulator.
7. Discuss about P-N junction diode under zero biasing condition.
8. Distinguish Type-I and Type-II superconductors.
9. Discuss the formation of cooper pairs and energy gap in superconductors on the basis of the BCS theory.
10. Write down the applications of superconductors.
11. Write down the characteristics of superconductors.
12. Explain the BCS theory.
13. Derive London first and second equation.
14. From London equation derive the expression for penetration depth.
15. Explain in details synthesis of nanomaterials by ball milling techniques.
16. Explain any method for synthesis of nanomaterials by bottom up approach.
17. Write down the applications of nanomaterials.

* * * * *

www.ingramcontent.com/pod-product-compliance
Lightning Source LLC
Chambersburg PA
CBHW041732100726
47973CB00011B/183

9798896108450